War Is Hell

War Is Hell

Studies in the Right of Legitimate Violence

C. Douglas Lummis

ROWMAN & LITTLEFIELD
Lanham • Boulder • New York • London

Published by Rowman & Littlefield
An imprint of The Rowman & Littlefield Publishing Group, Inc.
4501 Forbes Boulevard, Suite 200, Lanham, Maryland 20706
www.rowman.com

86-90 Paul Street, London EC2A 4NE

Chapters 5 and 6 were originally published in *Ashis Nandy: A Life in Dissent*; reproduced here courtesy of Oxford University Press, India.

An early version of the section on Gandhi in chapter 12 was published in *Alternatives*, vol. 31, no. 5; reproduced here courtesy of Sage Publications Inc.

The quotations from Max Weber (chapters 2 and 12) are from the Rodney Livingstone translation of *The Vocation Lectures*; used here courtesy of Hackett Publishing Co.

The "Soldiers' Ditty" in chapter 5 is from the David Luke translation of *Faust, Part 1*, reproduced here courtesy of Oxford University Press.

Copyright © 2023 by The Rowman & Littlefield Publishing Group, Inc.

All rights reserved. No part of this book may be reproduced in any form or by any electronic or mechanical means, including information storage and retrieval systems, without written permission from the publisher, except by a reviewer who may quote passages in a review.

British Library Cataloguing in Publication Information Available

Library of Congress Cataloging-in-Publication Data

Names: Lummis, C. Douglas, 1936- author.
Title: War is Hell / Charles Douglas Lummis.
Description: Lanham, Maryland : Rowman & Littlefield, 2023. | Series: World social change | Includes bibliographical references and index.
Identifiers: LCCN 2022038011 (print) | LCCN 2022038012 (ebook) | ISBN 9781538174203 (cloth) | ISBN 9781538174210 (paperback) | ISBN 9781538174227 (epub)
Subjects: LCSH: Peace--Philosophy. | War–Philosophy.
Classification: LCC B105.P4 L86 2023 (print) | LCC B105.P4 (ebook) | DDC 172/.42–dc23/eng/20230124
LC record available at https://lccn.loc.gov/2022038011
LC ebook record available at https://lccn.loc.gov/2022038012

Contents

Acknowledgments	vii
Introduction	xi
Chapter 1: Peace as the Original Position	1
Chapter 2: The Violent State	13
Chapter 3: Godlike Violence	29
Chapter 4: Distance and Distance-Collapse	43
Chapter 5: (Just) War Is Hell: Part I	57
Chapter 6: A Container for a Universal Solvent: (Just) War Is Hell: Part II	71
Chapter 7: The Ecstasy of War?	87
Chapter 8: SuperLeviathan: A Peaceful Use of Hell?	103
Chapter 9: SuperLeviathan Now	123
Chapter 10: Japan's Impossible Constitution	137
Chapter 11: Article 9 Meets Humpty Dumpty	149
Chapter 12: Commonsense Peace	169
Chapter 13: Final Rumination	201
Appendix: The Phenomenon of Violence	211
Bibliography	217
Index	223
World Social Change	233

Acknowledgments

I am writing this just a couple weeks before the birthday on which I will turn eighty-six. I write with mixed emotions. One of these is sadness. Most of the people to whom I owe gratitude for the things they taught me, positive or negative, have passed away long ago, before I had the opportunity to express that gratitude in proper form. But another emotion is wonder at how many worlds a person can pass through in a lifetime. My friend Jeff Lustig used to repeat the allegedly Chinese ironic curse "May you live in interesting times." The "times" from the year of my birth (1936, when Hitler was on the rise and there were show trials in Moscow) to the present (when fascism is again on the rise) have indeed been cursed, but yes, they have certainly been interesting, and I am grateful at least for that.

Here, I want to express my gratitude.

To my father, Keith Lummis, who never went to war, but whose eloquent, romantic riffs on the glories of battle talked me into the United States Marine Corps, but then over the years built up within me an immunity to such talk.

To Sergeant Mac, Sergeant Ski, and the other military instructors at Marine Corps Base Quantico in Virginia, from whom I was able to learn directly what drill instructors teach.

To Eugene Burdick, who, after I graduated from the University of California, Berkeley and entered the US Marines, kindly continued to exchange mail with me, and who for a while persuaded me that there was a liberal way to serve in the US military, for which his model was Colonel Edward Lansdale (the "Ugly American" himself). I have since developed an immunity to that sort of thinking as well.

To Sergeant Guido, and Sergeant Henley, my platoon sergeants in Okinawa from 1960 to 1961, Korean War veterans and model marines, who quietly made it clear that all they wanted was to retire before the next war started.

To then-US president Dwight Eisenhower, for his wise decision to scuttle the plan to dispatch our 1st Battalion 3rd Marines, then floating just off Saigon in a combat-loaded helicopter carrier, into Laos to join in the civil war there. This was in the first weeks of January 1961, just as he was writing his military-industrial-complex speech, and it was probably the next-to-last major decision of his presidency. The last would be his decision to send in the CIA instead, thus avoiding one disaster by setting off another.

To the students of the 1960 Anti-AMPO Struggle Generation who I met at Osaka University of Foreign Studies in 1961, who showed me what peace as common sense looks like.

To the students of the 1964 free-speech movement at UC Berkeley, who carried me with them as they became the Berkeley anti–Vietnam War movement.

To Sheldon Wolin, John Schaar, Norman Jacobson, Michael Rogin, Hanna Fenichel Pitkin, and a few others who comprised the never-quite-existent Berkeley School of Political Theory and who, among other things, developed a concept of politics not dependent on war.

To Robert Scalapino and Chalmers Johnson, whose influence was an important factor in my decision to seek employment in the Land of the Peace Constitution, not in the US.

To the loosely thrown together, unorganized organization called Beheiren (Japanese acronym for "Vietnam for the Vietnamese! Citizens' League"), which provided the subculture within which I "lived" for a number of years after 1968, and which inadvertently demonstrated that "another Japan is possible." And to mention only two members by name, to Tsurumi Shunsuke, who taught us that the movement to enforce the Japanese Peace Constitution is a movement for radical democracy, and that radical democracy is the only ideology that is radical in all existing political systems. And to Oda Makoto, who demonstrated how peace action can become a way of life.

To my colleagues and students at Tsuda College (now Tsuda University) in Tokyo, where for twenty-five years I was allowed complete freedom to teach as I liked, and where in the resulting lectures and seminars many of the themes in this book were developed.

To the people, mostly women, whom I have seen driven to tears by direct encounters with military reasoning.

To the members of the editorial committee of a volume of essays (in Japanese) on peace studies who, when I suggested that they include a study on just war theory, responded almost in unison, "What's that?" This provided the occasion for my first study on that subject, a much-expanded version of which is chapter 5 of this volume.

To Ivan Illich and the group of nonconformist scholars—gadflies all—who would gather at the study sessions he occasionally called together (in Montreal, Puerto Rico, Houston, Oakland, Tokyo, and Bremen and at Pennsylvania State University), some of which I was privileged to join. From them I learned, among other things, that "stepping outside the box," while already a trite expression, is, taken seriously, no small matter.

To the Centre for the Study of Developing Societies (CSDS), where I spent thirteen months as Rajni Kothari chair in democracy, and where I did the basic work on Gandhi that makes up most of chapter 12 of this book. I am especially grateful to the then-director, Suresh Sharma, for his patience with me, and to Ashis Nandy for his wonderful combination of passion, irony, and ability to make sense of things by standing them on their heads. And special thanks to Meeta Nath for teaching me that Gandhi was by no means a may-the-consequences-be-damned pacifist.

To Hanna Fenichel Pitkin, mentioned above, who critically read early versions of this manuscript, and whose advice to "un-blob your state" is followed in chapter 2.

To Roger Haydon of Cornell University Press, who made me aware of the importance of the United Nations Responsibility to Protect (R2P) program.

To Maja Vodopivec of Leiden University, who pointed me to the work of Roland Paris on the above subject.

To John Gittings, who carefully read this manuscript in its almost-complete form, and who informed me of the work by classicist and counselor Robert Emmet Meagher on Heracles's PTSD.

To Mark Selden, for his unfailing support and fearsome editing.

To Jeff Lustig, whose steady stream of rich wisdom and awful jokes I miss terribly.

To Frank Bardacke, who has read many versions of this manuscript, and whose advice and encouragement have been the meat and bread that kept this project going.

To Rowman & Littlefield editors Ashley Dodge, Haley White, Laney Ackley, and Chris Fischer, whose cheerful and businesslike manner of leading me through the final preparation of the manuscript has transformed that burdensome piece of work into a pleasant way to spend the time.

To Chinen Ushi, my wife, an unfailing source of good advice on all aspects of this project.

In particular, the argument at the end of chapter 11, on how Japanese illusions of peace have become entangled with their partly unconscious discrimination against Okinawans, is a perspective that she has largely developed in her writings. I am not going to thank her for "patiently bearing" my writing habits. She spends more time writing than I do.

Introduction

HELL

War is Hell.

—William Tecumseh Sherman

Day was departing, and the darkening air
   Called all earth's creatures to their evening quiet
   While I alone was preparing as though for war.

—Dante, at the entrance to hell

It was as though Christian men had turned to fiends, and hell itself had usurped the place of earth.

—Horace Porter, describing the Battle of the Wilderness

"I'm in hell," Goodrich sobbed over and over. "I'm in hell I'm in hell I'm in hell."

—James Webb, *Fields of Fire*

General Sherman's "War is Hell" is an aphorism that can be used by warriors, pacifists, and anyone in between: Like it or not, war is hell. When I was in the US Marines, I heard it often. It was a favorite among the clichés repeated by officers, serving both as a macho boast—"I have the grit to take it"—and, alternatively, as a free pass—"When war begins, we do whatever it takes to win." At the same time, by a hater of war, it can be used to express with wonderful brevity why war ought to be abolished. What is it about this expression that allows such different uses?

A "war" is a situation in which actions normally forbidden are permitted. In times of war, people are made to suffer horrors, while those who make them suffer, though subjected to danger, are not treated as criminals. Many anti-war people believe that when the horror of war has been shown, the case for pacifism has been made. The argument may be effective with people who imagine war as glorious adventure. But to say to a military man like Sherman (or an unromantic analyst like Clausewitz) that war is a horror is to repeat back to him one of his own axioms. In his address to the graduating class of the Michigan Military Academy in 1880, Sherman said, "There is many a boy here today who looks on war as all glory, but boys, it is all hell. You can bear this warning voice to generations yet to come. I look upon war with horror, but if it has to come, I am there."[1] Notice the contradiction. The "horror" of war includes the fact that it requires of us behavior we ordinarily think of as despicable. But as his "if it has to come, I am there" makes clear, Sherman considers volunteering a virtuous act.

To the military mind, the utterance "War is Hell" does not simply mean "War is all horrors." It means, "We know (better than anyone) about the horrors. The point is that war (as with hell) is the place where these horrors are permitted." It means you cannot make criticism, legal or moral, against soldiers for carrying out these acts. For Sherman, this leads, for example, to the corollary "Therefore you cannot criticize me for burning Atlanta." It is not only a negative matter, a suspension of a large part of ordinary criminal law and a large part of ordinary common sense. Volunteering to go to war and to carry out these acts is to be seen as a positive manifestation of virtue, for which one may be awarded medals.

The identification of war with hell embodies this duality; the meaning hell has for us presupposes two contradictory ethical systems, two contradictory sensitivities. To judge the behavior of hell's devils and fiends as horrific and evil presupposes an ethical sensitivity that almost all human beings share. At the same time, hell is depicted as the place where evil meets its worst enemy, which presupposes an entirely different ethical sensitivity. The ghastly tortures carried out by Satan and his subordinate fiends are authorized by the highest source of good in the universe. God can say, "Go to hell!" and the words will be sacred. But while the maker of these judgments is worshipped, those who carry them out are despised. Hell is a mechanism by which the highest good transmutes into the ultimate evil, while at the same time—mystically—maintaining its character as the highest good.

In this sense, hell represents the extreme model, the limiting case, of the concept Max Weber used to define the modern nation-state one hundred years ago: legitimate violence. This book seeks to examine, in various contexts, the structural similarities shared by these two self-contradictory (oxymoronic?) platitudes—"War is Hell" and "legitimate violence"—and to trace some of the effects that these have on our thought and behavior.

Having said that, this is a good place to allay the suspicion that this book is addressed mainly to pacifists. It is not. It is addressed to people who, though not necessarily pacifists, are yet troubled by war, and think we should have less of it or, better, none of it, if that is attainable.

That, in any case, is the thinking of its author. I respect many, though not all, of the people who call themselves pacifists. At the same time, I have never fully understood what the term means. It is not clear to me what happens to the word "peace" when you attach "ism" to it. "Peace" is the name of a certain state of society. Does adding "ism" to the word indicate a preference for that state? But you don't need to be a pacifist to entertain that preference. Does it mean the commitment to avoid violence no matter what? But if you want to build an actually existing state of peace rather than war, you will not want to use the logic of "no matter what." The preference for peace is a common-sense judgment, shared I believe by most soldiers, and realizing peace is a practical matter, something to be achieved not in abstraction, not just in one's soul, but on the ground.

THE RIGHT OF LEGITIMATE VIOLENCE

In this work, I hope to make a contribution to this project by examining, from a number of angles, the concept of legitimate violence. The right of legitimate violence, more specifically the right of belligerency, is modern warfare's grand enabling clause. But it is seldom examined in depth by political scientists, including political theorists, for whom the notion that the state is defined by its monopoly of legitimate violence is an axiom, a truth prior to examination, almost equal in certitude to "A circle is the locus of points equidistant from a given point." But its alleged certitude is of a different sort from that of a geometric axiom. The adjective "legitimate" is a value judgment, a vague one at that, that can be measured against a variety of standards. By applying to "violence," a behavior our common sense knows to be capable of great harm, the human judgment "legitimate," and then granting to that joinder the status of "axiom," we risk rendering a major sector of human experience immune to doubt, which in turn renders it immune to thought.

The definition of the state doesn't have the stability of an axiom. You can do a mental experiment. Take apart those two words that describe the state's defining characteristic, and then see what happens when you try to put them back together. What happens to the word "violence" when the adjective "legitimate" is attached to it? Does being called "legitimate" affect the nature of the action named? Does being called "legitimate" make violence less violent? Is there not something about "violence" that rejects the modifier "legitimate," like a body rejecting an inappropriate kidney transplant?

This work takes up various aspects of the concept of "legitimate violence" and the damage we do to ourselves by granting it axiomatic status.

The following is a summary of the chapters.

Chapter 1 reviews Thomas Hobbes's classic grounding of the state's right of legitimate violence on the argument that there is no other way to bring an end to the War of Each Against All. In doing so, he (and, less clearly, his predecessors) effectively defined peace as dependent on state violence: In the context of this formulation, the more fervently you want peace, the more dedicated you become to the violent state. But Hobbes's depiction of the Original Position as a state of war unintentionally points back to a yet prior position, a state of peace, taken for granted. This justifies us in positing another model to supplement that of Hobbes: the Peaceful Village as the Original Position. Taking this as an alternative "where to stand" opens up an entirely different world picture. In this picture, the acts required of us in war are not rooted in our original character as "natural man" but are entirely unnatural. Also, the state's founding myth, depicted by Hobbes as a rational choice made by people in the state of war, is seen as something imposed on the Peaceful Village by the Robber Band. This image of peace as the natural state appears in different form in Gandhi's *Hind Swaraj*.

Chapter 2 begins with a discussion of Max Weber's use of the term "legitimate violence" in his classic definition of the state, and some of the effects this has had on our political thinking and perception of political reality. In rational choice theory, "legitimate violence" can be rendered as this hypothesis: If we give that right to the state, the state will use it to reduce the number of violent deaths suffered by its people. A statistical analysis of the twentieth century suggests that this experiment has not been going well.

A linguistic analysis of the second key term in the formula—violence—in three languages shows that while the concept is used differently in these different cultures, it shows a common core in all three, as something that essentially ought not to happen. *(Being technical, the full version of this study is included as the appendix.)* This is followed by an analysis of the (very slippery) third term in Weber's definition: the state. The chapter closes with the first of two brief analyses of Weber's "Politics as a Vocation."

Some believe that contact with the sacred will reduce the amount of violence in human life. Chapter 3 reminds the reader of some of the difficulties this project faces. The poem that stands at the base of Western literature, *The Iliad*, is a tale of brutal war that the gods both watch and participate in but make no effort to bring to a peaceful end. They seem badly qualified to promote peace, as they are themselves immune to the main bad effect of war, being immortal *(athanatos)*, and enjoy mocking the warriors for being mortal *(thanatos)*. Warriors with a long string of victories entertain an illusion of *athanatos* and are described as "like gods," but when their luck ends, they experience "green fear" and "sheer death."

The main protagonist of the Old Testament, Yahweh, is an unabashed War God who gives his followers careful instructions in the rules of just massacre. The New Testament gives us precious principles of peacemaking, but soon enough the religion is transformed into a most dependable *jus ad bellum*, with Saint Augustine as the most brilliant theorist of just war.

Taking peace as the original position for our standing point enables us to see that for most people, to be able to do the work required by war, they must be changed. Enemies can be made easier to kill by elevating oneself and one's comrades to something approaching gods, or by degrading one's enemies to something less than animals (distancing). Chapter 4 takes up the latter idea. Instructing recruits in distancing is the special skill of the drill instructor (DI). Distancing is effective but fragile and, being based on a falsehood, may collapse. The terrifying discovery that the enemy is an ordinary human is a story one often hears from combat veterans. This chapter retells and analyzes a variety of such stories, both from fiction and from memory. It concludes with an account of Euripides's *Herakles*, recently rediscovered as a classic of post-traumatic stress disorder (PTSD).

If, among human behaviors, war most closely resembles hell in its horror, it is just war that most closely resembles hell as *just* horror. Chapter 5 takes up Michael Walzer's classic defense of just war against Clausewitz's (and Sherman's) critique. Can war, like a duel, be made to follow rules, or is it destined, like the pillage of a city, to explode all rules? Eloquent descriptions of both models can be found in Shakespeare's *Henry V*. The poet also shows a clear understanding of the integral role that domination of women plays in the deep structure of war.

Since Grotius, legal experts have sought to devise rules to limit war to just purposes *(jus ad bellum)* and just methods *(jus in bello)* while at the same time not spoiling the chances of their sides winning. Chapter 6 introduces some samples of the result: a hodgepodge based on differing principles (chivalry, custom, humanitarianism, rationalization, etc.) derived from different ages and always struggling against the technological improvement of weapons. We have treaties outlawing dumdum bullets but not nuclear missiles. Walzer's brave attempt at providing just war theory with a firm basis shipwrecks on his assertion that as Nazism is "absolute evil" and the British had no other effective weapons, they were justified in the area bombing of German cities at the beginning of World War II. That is, he shows us that as the value of the *jus ad bellum* increases, the motivation to place *jus in bello* limitations on your military tactics declines, to the point that it can disappear altogether. This is the reasoning of Clausewitz that Walzer had set out to refute. "Absolutely" just war is revealed as the most hellish of all.

Chapter 7 looks at the claims that war sometimes produces an ecstasy that one cannot experience in peaceful daily life. Some of these claims turn out, upon examination, to be something else: the pleasure of looting, the pleasure of a cease-fire, the pleasure of comradeship, the pleasure of reading about war, and so on. More persuasive is the argument that troops may experience a pleasure in collectively making history (especially when winning). I suggest that *if* there is a special pleasure in combat itself, it may be in the very duality of "legitimate violence." War, like martial law, is a state of exception. Giorgio Agamben points out that in the state of exception, law is not absent but present like mana—that to which this is the exception: LAW. To the soldier, killing is "the wrong permitted," a case of "getting away with murder," a superhuman act sometimes in the heat of battle resulting in an ecstatic state. Years later (for those who survive this experience), this ecstatic state typically reappears as PTSD.

Many people have proposed plans for establishing perpetual peace; many of these hobbled by accepting Hobbes's "axiom" that peace is structurally dependent on war. Chapter 8 briefly describes proposals by the Abbé de Saint-Pierre, Rousseau, and Kant, and after World War I, by Charles Clayton Morrison, Clarence K. Streit, Emery Reves, Grenville Clark, and Louis Sohn, among others. The latter all influenced the League of Nations, the Kellogg-Briand Pact, the United Nations, and the various international instruments attached to the UN, with all their strengths and weaknesses. It's well known that both the UN and the League before it were and are weakened by the refusal of the member states to grant to either the right of legitimate violence. The refusal to support the proposal to grant the UN a monopoly not only of land, sea, and air power but also of nuclear technology is understandable. In the 1930s, the conservative German political theorist Carl Schmitt argued that under such a regime, there would indeed be no war, only executions.

Chapter 9 depicts our present era as one in which the UN and the US are each seeking to evolve in the direction of SuperLeviathan, the former through treaties and initiatives such as the Responsibility to Protect (R2P) program, and the latter through military actions such as the War on Terror, neither with much success. Where this will lead us is unclear.

Chapter 10 takes up the Japanese constitution's war-renouncing Article 9, one of the most radical peace initiatives of the postwar period (and which put "legitimate violence" at the top of my list of political puzzles that need solution). Though forced on the imperial Japanese government by the Allied occupation, it was legitimized by the long struggle of the people to defend it, which, though much weakened, continues to this day.

Chapter 11 seeks to introduce some of the flavor of the prolonged struggle over the Japanese constitution: The government's "amendment by interpretation" aiming to render the rebuilding of the Japanese military legal (leaving the basic rules of language in shambles) versus the self-inventing civil society's efforts to prevent that resulted in the bizarre phenomenon of a huge, well-trained, expensively armed "military" still prevented from carrying out full-scale military action.

In the first eleven chapters, I have tried to show that the trouble with war is not that it is immoral but that all too often, the more persuasive its moral justifications, the worse it gets. While it's an excellent way to wreck everything, it's a poor way to get things done. In chapter 12, I support this argument by comparing the theories of power of two unlikely partners in theory, Hannah Arendt and Mohandas Gandhi. Arendt's *On Violence* is well known; Gandhi's *Hind Swaraj* is less so, at least in military studies. The former supports her story of civil disobedience against the Nazis in Denmark; the latter supports Gandhi's invention of the Self-Limiting Revolution in India. As the best way to express Gandhi's notion of power, I have put it in the form of a story focusing on some of the lesser known events of his life: his beginning as a British-trained lawyer, his experiment with self-limiting revolution (1921), his virtually unknown constitutional proposal (autonomous village republics), his refusal to take any role in the independent government of India being planned by his disciples, and his proposal that the Congress Party dissolve and its members return to the countryside to build a nation of village republics (formally proposed just hours before he was assassinated).

Chapter 13 consists of a discussion of some of the conclusions that can be drawn from the points made in the first twelve chapters. Peace is not something we learn from the gods, nor is it one of the Ten Commandments; rather, it is plain common sense, the human thing.

The chapter—and the book—concludes with a second brief essay on Weber, arguing that it was his misunderstanding of the nature of public power that led him to "legitimize" the monopoly of violence of the state.

NOTE

1. William Tecumseh Sherman, *Columbus Mileposts*, August 11, 1880, quoted in *Columbus Dispatch* (August 11, 2012).

Chapter 1

Peace as the Original Position

> *[In the Natural State, men]* use violence, to make themselves masters of other men's persons, wives, children, and cattle.
>
> —Thomas Hobbes

PEACE AS SUCCESSFUL PACIFICATION

To understand the phenomenon of war, one must also understand the situation called peace. In the word's most ordinary usage, to be at peace means military action is neither taking place nor immediately expected. In that meaning, there are large areas of the world that are at peace. Peace thus understood can be described as "that state of society that exists between wars." It is the state of society that, as the military planners promise, is *created* by war—either by the signing of a peace treaty or by the successful "pacification" of an enemy—and is *maintained* by the threat of war. And while there are a few people who disagree with this (weapons merchants or those who enjoy wars vicariously), most people see the periods between wars as preferable to the wars themselves, and consider the efforts to make them last honorable work.

However, Thomas Hobbes, surely one of the greatest philosophers of peace (I'll defend that assertion below), gave us a definition that, while still defining peace as not-war, is more detailed. "For WAR, consisteth not in battle only, or in the act of fighting, but in the tract of time wherein the will to contend by battle is sufficiently known. . . . So the nature of war, consisteth not in actual fighting, but in the known disposition thereto, during all the time there is no assurance to the contrary. All other time is PEACE."[1]

To which we may ask, *What* other time? For us living in modern states, there is no such time in living memory, nor was there in Hobbes's seventeenth-century England. If we wish to study peace, where can we look?

True, there have been periods when people believed they were living in such an "other time," and the belief gave them happiness and hope, but as the historical record shows, the belief has repeatedly proved an illusion. Within the society believed to be peaceful, the seeds of war were germinating. In Hobbes's words, "the will to contend by battle" had never gone away nor had preparations been abandoned. The operating principle is expressed in the ancient Roman adage "If you want peace, prepare for war." In this time of peace, soldiers drill, weapons are manufactured, strategies are planned, military-style patriotism is propagated, past wars are glorified, and children (mostly boys) are given toy soldiers and guns to play with.

Hobbes, allegedly the most realistic of realist philosophers, defined true peace as a state in which all of this has gone away. Was he, behind all his tough-minded, sometimes chilling reasoning, a secret dreamer? Or was his intention by defining peace in its pure state to relegate it to the land of fantasy and render it unworthy of serious consideration? Or was it that this philosopher who placed such great value on reason was forced to adopt this definition for the sake of logical consistency? Whichever the case, what is interesting here is that when the word "peace" takes on this meaning, it evaporates. For if there were no war and no rumors of war, the word "peace" would not be needed; some expression like "daily life" would do.

THE ORIGINAL POSITION

There is no danger, however, of the word "peace" falling out of use anytime soon; in the world we live in, the absence of war and how to achieve that absence are issues of desperate importance and need a name. But given the importance of peace, it's remarkable that the subject is surrounded by taboos. What is it that people find frightening about the notion that peace could be made into a lasting system, rather than "the time between wars"? The resistance is not against the idea that war is a horror—everyone (well, almost) knows that. The resistance is against the idea that it might be unnecessary. But rather than taking up the question of whether perpetual peace is a realistic possibility, here I want to begin by proposing that there is value in conceiving a model of a stable warless state, apart from whether such a state can easily be achieved.

There is precedent for this. There are many concepts in political theory that depict model situations that in their pure form do not, never did, and never could exist, yet teach us important things about the world that does exist. There is Plato's image of the ideal polis in *The Republic*; there is Thomas More's utopia; there is the state of nature of Thomas Hobbes and that of John Locke; there is Rousseau's natural man; there is Adam Smith's economic man; there are the models and ideal types used by contemporary sociologists, economists, and political scientists. On the subject we are addressing here, war and peace, probably the most influential model has been Hobbes's image of the state of nature as a war of each individual person against every other, an utterly intolerable situation that can, Hobbes argues, be escaped only by establishing a Leviathan state with power enough to "keep the peace." Hobbes depicts this state of war as both miserable and ignominious. As he famously put it, people in that situation will have "no knowledge of the face of the earth; no account of time; no arts; no letters; no society, and which is worst of all continual fear, and danger of violent death."[2] His eloquence is persuasive, but labeling this "the state of nature" is misleading. In analyzing the human, the distinction between nature and artifice is important, but to suppose that the boundary between them corresponds to the boundary between war and peace is too simple. If the human has such a thing as a "nature," it is, as we can learn from Locke or Marx (or from daily experience), that of worker, whose work produces an environment of nature and artifice mixed together with complexity that defies disentangling. War itself, after all, is fought with weapons, which are not found in nature. A tree branch is not a club until someone wields it as such.

Put differently, Hobbes's list of things people in the natural state (assuming there ever were such beings) would lack is not a list of things they would miss. It is, however, a list of things knowledgeable people in the seventeenth century (for example, Hobbes's readers) were likely quite proud of and would have hated to lose. Consider these: "No knowledge of the face of the earth" (this was the middle of the age of exploration; Jamestown was founded when Hobbes was nineteen); "no account of time" (Hobbes met and conversed with Galileo in the 1630s, just when the latter was constructing the world's first clock escarpment); "no arts" (Rembrandt was Hobbes's contemporary); "no letters" (Shakespeare's works were completed and the King James Bible was published in Hobbes's lifetime). As for the "danger of violent death," this was certainly something the seventeenth-century English had very much to fear, but the civil war that caused that fear was motivated by a sophisticated set of ethical and theological distinctions produced through centuries of debate, very much a product of society.

Demonstrating that the war of each against all never existed and never could in any lasting form is no refutation of Hobbes. What matters is that we can imagine it "breaking out," like a riot perhaps, which strikes fear in us and provides the nudge that begins a mental experiment. We can then ask: How do things look from there? Or ask Hobbes's specific question: How would a peace enforced by an all-powerful Leviathan state look from there? And the answer is: Not bad at all. Not by any means an idyllic utopia; sovereign power, Hobbes shows persuasively, can be hurtful but, he says with his wonderful bluntness, "not so hurtful as the want of it."[3]

This way of framing the question—how can we establish a state of peace?—and then answering it—only by establishing a sovereign power that will force us to be peaceful—has had immense influence in shaping the modern world. Hobbes did not invent it, but he put it into a nightmarish form that seems to obliterate all other considerations. This image—call it the Leviathan solution—is at the foundation of the modern state, at the foundation of the science of that state (political science), at the foundation of both the study and the practice of international relations as well as the rules intended to regulate those relations (international law). In each of these spheres, "not so hurtful as the want of it" is the principle that sweeps away all objections.

The notion of legitimate violence has existed from ancient times, in a multitude of forms, religious and secular. In modern Western political theory, it takes its shape from Hobbes's image of "war of each against all." Hobbes didn't use the term "legitimate violence," but he used a version of the concept. In his logicomythic account of the transition from the state of nature to the state of society, the state of nature is prior to the introduction of enforceable law, and is therefore a situation in which, legally, nothing is forbidden. With nothing forbidden, each person has a right to everything, which is another way of describing the state of war among everybody. But, Hobbes tells us, while there is no positive law to regulate people's behavior, God's law still applies, and human beings, being endowed with reason, are aware of this. Not being wild animals, they are cursed with the knowledge of good and evil, and this is a big part of what makes the state of nature miserable. The situation is impossible: The "forbidden" is not only permitted but also unavoidable. To escape this situation, the people must hand over their "right to everything" to a single person or body, empowering that person or body to make positive law and to enforce it: This act establishes Leviathan. This right is not something new; it's the right everyone already had in the state of nature, which everyone but Leviathan gave away. Thus, it preserves the dual character of behavior that prevailed in the earlier condition: the forbidden permitted, but now permitted to only Leviathan and those people acting under Leviathan's authority (police, soldiers, judges, jailers, and executioners): It is their violence that is legitimate.

It is clear from Hobbes's description that his natural man has been blooded. He has done what it takes to enable himself to kill other humans. Hobbes doesn't argue that killing comes naturally and easily to natural man. God's law applies in the natural condition but is impossible to carry out if you want to survive. The people know what is good behavior, but the situation makes it impossible to act on that knowledge. Thus, the war of each against all begins to look less like the "original" human situation; it has within it the vestiges of a previous situation, the situation people were in before they changed themselves into beings capable of killing their own kind.

Was it intentional or in a fit of absentmindedness that Hobbes, in *Leviathan*, mentioned in passing that "natural man" has a wife and children?[4] From this, we learn that in the war of each against all, the combatants are male heads of households, and that behind each is a family. And we are reminded that each head of household was fed and raised from infancy mainly by a mother and presumably initiated by a father into the methods of killing. If the war of each and all had been between men and women, or between mothers and their children, the human race would have been long extinct.

THE RIGHT TO MAKE PROMISES

In his "Genealogy of Morals," Nietzsche asks, "To breed an animal with the right to make promises—is that not the paradoxical problem nature has set itself with regard to man?"[5]

Without getting entangled in the bramblebush of the "Genealogy," we may ask, Is this not also the paradoxical problem raised by Hobbes's model of the transition from original war to Leviathan peace? In his telling, the transition is achieved by means of a contract, that is, a promise. But if the original position is as Hobbes describes it—no arts, no culture, no society, and certainly (though Hobbes doesn't use the word) no civility—why would the people living in it be qualified to make promises, or even have any understanding of what the word "promise" means? Promises presuppose language ("doing what you said you would do," "keeping your word") but how would it be possible for people with "no society" to have language?

To this, Hobbes does have an answer. In *Man and Citizen*, he states that language gives us, among other things, the ability to "command and understand commands."[6] We can imagine how a population in a state of war of each against all might develop into a "society" organized on the master-slave principle and in turn develop a language of command and obedience. But such a society would have no need of a word for "promise," not having the practice, described by Nietzsche not as obeying under coercion but as "a continuing to will what one has willed, a veritable 'memory of the will.'"[7] To people living in the state of nature as Hobbes described it, the proposal to form a social contract would be incomprehensible. Or perhaps they would take it to mean, "Let us all make ourselves slaves under a Great Master." Of course, in some actual cases, that reading might accurately reflect the nature of the contract. But if we assume that Hobbes intended to propose a society based on a contract or promise properly so called, that means he assumed that the people in the state of nature understood what that would entail, which they could do only if they had had the experience of making promises and—at least sometimes—keeping them. Promises, after all, are a method for creating and maintaining order without use or threat of violence—a method of peace essential to the forming of society needed, as Plato pointed out, by even a robber band.

These considerations make it possible for us to posit another original position, logically and developmentally "prior" to the war of each against all. We can propose that, at least as a model, the transition that matters is not that from war to peace but that from peace to war. An image (primal memory?) of that experience is preserved in the myths of the expulsion from the Garden of Eden, the transition from the Golden Age to the Iron Age (as well as the memory each of us has of our early childhood), where an "original position" is depicted as a place where violence is unknown.

Hobbes's image is not a myth but a model. Though he says the people living in his state of nature have "no society," we see that they must. Without the experience of peaceful human relations, the people he depicts as living in the state of nature could not understand the things he wants them to understand or do the things he wants them to do. It is not a peace that depends upon the violence of Leviathan but rather a peace that is the necessary condition for this two-legged animal to develop itself into a human being. To the objection: Impossible! I have already given my answer. This is not a historical description but a model, as is Hobbes's war of each against all. The fact that Hobbes's model is flagrantly impossible has not prevented it from becoming a foundational concept in modern political theory. So, the impossibility of a naturally peaceful human society *(should it indeed turn out to be impossible)* does not detract from its usefulness as a model. It makes possible certain mental experiments: To people in that situation, what would our world look like? Might they not see things in it that are hidden to us or at least difficult to notice? How would the modern state appear to them? What would international relations, international law, look like? What would the soldier look like? And from that position, what would those people choose? Would they choose Leviathan? And were Leviathan to be established, what would they need to do to themselves to become its citizens?

Imagining peace as the original position raises other questions. If one takes as the starting point Hobbes's image of a war of each against all, establishing Leviathan is, for him, establishing a state of peace. This peace is achieved when Leviathan succeeds in monopolizing the right of legitimate violence. But the question arises, Who or what legitimizes this legitimacy? On what authority can Leviathan claim to possess the right to kill? Hobbes argues that it is the social contract: The people in the state of nature have the right of violence, which they hand over to Leviathan. But in his telling, in the state of nature, the people have no *positive* right, it's just that without law, there is nothing to forbid them. There is no person or body with the authority to pronounce their killing each other just, nor is there one with the authority to pronounce it unjust. People surely know well the suffering this situation produces, but on the ethical and legal question, there is only nothingness. Hobbes says that each person "has" the right of self-defense, but if we look carefully at each of these "rights," we see that what they amount to is, in Hobbes's felicitous phrase, "the silence of the law." Collecting all these silences and handing them over to Leviathan may produce a great clamor, but still cannot be heard. Hobbes understandably supplements this by saying that God's law applies in the state of nature, but only in conscience, so that no one is actually obligated to obey it. In the state of nature, anything goes, but God's law is there, waiting in the wings as it were, looking forward to the day when Leviathan appears and creates a situation in which law can be safely obeyed—and in the meantime torturing the consciences of the natural men and women.

On the other hand, if we posit peace as the original condition, the picture changes. First of all, the legitimacy problem disappears. We needn't search for an authority to establish peace. We don't need to justify it. We don't need the expression "legitimate peace." Secondly, seen against the background of the state of peace, the founding of Leviathan reveals another side. Rather than the establishment of peace, it becomes a declaration of war—the establishment of peace *itself* becomes a declaration of war: the primal war of the state, the war by which Leviathan "pacifies" the territory over which it is to rule. In this primal war, the rules are different from those that apply in a war between states, but the goal of Leviathan is to establish itself as the sole possessor of the right of legitimate violence, which if successful establishes it as "the state."

In this telling of the story, "legitimacy," rather than something the people create, becomes something of which the people need to be persuaded, and the social contract becomes a PR device useful in persuading them: It becomes propaganda. Incidentally, this brings the story closer to the way Max Weber, who gave us the term "legitimate violence," tells it. Weber is careful to avoid seeming to claim that the state's violence *is* legitimate, and he prefers the expression "(believed to be) legitimate." (See chapter 2.)

In the real world of state-building, these two differing stories unfold together: Typically for some, the state is the welcome result of a contract, or at least of consent, while for others it is the force by which they have been defeated. In the years since World War II, as peoples carved up by colonialism struggle to organize themselves into units that all or most can accept, this contradiction has resulted in bitter and bloody wars between the state and the people. But even the 1776 independence movement in North America, celebrated as the birth of government by consent, had both aspects. The Declaration of Independence amounted to a declaration that the colonies were assuming the right of legitimate violence against England, which could also be used against royalists (it is said that 30,000 refugees fled the country), whiskey tax rebels, anti-federalists, slaves, and native Americans.

But here the discussion is focused not on the historical record but on the peace-as-original-position model. To picture that model, we need a more vivid image. Let me propose two: the first, the Peaceful Village; the second, the Peace of Daily Life.

THE PEACEFUL VILLAGE

Imagine a village sufficiently isolated that the government of whatever state (or kingdom or duchy or caliphate or empire) it is located in has not paid it much attention, or perhaps lost track of it altogether. It is not a utopia; the people there are ordinary—think of them as being much like the people you know. They quarrel, they gossip, they say nasty things about one another sometimes, they apologize and make up. It is also not Eden; they are aware of the existence of war. But they haven't experienced war or fear of war in living memory. I won't offer an analysis of why that is so, except to say that it is not because they believe in some extreme anti-war religion or philosophy. They just haven't had a war, either among themselves or against an outsider. Perhaps they find war vulgar. Perhaps they think of it the way we think of cannibalism, as simply out of the question. Perhaps they understand that it is an inefficient way for people to settle their differences. Perhaps it is just part of their unexamined common sense. Or perhaps it was an accident of history; they just never thought of it. But for whatever reason, it looks as though that situation is going to continue for them in the foreseeable future.

Again, whether such a village ever existed is not the issue here. What matters is that we can imagine it without violating our understanding of what human beings are. We can imaginatively people it with men and women we know, and we can imagine the villagers having experiences that overlap, to some degree, the experiences of our own daily lives.

Think of these villagers as witnesses to the situation we find ourselves in today. Think of them as located in a valley from which they can observe our mountain. In the following chapters, I will discuss some of the ways that war has pervaded our society, our institutions, our ways of thinking, our souls. In doing so, I will try to describe these as they might appear under the villagers' naive, severe gaze. I ask the reader to help me by keeping that gaze in mind.

One way the above model differs from that of Hobbes is that it is static. His is constructed so as to develop "naturally" into the stage that follows. The seeds of the next stage are planted within it. It inexorably yields Leviathan. The Village, the state of peace described above, is not going anywhere. It is not an unfolding story. To give it story form, we must give it an additional actor.

THE PEACEFUL VILLAGE (2): ENTER THE ROBBER BAND

To the valley where the village lies, there comes a robber band. As robbers, these people produce nothing and depend for their livelihood on stealing. Of course, to survive and be effective, they will have agreed to some rules of fair dealing internally—rules for distribution of the loot and so on. But their relationship with the villagers is that of robbers: The villagers are there to be stolen from. As the robbers are rational robbers, they don't massacre the villagers or destroy the village. To do so would be to destroy their economic base: Without a reasonably prosperous village, there would be little to steal.

For their part, the villagers, being peaceable, hide their grain and other wealth as best they can, and flee until the robbers leave. When the robbers are gone, the villagers return and go back to work.

In this world, there is no such thing as "legitimate violence." The villagers don't use violence, and both the villagers and the robbers understand the robbery and its accompanying violence as "robbery" and "violence" (again, within the robber band, both are forbidden).

One can imagine these two forces striking a balance and continuing indefinitely—an ecology of productive labor and robbery. But there are several ways it might change. The robber band might decide that rather than periodic raids, it would be more efficient to conquer the village and rule the villagers directly. We could call this the institutionalization, followed by the gradual legitimation, of robbery (Johan Galtung's "institutional violence").[8]

Alternatively, several of the robbers might break with the band and offer to protect the villagers against the band's remaining members if the villagers will give them the food and other goods that they had been stealing, thus removing the need for disruptive raids. If the villagers accept this risky offer, they will be hiring robbers to protect themselves against robbers, counting on the violent to protect themselves against the violent. Later they will be told, and perhaps persuaded, that they are being protected from each other. In this way, violence takes over and works its way into what had been a peaceable world.

I am not interested here in making the case that the villagers ought not to accept this offer. I only want to point out some of the consequences that will follow if they do. With this move, something new will be introduced into their world, that paradox called legitimate violence. In Hobbes's version of this founding myth, in the beginning violence is all there is, and the social contract radically reduces it, creating a situation in which the sovereign's monopoly of legitimate violence is, while hurtful, "not so hurtful as the want of it." In the village version of the founding myth, the beginning is peace, and violence is an interloper and a destroyer, forcing changes in people's ways of thinking and acting, and disfiguring human society. Legitimacy has been bestowed on behavior that everyone had understood as crime. Calling it legitimate changes its status in society, but not its nature as human behavior. A terrible puzzle has been placed at the heart of their society that will plague their history from then on.

But of course where I write "their history," I mean "our history." Because however it got there, this oxymoron has worked its way into the very center of the institutions of modern life. What follows in this book will be an exploration of some of the variations this paradox has taken and some of the consequences it has produced.

THE PEACE IN DAILY LIFE

Mohandas Gandhi's *Hind Swaraj* takes the form of a conversation between the Editor and the Reader. When the Editor talks about nonviolent methods of problem-solving, the Reader asks (as people so often do) if there is any record in history of nonviolent methods actually succeeding. The Editor answers, "History, as we know it, is a record of the wars of the world. . . . How kings played, how they became enemies of one another and how they murdered one another is found accurately recorded in history, and if this were all that had happened in the world, it would have been ended long ago."[9] The beauty of this exchange is that it makes nonviolence into an everyday matter. In Gandhi's view, it is what most of us practice most of the time. Even in the most violent of times, it is our nonviolent customs and practices that enable us to survive those times. We have arguments and disagreements, but we don't often fight to the death about them. We talk, shout maybe, maneuver, and use all sorts of devices to get our way, but we don't typically kill each other. Hobbes would say that this is because we fear punishment by Leviathan, but is it? Are we really all murderers prevented from murdering only by self-interested fear of the law? In this passage, Gandhi is saying that we are not. The ordinary daily life of most human beings, most of the time, is nonviolent. This is his answer, or one of his answers, to the question I raised above: Where can we look to find peace? We can find it, or at least one form of it, in our own experience. It is that which makes social life possible.

This is the argument—or very close to the argument—that Socrates famously used to force the submission of the cynical Thrasymachus in Plato's *Republic*: justice among thieves. Thrasymachus argues that injustice is the source of power, against which Socrates asks, "Do you believe that a city, or an army, or pirates, or robbers, or any other tribe which has some common unjust enterprise would be able to accomplish anything, if its members acted unjustly to one another?" To which Thrasymachus can only answer, "Surely not."[10] The big difference is that Socrates is talking about justice while Gandhi is talking about nonviolence. But each in his own way is pointing out that it is not through war that Homo sapiens form themselves into human society, but rather through the infinitely complex network of habits and behaviors by which we learn to get along. Peace is the condition for being human at all. The trouble is we live inside large organizations that maintain themselves in a state of war—some of them states, some robber bands, and some hard to tell which—and transform us, or operate to transform us, into warriors.

Later in his life, Gandhi chose the Indian village as a possible model for a peaceful and self-sufficient society. I shall have more to say about this in the final chapter.

NOTES

1. Thomas Hobbes, *Leviathan: or The Matter, Forme and Power of a Commonwealth Ecclesiastical and Civil*, ed. Michael Oakeshott (New York: Collier Books, 1962), 100.

2. Hobbes, *Leviathan*, 100.

3. Hobbes, *Leviathan*, 141.

4. Hobbes, *Leviathan*, 99.

5. Friedrich Nietzsche, "The Genealogy of Morals," in *The Birth of Tragedy and the Genealogy of Morals*, trans. Francis Golffing (New York: Doubleday, 1956), 189.

6. Thomas Hobbes, *Man and Citizen*, ed. Sterling P. Lamprecht (Westport: Greenwood Press, 1982 [orig. 1642]), 39.

7. Nietzsche, "The Genealogy," 190.

8. Johan Galtung, *Peace by Peaceful Means* (London: Sage Publications, 1996), 187–99.

9. M. K. Gandhi, *Hind Swaraj*, eds. Suresh Sharma and Tridip Suhrud (New Delhi: Orient Blackstone, 2010), 72–3.

10. Plato, *The Republic of Plato*, trans. Allan Bloom (New York: Basic Books, 1968), 351a–352d.

Chapter 2

The Violent State

> Anyone can see that aggressive Princes wage war at least as much on their subjects as on their enemies.
>
> —Rousseau

THE OXYMORONIC STATE

The term "legitimate violence" was given us around a century ago by the German sociologist Max Weber. Weber characterized the state as a social organization that successfully claims, within a given territory, *"Monopol legitimer Gewáltsamkeit,"* generally translated as "a monopoly of legitimate physical violence."[1] The formulation is puzzling. On the one hand, "legitimate violence" reads like a contradiction, leading some translators to soften it by rendering *Gewalt* as "force." On the other hand, the notion has become so widely accepted that doubting it seems like doubting reason itself, and even trying to think about what it means requires mental effort. That the state is a violent organization, and that its violence, when exercised according to the law, is legitimate, is the axiom upon which modern politics is built. This axiom has worked its way into the consciousness of the general public (except for a few anarchists and pacifists) as common sense. We all know that when, in the name of the state, authorities force people to pay fines, the police beat people with clubs in the line of duty, the judge orders people to prison, the executioner hangs or poisons people, and the military drops bombs on cities, none of these is a crime.

We know these things, but what does this knowing mean? If knowing is an act of the mind, what sort of act is it to "know" that a military bombing is not murder? What are we *doing* (and *doing to ourselves*) when we "know" these things? Is not this "knowing" a form of "not knowing"? Is it not a "knowing" that requires a forgetting? A "knowing" that, instead of putting us in touch with the reality of the world, renders part of that reality invisible?

In the 1934 edition of the *Encyclopedia of the Social Sciences*, the entry "Violence"—written by Sidney Hook—begins with the sentence, "In the social context violence may be defined roughly as the illegal employment of methods of physical coercion for personal or group ends." If so, Weber's term becomes an oxymoron—"legal illegality." Replacing "violence" with "force" would ease the contradiction: Force is not illegal by definition. Strictly speaking, neither is violence—Professor Hook was wrong about that—but still, "force" is the milder term. Using it reduces the shock value of Weber's expression. I believe that the contradiction—the *absurdity*—of the expression was intentional. Weber—who with his extraordinary ability to view things from multiple perspectives surely knew well how things look from the Village—saw a contradiction in the politics of the state and coined a term that would correspond to that contradiction. The absurdity in the term reflects the absurdity in the thing. He hoped thereby to help us see that absurdity.

The legitimate violence allowed the state takes three forms: police action (to be used to prevent crimes), punitive action (which the police shouldn't have, though some police agents seem not to realize that), and belligerency. This right to beat, shoot, detain, and sometimes hang or gas people is held not by the individual officer of the law, judge, jailer, executioner, or soldier but rather by his or her office; it is a right that the individual government employee exercises as the state's representative. Through the magic hidden in the words "office" and "representative," the individual government functionary is rendered guiltless for what he or she has done, and that five-word sentence that defines the age of bureaucracy is born: "I'm just doing my job." This innocence is legal, social, and moral: The officer is not to be arrested, is not to be socially condemned, and need not feel guilty.

THE MAGICAL STATE

Let's walk more slowly through some of the effects of this "legitimate." Under the state's power of punishment, the state's representatives may force people to hand over money (fines), lock them up in metal rooms (imprisonment), or, in many jurisdictions, kill them (execution). For a private person, taking money by force would be robbery or extortion, confining a person against his or her will would be kidnapping, and killing someone would be murder. And while it is "the state" that has the authority to do these things legally, the state is an abstraction that can't "do" anything; the acts themselves must be carried out by people. In the case of execution, someone must pull the trigger on the gun, push the button that releases the trap door under the noose, or close the switch that sends the electricity or the poison gas. In the case of firing squads, sometimes one rifle is loaded with blanks so that each of the executioners can take comfort in the possibility that his or her rifle was the one not loaded. Similarly, it is said that in the case of hanging, electrocuting, or gassing, sometimes several dummy buttons or switches are prepared in addition to the one that actually brings about the death. But however the execution is done, in governments that have not abolished the death penalty, there are public employees whose job descriptions include killing people, and these employees are not to be condemned legally or morally. Still, the use of dummy buttons and blank ammunition suggests that even though the action is taken under the authority of the state, executioners may sometimes have trouble sleeping at night.

The right of belligerency is the right of soldiers to kill, wound, and capture people, and to destroy property, in wartime. It may sound strange to call this a right, but from the standpoint of the soldier, it is a right of vital importance. It is what makes war possible. Imagine the situation of the soldiers if, after obeying their government's order to go off to a foreign country and make war, upon returning they were arrested for murder. Under working conditions like that, who would go to war? The right of the soldiers to kill is protected by domestic and international law. Soldiers who are captured by the enemy cannot legally be punished for what they did, so long as they have followed the laws of war, committing no war crimes. If you are a soldier and capture the enemy soldier who threw the bomb that killed your brother, you may not harm that person, but must protect, feed, and give medical care to him or her as a prisoner of war. And when the war ends, prisoners of war are to be returned to their home countries unharmed, where they are usually welcomed as heroes. (I understand that these rules, never fully enforced, have largely collapsed since the beginning of the "War on Terror." I shall discuss that in chapter 9.)

This is the magic of the state, the magic by which evoking "the state" transforms action A into action B, without changing its nature as an act. It is a magic that has worked its way into the consciousness of each of us. When we read in the newspaper that some high school students have brought guns onto their school campus and shot dead four or five people, we are horrified. What, we wonder, could have motivated them to do such a thing? Were they mentally ill? Were they possessed by a demon? Were they captured by some evil ideology? Such behavior makes us feel despair for the human race. But when we read in the next day's paper that our troops (also mostly teenagers) killed a few score people in whatever war we are presently fighting, we may sigh, but we feel no such horror. When the troops return from this work, we do not shun them but welcome them and wish them well. And we have in the world today presidents, prime ministers, and generals responsible for the deaths of thousands and tens of thousands of people; when they appear smiling on television, we are not revolted; we do not call up the station and protest the presentation of mass murderers as if they were respectable citizens.

This is the magic by which the name of the state transforms horrors into administrative acts. I do not understand how this works; that is, I do not understand the psychological mechanism, the magic, by which the state persuades us, when we are looking at phenomenon A, to see phenomenon B. Yet it works, though never perfectly: There are times, often years later, when the people who were persuaded to take what they believed were administrative acts find those acts returning in their dreams, as horrors.

LEGITIMATE VIOLENCE: THE HYPOTHESIS

There is another question here that is easier to answer: Why do we give this right—the right of legitimate violence—to the state in the first place? I say "we" because according to the dominant political theory today, state power is derived from the consent of the people, which would mean the state has only the powers given it by the people, and no more. Or if you don't believe that, as a historical fact, the people "gave" the state its powers, the question can be rephrased: How did we come to be persuaded that the state's violence is legitimate? The answer is simple and, in both political theory and common sense, well known. We are persuaded that this arrangement will make the world a safer place to live in. According to this idea, the state will use its right of violence to protect us, internationally from foreigners, domestically from one another.

In chapter 1, I gave a brief outline of what I believe to be the clearest statement of that position, that of Thomas Hobbes, and there is no need to repeat that here. But it is important to remember that at the time Hobbes wrote this, he was not describing empirical fact but proposing a hypothesis yet to be tested. According to him, no state of the sort he described as Leviathan, built on the theoretical foundation he presented, yet existed.

> There be also [those] that maintain, that there are no grounds, nor principles of reason, to sustain those essential rights, which make sovereignty absolute. For if there were, they would have been found out in some place, or other; whereas we see, there has not hitherto been any commonwealth, where those rights have been acknowledged, or challenged. Wherein they argue as ill, as if the savage people of America, should deny there were any grounds, or principles of reason, so to build a house, as to last as long as the materials, because they never yet saw any so well built.[2]

It is possible to interpret world political history since then as the gradual penetration of Hobbes's "grounds and principles of reason" into every corner of the globe. Following his metaphor, the twentieth century was a veritable housing boom of modern sovereign nation-states. At the beginning of that century, there existed some fifty sovereign nation-states; today there are around two hundred (depending on how you count). There is hardly a community or an individual anywhere who does not live under the rule of a state claiming this monopoly of legitimate violence. Of course, there are a few states that have not been successful in this claim. These are what have come to be called, in recent years, the "failed states." What exactly have they failed at? In Hobbes's terms, they have failed to make state sovereignty absolute; in Weber's terms, they have failed to achieve a monopoly of (believed-to-be) legitimate violence. There, "the primal war of the state," the war by which the state seeks to achieve its domination over the people, continues. Some may say these are the very cases that prove the wisdom of Thomas Hobbes: However it is achieved, absolute sovereignty is the only road to peace. But the matter is not so simple.

LEGITIMATE VIOLENCE: THE GRAND EXPERIMENT

The twentieth century, then, can be thought of as a one-hundred-year, world-scale experiment to test Hobbes's hypothesis. Restating the hypothesis in its simplest form—the form in which ordinary people are persuaded by it—it is that if we allow the state the exclusive right to use violence, it will use that right to protect us. It will use the right of belligerency to protect us against foreigners, and it will use the police and judicial powers to protect us against one another. This is the "social contract" that produces the modern state. It is not a social contract that asks much. It does not aim to found a utopia, or to rid the world entirely of violence. What we hope is only that the number of violent deaths be reduced. It seems like political realism itself.

In the twentieth century, based on this hope, nation after nation, including those liberating themselves from colonialism, established sovereign states, giving—or allowing—those states the right of legitimate violence. In hindsight, how does it look?

In the twentieth century, did the state succeed in protecting its citizens?

Did the level of violence go down?

Did the number of violent deaths decrease, compared to previous centuries?

You do not need to be a scholar of history to know the answers to these questions. They are written in giant letters across the face of history. They are known to virtually everyone, though their significance is acknowledged by few. The three relevant facts are as follows.

1. More people died violent deaths in the twentieth century than in any comparable period in the history of the human race.
2. The big killer has not been the Mafia, not the yakuza, not robbers, not jealous lovers, not even psychopathic serial killers. The big killer has been the state. According to the research of R. J. Rummel, the courageous political scientist who assigned himself the grisly task of counting the bodies, the state (as of 1994) had killed 169,198,000 people in the twentieth century.[3] I have not attempted to verify this astounding statistic. Perhaps Rummel was a great exaggerator, though his statistical methods, as he describes them, seem sound. But even if you reduce his figure by half, the conclusion is the same.
3. Most of the people the state has killed are its own people. If the state killed mostly foreigners, then even though the death toll is fearsome, we could at least say that the state is trying to fulfill its promise to its citizens. But this is not the case. According to Rummel, in the twentieth century (again, up to 1994), the state had killed 134,756,000 of its own citizens, as compared to 68,452,000 foreigners.[4] Of course, in the twentieth century, there were some monster governments—notably Stalinist USSR, Nazi Germany, and Mao's China—that skew the statistics. But again, even adjusting for that, the conclusion does not change. As we know from the daily newspaper, most of the wars going on today are between states and their people, or a part of their people, or people they want (or don't want) to be their people. There are countries in the world whose militaries seem to have no other purposes, no other strategies, and no other hypothetical enemies. Why, we wonder, should a small country have a military at all when it hasn't got the resources to build one that could win a foreign war? Rummel's statistics suggest an answer: The primary target of the state's military is not some other country. The primary war is against the state's own people.

The experiment is not going well.

As I wrote in the introduction, I believe that in thinking about peace, it is best to steer clear of utopian idealism and assume the position of political realism. When it is a question of protecting ourselves from violent death, most of us will want to adopt the strategy that has the best chance of success. By all means, let us be realists. To be a realist, the first thing one need do is look at reality. In this case, the reality that matters is the historical record. The historical record tells us that by giving the state the right of legitimate violence—the license to kill—we have created the greatest mass killer in the history of the human race. Can it be called realism to imagine that this mass killing machine, given its record so far, can be trusted to protect us in the future? Or is this not the most dangerous form of starry-eyed romanticism, *state-romanticism*?

It is true that there are differences among states. As Rummel's statistics show, authoritarian states kill more than representative democracies, and totalitarian states kill more than authoritarian states. Moreover, the representative democracies don't often fight wars with one another.[5] For Rummel, this is the important lesson to be learned from the statistics, and I agree with him that this is a good reason to continue the struggle for democracy everywhere in the world. But it is important not to get starry-eyed about the representative democracies. After all, in the twentieth century, the representative democracies did not hesitate to carry out mass killings in their colonies, and against countries with other forms of government, and it is only representative democracies that have carried out firestorm and atomic bombings of cities.[6]

It should be mentioned that in the twentieth century, some revolutionary and independence movements, groups that are not states, claimed for themselves the right of belligerency, and that in some cases this right has been recognized internationally. But these groups expect either to seize the state or to form a new state in the future; their right of belligerency is the state's right, which they are applying to themselves in advance, as it were.

It also is true that in the twenty-first century, we have seen not a new form but the reappearance of a very old form of the claim to legitimate violence. This is the violence of religious groups that claim the authority of their god. I think the Villagers will find it strange that people who believe they have been commanded by a supernatural being to kill people should conclude that this being is a god rather than a demon. But the tradition is old, in the West going back to the Old Testament and before. It may be, as Carl Schmitt has suggested, that the state borrowed its mysterious power called "sovereignty" from the Sovereign of monotheistic religions. If so, then the violence of the state, the violence of holy war, and the most holy violence of all—the imagined violence of hell— might not be as categorically different as they at first appear.

In each of these cases, the problem anyway is the same. By creating this remarkable notion of legitimate violence, we hope we are empowering ourselves to bring about peace, freedom, and order, but all too often it brings us oppression, chaos, and violent death. How does this happen? As a step toward answering this, I want to return to the question with which this chapter began: What can the expression "legitimate violence" mean? As a step toward answering that, we need to ask: What exactly is this action we call violence?

Chapter 2

THE PHENOMENON OF VIOLENCE

To get a grasp on this many-faceted set of behaviors, I made a comparison of the words for "violence" in three languages, English, German, and Japanese. English because that is the language in which this book is written, German because that is the language Max Weber wrote in, and Japanese because when I originally did the research for the paper on which this chapter is based, the paper was to be published in Japanese. Interestingly, each sees the phenomenon from a slightly different angle. (The following is an abbreviated version. The full report is included as the appendix.)

The Oxford English Dictionary (OED) mainly emphasizes the result: the damage caused by the violent force. Something of value is damaged, disrespected, or destroyed. It could be a human being, a humanly built artifact, an animal, a plant, or an orderly developmental process. The word can describe confining a human or animal against its will. It can describe bad grammar. We speak of violating the law, one's oath, one's principles, or a sacred space. And we speak of violating a woman.

Use of the word seems to presuppose that the world around us contains boundaries that ought not to be crossed (violated); when they are, we call it violence.

The Japanese dictionary *Koshien* defines *boryoku* with wonderful simplicity: *"wild force, illegal force."* The emphasis is not on the effect but on the character of the action. It is seen as an explosion, a breakdown of order, a descent into chaos. It can be used to describe typhoons, wild rivers, rogue horses, children—and bad grammar. When used to describe the action of human beings, this almost always means the speaker is describing the action as illegal. One would think this would make it an inappropriate word to use in translating Max Weber's definition of the state, but many Japanese political scientists do so use it.

The Oxford-Harrap Standard German-English Dictionary defines *Gewalt* focusing first of all on the relationship it establishes between the actor and the acted-upon, generally one of domination: The first example of usage is *göttlich Gewalt*, divine power. There are examples of evil actions as well, by tyrants, dictators, and the like, but also of kings, feudal lords, teachers, and parents seen as using their power not to destroy order but to create and preserve it. *Gewalt* is used to describe the force that brings human emotions under the control of the will in the case of the individual, of the teacher in the case of the classroom, of the army in the case of the occupied city. It would not be easy to form a sentence expressing these ideas using the words "violence" or *"boryoku."*

Despite the differences among these three words, the words do share enough to stand as approximate translations of each other. What they share is a picture of the world we live in as having multiple ethical structures built into it, some written into positive law, some understood as common sense, some requiring good intentions to maintain, and some developed by natural processes in the natural world that supports us. When we call an action violence, we are asserting that something valuable is being harmed by it—asserting that even if we are persuaded that there is sufficient reason to carry out that action anyway. If a corpse is found riddled with bullets, no matter whether those bullets were fired by a burglar, a policeman, a psychopathic killer, a jealous lover, or a president's bodyguard, the coroner will pronounce it a violent death.

THE STATE AS BLOB

When I first wrote the article on which this chapter is based, Hanna Fenichel Pitkin kindly read it and, among many other comments, wrote, "I wish you would somewhere in your essay un-blob your state." This was just when she had published her *Attack of the Blob*, in which she argues that Hannah Arendt's concept of "the social," depicted as shapeless, definition-resisting threat to freedom, is best seen as a blob, calling up the image of the various alien beings Hollywood uses to attack us from outer space. Her point is not to dismiss or trivialize Arendt's argument but to show that only when the blob is demystified, or, better, only when "the social" is un-blobbed, does it become clear what Arendt was trying to say.

There are many differences between Arendt's "the social" and the notion of "the state," not least of which is that the former is Arendt's neologism, whereas the latter is an ancient term. Attempting to sort out the similarities and differences between the two would take us offtrack. However, if we take Pitkin's notion of the blob in its broadest sense, "the state" definitely possesses blob-like qualities.

First of all, "the state" not only is shapeless but also changes shape every time you blink. The OED devotes five and a half pages to defining "state." The first two pages list such meanings as "a combination of circumstances" (e.g., state of nature, state of the weather, state of my finances), "a mental or emotional condition" (e.g., state of mind, hypnotic state), and "a phase or stage of existence" (e.g., "in a solid or a liquid state"); several usages related to high rank or exalted position (e.g., "a life of state and pleasure," "stateroom," "lie in state"); and a number of other variations mostly rare or obsolete. These all seem different, but what they share is that, unlike words like "characteristic" or "essence," each refers to a situation that can and probably will change into something else. Definitions of "the state" as a political form begin with number twenty-nine:

> The body politic as organized for supreme civil rule and government; the political organization which is the basis of civil government (either generally and abstractly, or in a particular country); hence, the supreme civil power and government vested in a country or nation.

This sounds right, but blink and you have number thirty, where "the supreme civil power and government" becomes the people ruled by that supreme power:

> A body of people occupying a defined territory and organized under a sovereign government.

Then there's number thirty-one A, where it becomes the location of all this:

> The territory, or one of the territories, ruled by a particular sovereign.

And number thirty-two, where it becomes "what they do":

> All that concerns the government or ruling power of a country: the sphere of supreme political power and administration [e.g., state secrets, reason of state, affair of state, state power].

Thus "the state" can change its form from "the people" to "the people and the government taken together" to "the government" to "the people who hold the real power in the government" and hence, in some cases, to "a single person" (*l'état, c'est moi*).

In the context of this discussion, our question is: Which of these various entities "claims" the monopoly of legitimate violence? It can't be the territory where the people live, but also it can't be "the people" themselves, simply understood. For monopoly means that the people do *not* have the right of legitimate violence, except in cases of personal self-defense. Perhaps it is the people not taken individually but organized as a body politic. But again, it would be strange that the people would "claim" a right that, if their claim is successful, they will not have. On the other hand, if we follow Hobbes and say that the people "grant" the right of legitimate violence to "the state," that will presuppose that "the state" is something distinct from the people. The thing would be much easier to understand if "the state" were defined as Louis XIV understood it: the sovereign ruler shouts, with Shakespeare's Queen Margaret and Lewis Carroll's Red Queen, "Off with his head!" and that's the law. But that is supposed to be unacceptable in the so-called modern nation-state. When the US president makes an "off with his head" decision to use a robot airplane to assassinate a suspected enemy combatant, the authority to make that decision, if it existed (in fact it does not), would reside not in his person but in his office. (Ex-presidents, thank heaven, do not have the authority to command executions.) But where exactly is that authority located? If it is not in the state-as-the-whole-people, is it in the state-as-government? But here we have an odd circularity. The government is made up of people. If all government officials were suddenly to quit and go home, the empty buildings would not be a government. But if those officials stay on their jobs, their authority, like that of the president, derives not from their persons but from their positions; it is "government authority." If their authority "comes from" the government, where was it before it came to them? Put differently, how can their authority "come from" the government if the government is nothing other than themselves? Here we see the blob-like character of "the state." Government authority appears to be "granted" by an entity that we can neither define nor visualize.

In the present context, the issue is "the right of legitimate violence." According to Weber, the state "claims" this right. The first definition of the verb "claim" in the OED is "To demand as one's own or one's due; to seek or ask for on the ground of right." It comes from the Latin *"clamare"*: "to cry out." So for "the state" to "claim" a right, the state not only must have breath, vocal cords, and a mouth capable of forming words, but it also must be qualified to utter the sentence "I claim this right." That is, it must be an "I." But while we are accustomed to thinking of "the state" as if it were such (capable of action, capable of making promises, etc.), in fact it is not. Just as the corporation's personhood is what they call a "legal fiction," so the state's personhood is both a legal and a political fiction. Weber's "the state claims this right" simplifies an immensely complex set of actions of numerous government officials by portraying the state as a person. The most realistic and least blob-like image of this "claiming" is to visualize the claimant as (in the OED's words) "the people who hold the real power in the government." As for where the right comes from, the answer would be, "Thin air." They "have" the monopoly of legitimate violence when the people are persuaded that they do. At least, that seems to be Weber's view of the matter.

MAX WEBER AND THE EVIL MOMENT OF THE STATE

Max Weber's definition of the state as the association that successfully claims a monopoly of legitimate violence appears at the beginning of his essay "Politics as a Vocation." This essay was originally a lecture delivered to university students, some of whom were interested in political careers. He follows the definition with an account of how that monopoly came about, an account strikingly different from the picture given by Hobbes. This is not only because Hobbes was writing at the beginning of the process while Weber was writing after it was partly completed. It is also because Hobbes was writing political theory, while Weber was basing his account on the historical record. That in history there has been no case of a people pulling itself out of the state of nature by making a social contract and founding a state to enforce it is one of the first doubts that occur to people after reading Hobbes. But this doubt is answerable. The state of nature is an abstract model on the basis of which we can carry out a mental experiment, enabling us to see things that might otherwise remain invisible; it is a myth designed to explain why people consent to state violence, to persuade the seventeenth-century English to give up their revolutionary ambitions, and to persuade others, including us, to do the same. None of these fits well with Weber's account of how the state actually did or does succeed in monopolizing legitimate violence. In discussing this legitimacy, Weber focuses not on "consent" but on "obedience":

> Every ruling apparatus that calls for continuous administration has two prerequisites. On the one hand, it requires that human action should be predisposed to obedience toward the rulers who claim to be the agents of legitimate force. On the other hand, thanks to this obedience, the rulers should have at their disposal the material resources necessary to make use of physical force where required.[7]

And rather than "social contract," which would be voluntary, he uses the terms "dispossession" and "expropriation." In a passage that shows Weber as a careful reader of Marx, he writes,

> The modern state begins to develop wherever the monarch sets in train the process of dispossessing the autonomous, "private" agents of administrative power who exist in parallel to him, that is to say, all the independent owners of the materials of war and the administration, financial resources, and politically useful goods of every kind. The entire process provides a perfect analogy to the development of a capitalist enterprise through the gradual expropriation of the independent producers.[8]

This description of the process fits the robber-band model better than it does the social-contract model. Weber neither criticizes nor defends it. It seems he wants the ambitious young people to whom he is talking to understand, if they embark on political careers, the nature of the beast they will be dealing with.

> This is not an issue on which I shall comment today. I shall confine myself to the purely *conceptual* point that the modern state is an institutional form of rule that has successfully fought to create a monopoly of legitimate physical force as

a means of government within a particular territory. For this purpose it has concentrated all the material resources of organization in the hands of its leaders. The modern state has expropriated all the autonomous officials of the "estates" who previously controlled such things as of right and has put itself in the shape of its highest representative in their place. (italics in original)[9]

Weber's objectivity here should not be taken to mean that he is unconcerned with ethics. On the contrary, he is describing a situation that presents, to the political actor, a terrible ethical dilemma. It is this dilemma that is the main theme of the lecture.

In the latter part of the essay, Weber argues that "all ethically oriented action can be guided by either of two fundamentally different, irredeemably incompatible maxims: it can be guided by an 'ethics of conviction' or an 'ethics of responsibility.'"[10] The former is the ethic of the saint. Its text, according to Weber, is the Sermon on the Mount.

> The Sermon on the Mount (and by this is meant the absolute ethics of the Gospel) is a far more serious business than is imagined by those who like to quote its commandments nowadays. In truth, it is no laughing matter. . . . It is no hansom cab that can be stopped anywhere, to jump into or out of at will.[11]

It teaches that a person must never commit a sinful act, even in circumstances where avoiding a sinful act will have terrible consequences. The saint thinks not of consequences but of the act itself. The ethic of responsibility, on the other hand, is concerned with consequences. In the real world, it simply is not true, Weber argues, that evil acts always bring evil consequences and good acts good consequences. The moral quality of an act does not carry through unchanged down the long chain of actual cause and effect. The saint's behavior may be good for the saint, but for our political leaders, we want people who care for the consequences of what they do. Weber agrees with Machiavelli that a politician who seeks to follow only the ethic of conviction will be useless at best, dangerous at worst.

> The early Christians too, were well aware that the world was governed by demons and that whoever becomes involved with politics, that is to say, with power and violence as a means, has made a pact with satanic powers. It follows that as far as a person's actions are concerned, it is *not* true that nothing but good comes from good and nothing but evil from evil, but rather quite frequently the opposite is the case. Anyone who does not realise this is in fact a mere child in political matters. (italics in original)[12]

The expression "legitimate violence" corresponds to this distinction. "Legitimate" means "Legitimate in the context of the ethic of responsibility."

It means that the perpetrator of an act of legitimate violence (1) has not broken the law and should not be arrested, and (2) has acted with good intentions (or in the case of the bureaucrat or soldier, has acted with no intentions) and should neither be condemned nor feel guilty. On the other hand, calling the action "violence" means that, according to the ethic of conviction, it is an action that ought never to be taken by human beings. It is clear from the thrust of the essay that when Weber chose the word *"Gewalt,"* he did not mean something inherently benevolent, like the protection of a parent over a child. If he had, he would not have needed to add the adjective "legitimate"—and anyway, that is by no means Weber's view of the state. In saying that to enter politics is to make a pact with the "satanic powers," he makes that as clear as clear gets.

But when Weber argues that the political actor must choose the ethic of responsibility, he does not mean that the ethic of conviction is mistaken. Rather, it means that "we find ourselves placed in different cultures [Gerth and Mills translate *Lebensordnungen* as 'life-spheres'] each of which is subject to different laws."[13] The fact that the two ethics contradict each other does not mean one of them is wrong: The contradiction, for Weber, is in the nature of the world; it is the "tragedy" of political action. The ethic of responsibility is also properly called an "ethic." The violent acts taken by the representatives of the state are, from the standpoint of one ethic, acts that no person ever ought to do. But from the standpoint of another ethic, they may be acts that we very much want the representatives of the state to carry out.

Weber's lecture "Politics as a Vocation" has a double purpose. On the one hand, he wants to refute what he considers to be naive pacifism: that it is possible to enter politics and continue to follow the ethic of conviction. He is not, however, trying to persuade those young people to become political cynics. His other purpose is to relativize the state, to reveal it as far from perfect and by no means to be worshipped, to force it, as it were, to confess its sin. The self-contradictory expression "legitimate violence" not only was intended to shock the students but also was a contradiction both sides of which he hoped they would remain constantly aware. For Weber, the sign of a mature political actor is the ability to understand both of these truths, and never to adopt one to the degree of forgetting the other. The fact that an evil act may be necessary does not prevent it from being evil; the fact that a necessary act may be evil does not prevent it from being necessary. It is this that Weber calls "the tragedy in which all action is ensnared, political action above all."[14]

Weber, I believe, hoped that by forcing "the evil moment of the state" into the open, he could contribute to a politics that used this evil with care, circumspection, and humility and as rarely as possible. Ironically, his formulation has come to be used in the way he most hoped to prevent: If the violence of the state is legitimate, then there is no need to worry about it, no need to call it violence (call it "enforcement" or "pacification" or the like), no need even to see it. When Weber labeled the state a violent organization, it was by no means his intention to make it more so; like Hobbes, he hoped the state would use its violence to reduce the overall amount of violence in the world.

As history since Weber's time has shown, this hope has not been fulfilled. I will take up Weber again in the final chapter.

NOTES

1. Max Weber, "Politics as a Vocation," in *The Vocation Lectures*, ed. David Owen and Tracy B. Strong, trans. Rodney Livingstone (Indianapolis: Hackett, 2004), 33.

2. Hobbes, *Leviathan*, 248. This is not the only place where Hobbes reveals how little he knew about native American peoples.

3. R. J. Rummel, *Death by Government: Genocide and Mass Murder since 1900* (London: Routledge, 1997), 15.

4. Rummel, *Death by Government*, 15.

5. Rummel, *Death by Government*, 14.

6. For a critique of the notion that representative democracies are a force for peace, see Hans Joas and Wolsfanf Kuobl, *War in Social Thought*, trans. Alex Skinner (Princeton: Princeton U. Press, 2013), 220–8.

7. Weber, "Politics as a Vocation," 35.

8. Weber, "Politics as a Vocation," 37.

9. Weber, "Politics as a Vocation," 38.

10. Weber, "Politics as a Vocation," 83.

11. Weber, "Politics as a Vocation," 81.

12. Weber, "Politics as a Vocation," 86.

13. Weber, "Politics as a Vocation," 87. For the alternative translation, see Max Weber, *From Max Weber: Essays in Sociology*, eds. and trans. H. H. Gerth and C. Wright Mills (New York: Oxford, 1958), 123.

14. Weber, "Politics as a Vocation," 78.

Chapter 3

Godlike Violence

Thou shalt not kill.

—Exodus 20:13

Thou shalt not murder.

—Alternative translation

VIOLENCE ADORNED

The right of legitimate violence, it is alleged, justifies certain acts of violence legally and ethically. Again, "justifies" means that the perpetrator of such violence may not be subjected to criminal prosecution, ought not to be subjected to ethical criticism, and need not feel guilty (or carry "bloodguilt," as the saying goes) for what he or she did. But, as I argue above, the claim also has the deeper effect of seeming to alter the nature of the behavior itself. Acts of legitimate and illegitimate violence seem different, not only in our legal and moral evaluation of them but also in their physical character as acts. Hearing about the one or the other, our bodies react differently, a different set of emotions is triggered, a different train of thought is set in motion. The claim of legitimacy is made with the intention of making certain actions easier to carry out, and is often partly successful in this.

It is notoriously difficult to persuade most people that killing fellow persons is a wholly virtuous act. When you are faced with the prospect of having to do it, or to watch someone do it, especially when you are the one to whom it is being done, it just doesn't appear to be the right way to treat another human. For the "legitimate killer," there is always the danger, despite what the law says, that violence will reveal itself, as it were, unadorned. Thus violence, to maintain its legitimacy, may require additional adornments. One effective solution is to attach it in one way or another to whatever god or gods your society may believe in. In this chapter, I will give a few samples of ways this has been done in ancient and more modern times.

WHY GODS CAN'T BE HEROES

In Homeric Greece, the gods were quarrelsome. They fought among themselves on Olympus, and they descended to earth to participate in the wars of human beings. Or it was by so imagining them that the Greeks were able to think of their wars as infused with godliness. In *The Iliad*, that ghastly war story that stands at the head of the Western tradition of letters, the greatest killer is Achilleus, who is descended from the goddess Thetis. When he goes roaring and flailing through the enemy's ranks, chopping up young men left and right, he is accompanied by the goddess Athene, and his every motion seems filled not only with glory but also with mystery; he is described as "shining."[1]

This does not mean that simple, unadorned death is hidden from the reader of *The Iliad*. On the contrary, it is because it shows war in both its adorned and unadorned forms that it is the right place to begin this chapter. Simone Weil famously characterized *The Iliad* as a "poem of force"; I think it is better understood as a poem of killing. In it, war is reduced to its essence: the killing of persons. Killing is the main form of action (or, as in the case of Achilleus's great sulk, not killing is the main form of inaction). It differs from most war descriptions in that the name of the person killed is regularly given. Sometimes there is also a brief personal history—the names of his parents, where he lived, what his special skills were (breaking horses, entertaining guests, archery), all this mentioned just before the vivid description of the nature of the wound that kills him.

In *The Iliad*, the chief way of praising the greatest of the heroes and heroines is to say that they are godlike. Some are likened to gods for their beauty (Paris), some for their voices (Talthybius), some for their dignity (Priam), some for specific body parts ("Agamemnon, with eyes and head like Zeus . . . like Ares for girth, and with the chest of Poseidon" [2, 477–9]). Many are described as descended from gods, but while beauty and strengths are thus transmitted to them, they do not inherit the power to defy laws of nature (though they sometimes ask a god to do this for them). The powers that matter in the context of *The Iliad* are two, which in war are closely related: the ability to kill at will, and the ability to avoid being killed. But in the case of the gods, this is not an "ability"; it is what defines them as gods: beings that can kill without being killed. It gives them their name, the immortals *(athanatos)*. Humans, on the other hand, are named for their lack of that characteristic. They are the mortals *(thanatos)*, the ones who die. Reading these ancient stories, one is tempted to wonder whether from the standpoint of the war gods, dying is what we are here for. War seems to be one of the gods' favorite pastimes, but war properly understood is a game that can be carried out by only mortals. In a world only of gods, there are quarrels but no wars. Wars need someone to do the dying.

As Robert Emmet Meagher has pointed out, this has an ironic consequence: As beings who never face death, the gods are disqualified from the status of heroes.[2] They have little need of courage, and little interest in that large sector of our commonsense ethics that we call "humanity," which is grounded in our understanding that we are born to die.

Still, those mortals who have identified themselves as warriors dream of being like them, and *The Iliad* can be read as a long, and ultimately futile, series of challenges to the gods' monopoly of immortality. In one-on-one combat, not dying and killing are the same thing; the hero who survives killing one opponent after another has achieved, at least for that brief period, *athanatos*. Thus, the killing partakes of godliness, and the killer who survives becomes godlike. Menelaos is "a man godlike" (4, 212), Pandarus is "the godlike" (5, 168), Thrasymedes is "godlike" (16, 321), Meriones is "a mortal like a god" (16, 632–3), Patroklos charged three times "with the force of the running war god, screaming a terrible cry, and three times he cut down nine men" (16, 784–5), Polydorus is "godlike" (20, 407), Achilleus is "a man like the murderous war god" (20, e46), and of Hektor, the man Achilles most famously killed, Hektor's mother, Hake, says, "They adored you as if you were a god" (22, 434–5). Like all the greatest works of ancient Greece, *The Iliad* is a tragedy, not so much because both Hektor and Achilleus die (actually, Achilleus is still alive at the end of the poem, but we know that his end is soon), but rather because its theme is the tragedy of the human condition of mortality. All those heroes, with courage, skills, and strengths we could never imagine matching, carrying out what are called "death-defying deeds," knock-knock-knocking on the immortals' door, and not a one gaining entrance.

The gods find the whole thing wonderfully entertaining. As the battle moves toward a climax, Zeus says, "I shall stay here upon the fold of Olympos/ sitting still, watching, to pleasure my heart" (20, 22–3). The other gods continually interfere in the battle, sometimes to ensure victory for a contestant they like, sometimes apparently just to prolong the contest, regularly using dirty tricks. And from time to time, they mock the mortals' futile aspirations. When Diomedes attacks one of Apollo's favorites, Apollo "cried out to him in the voice of terror / 'Take care, give back, son of Tydeus, and strive no longer to make yourself like the gods in mind, since never the same is / the breed of gods, who are immortal, and men who walk groundling'" (5, 439–42). And when Hektor, having stolen Achilleus's armor, begins putting it on, Zeus mocks him: "Ah, poor wretch! / There is no thought of death in your mind now, and yet death stands / close beside you as you put on the immortal armour / of a surpassing man" (17, 200–3).

To the real immortals, what we call the warrior's bravery appears as the self-deceiving illusion of immortality, the state of having "no thought of death in your mind." The same mini-drama is repeated over and over in *The Iliad*: Two combatants meet, each perfectly confident of victory and with no thought of death in his mind. One of them is proved to have been correct for the time being, and the other is forced to realize that there was something he had not properly understood. For while the successful killers in *The Iliad* are granted godlike killing, those who are killed experience only unadorned, human death—what in *The Iliad* is called "sheer death." Elegance of speech and grace of motion are denied them; they bellow like stuck bulls and claw the earth; they grasp at their internal organs spilling out of their bodies. We are shown the reality of "a tooth for a tooth":

> Idomeneus stabbed Erymas in the mouth with the pitiless bronze, so that the brazen spearhead smashed its way clean through below the brain in an upward stroke, and the white bones splintered, and the teeth were shaken out with the stroke and both eyes filled up with blood, and gaping he blew a spray of blood through the nostrils and through his mouth, and death in a dark mist closed in about him. (16, 345–50)

And of "an eye for an eye":

> Menelaos struck him as he came onward in the forehead over the base of the nose, and smashed the bones so that both eyes dropped, bloody, and lay in the dust at his feet before him. (13, 615–7)

Thus, while the winners are granted the experience of killing adorned with the illusion of godliness, what the losers experience is unadorned death. Or rather, no one knows what they experience, because all who have had that experience are dead. What the poet can show us is what that experience would look like to one standing nearby. And with that image clearly in mind, it is difficult to go into battle. As it is impossible to conceal that image from soldiers in actual combat, you need to use the trick of placing it in the context of the story of your victory: the image of what you are going to do to the other. But in *The Iliad*, sometimes this fails, and even the bravest of the warriors—even Hektor—fall into panic, what the poet calls "green fear." These are the moments when the warrior has a clear vision of death unadorned—unadorned by godliness, unadorned by glory, unadorned by being located in a heroic story, death in the form of guts spilling from the belly and blood spurting from the eyes: sheer death, bringing to a halt the miraculous functioning of a living, sentient organism, oneself.

HOLY WAR

In *The Iliad*, killing is depicted as godlike, but it is not holy. The Greek gods, being part bully and part trickster, hardly display what could be called human sensibility, let alone sensibilities that transcend the human. Holy war, at least as we know it in the Jewish, Christian, and Islamic worlds, begins in the Old Testament. There is no need to detail this chapter and verse; everyone even slightly familiar with the Old Testament knows that Yahweh was a great killer of his enemies, carrying out the first fire (and brimstone) bombings to get rid of same-sex love in Sodom and Gomorrah, destroying all but one family of the human race plus most of the animal life in the great flood, drowning the entire Egyptian army in the Red Sea, and so on. Moreover, the gift of land, which he had promised in his covenant with the Israelites, was in fact secured by them through some three hundred years of war, and then only temporarily.[3]

As the biblical scholars G. Ernest Wright and Reginald H. Fuller point out, adorning warfare with holiness does not mitigate its violence. On the contrary, it seems to turn the rational-interest-based violence of the robber band on its head. While pillage is forbidden, massacre becomes total.

> Israel at the time of the conquest and throughout the period of the judges believed in such a thing as holy war. That was a special institution with special customs and laws governing the practice of it. In holy war, God was believed to be the leader who would give the people the victory, provided that they followed him without any hesitation or lack of faith and with complete obedience to his will and law.... In holy war, the booty of the enemy was the property of God; as regards the cities taken in the land of Canaan, no spoil was to be allowed; Israel was to gain nothing except a place in which to live. The booty of the enemy was under the ban and was to be completely destroyed as a holocaust to God in order that the land might be purified for new occupation. No human being was to enrich himself by keeping any enemy property as his own possession. Yet in the case of the conquest, this ban against the taking of booty and the offering of all to God was extended to the pagan people in possession of the land. There were to be no captives whatsoever.[4]

No prisoners. As, for example, in the battle of Jericho:

> And it came to pass, when the people heard the sound of the trumpet, and the people shouted with a great shout, that the wall fell down flat, so that the people went up into the city, every man straight before him, and they took the city. And they utterly destroyed all that was in the city, both man and woman, young and old, and ox, and sheep, and ass, with the edge of the sword. (Joshua 6:20–21; biblical quotations from the King James bible)

As Wright and Fuller wrote, these were the special rules for holy war. Earlier, Moses had explained the difference between ordinary war and holy war to the Israelites:

> When thou comest nigh into a city to fight against it, then proclaim peace unto it. And it shall be, if it make the answer of peace, and open unto thee, then it shall be, that all the people that is found therein shall be tributaries unto thee, and they shall serve thee. And if it will make no peace with thee, but will make war against thee, then thou shalt besiege it: And when the LORD thy God hath delivered it into thine hands, thou shalt smite every male thereof with the edge of the sword.
>
> But the women, and the little ones, and the cattle, and all that is in the city, even all the spoil thereof, shalt thou take unto thyself; and thou shalt eat the spoil of thine enemies, which the LORD thy God hath given thee.
>
> Thus shalt thou do unto all the cities which are very far off from thee, which are not of the cities of these nations.
>
> But of the cities of these people, which the LORD thy God doth give thee for an inheritance, thou shalt save alive nothing that breatheth:
>
> But thou shalt utterly destroy them, namely, the Hittites, and the Amorites, the Canaanites, and the Perizzites, the Hivites, and the Jebusites; as the LORD thy God hath commanded thee. (Deuteronomy 20:10–17)

The Israelites did not invent the sacking of cities, nor were they the first to see massacre as sacred behavior. On the contrary, archeologists, when uncovering ancient mass graves filled with the bones of people who all died by violence, take this as evidence that the people of that era already had religion. But these Old Testament tales of holy and semi-holy war, attaching the authority of Yahweh to indiscriminate massacre, have had an immense influence on the history of much of the world since then. I know that there are theologians and worshippers in branches of Judaism, Christianity, and Islam who believe there are ways to interpret these texts as messages of peace. I respect those efforts, and would not dream of trying to refute them. However, those theologians who want to argue for a religion that infuses war with sacredness, and sees war as an activity ordained by the highest moral authority in the universe, can find a wealth of material in the Old Testament to support their case.

THE GODS VERSUS GOD

A word should be said here about the differences between the "godlike" wars of Greek mythology and holy war as described in the Old Testament. The differences are obvious, and immense. For the ancient Greeks, the gods were not an infallible moral authority; as the gods are depicted, they hardly seem moral at all. In the conversations people have with them, the people do not fall on their faces in abject submission, but rather sometimes voice criticisms and give them back talk; I know of no story from ancient Greece resembling the book of Job. The Greek gods are loved for their beauty, their splendor, their power, and especially their ability to violate the laws of nature, which can come in handy. They are also loved erotically, which is why there are so many children of mixed parentage in these stories, whereas in Christianity there is only one. When Greeks try to be like the gods, they are struck down for their hubris, but this doesn't mean they are hated as sinners. Icarus was foolish for trying to fly to the sun, and it was inevitable and just that his wax wings would melt and he would fall to the earth, but he is loved for the attempt, which is why the story is a tragedy. This is very different from the story of the people who tried to get to heaven by building the tower of Babel. Their tower was not a brave-but-doomed attempt; rather it was an abomination, and the people who built it were accursed, so that the story is not a tragedy but rather what is called a "moral tale."

Moreover, while the gods take a great interest in the battle for Troy, that does not make it holy war because they are not all on the same side; some of them even shift from one side to the other. In holy war, one side is seen as entirely holy and the other side entirely accursed. Yahweh may punish the Israelites for their "stiff-necked" behavior by arranging for them to lose a battle, but his covenant is with them and no one else.

And in *The Iliad*, warriors who are killed are first introduced to the reader: name, birthplace, character. In the stories of the Jewish wars, the killed are nameless, faceless masses. In a way, that makes it easier reading.

Wright and Fuller ask, "How can a terrible war of conquest be considered a gracious deed of God?"[5] How indeed? This is an important question for anyone who reads these stories, but for one who considers the Old Testament to be the holy word of God, it is an agonizing question. And it is a perennial question for believers in monotheistic religions: How can God be omnipotent but still not responsible for what happens in the world? Wright and Fuller give a classic answer:

> In the biblical point of view wars exist because of human sin, and God uses human agents to accomplish his purposes in history. . . . The agent is sinful, but nevertheless God uses it for his purpose. . . . Now we know not only from the

Bible but from many outside sources as well that the Canaanite civilization and religion was one of the weakest, most decadent, and most immoral cultures of the civilized world at that time. It is claimed, then, that Israel is God's agent of destruction against a sinful civilization, for in the moral order of God civilizations of such flagrant wickedness must be destroyed. . . . All this does not mean that Israel as God's agent is free of her responsibility.[6]

God, it seems, has plausible deniability; humans do not.

THE INNOCENT WARRIOR

There may somewhere be some exceptions, but it seems to me that it is a common characteristic of religions that they include some provision for (at least) regulating and limiting the killing of human beings. (If religion is defined as belief in a supernatural power entitled to obedience, without such a provision one would wonder wherein this entitlement lies.) But, especially when a religion is institutionalized as a governing body, some form of killing is usually allowed. Institutionalized governing bodies, as Max Weber argued, have trouble operating under only the ethic of conviction but also need the ethic of responsibility, the ethic that aims to achieve real results in the world. And the killing of human beings can be a very effective way to get results.

The fifth commandment of the Decalogue seems to rule out killing altogether—unless it is true, as some claim, that "Thou shalt not kill" is a mistranslation, the correct one being "Thou shalt not murder," that is, kill *illegally*. Be that as it may, as is shown in the examples above, when it comes to organizing and institutionalizing the Israelites into a political body that will exercise real power in the world, the Old Testament does not depict Yahweh as forbidding killing in all circumstances. And the reasons are perfectly understandable. When people stand in the way of your plans, such as by living on the land you would like to have for yourself, killing them all can be a decisive solution.

The Sermon on the Mount seems to revive the fifth commandment as an absolute. At least, that is the way many of the early Christians, and especially the generation of people who actually met Jesus, are said to have understood it. We are told that they shared their possessions and lived nonviolently. This was made easier by their belief that Jesus would be returning soon, and earthly life would be coming to an end; in such a situation, Weber's ethic of absolute ends serves well. But when Jesus did not return, things got complicated. As the first generation grew old, an institution was needed to pass on the gospel to the next generation: a church. And as the Christians were persecuted, institutions were needed with which to hold themselves together and to resist: institutions for governance. They found themselves living not only in a kingdom "not of this world" but also in institutions very much "of this world," and thus in need of an ethic taking responsibility for achieving actual results in this world. And when, three centuries after the death of Christ, the Roman Empire adopted Christianity as its established religion, things got more complicated still. The Roman Empire had violence built into its structure; it was founded on war and maintained by war; soldiers marching down the Roman roads were the blood circulating through its veins. What could it mean to make such an organization Christian? How can a band of robbers adopt a religion dedicated to peace, and go on robbing?

The first great solution to this puzzle was proposed by Saint Augustine (354–430) with his notion of the two cities. "Mankind," wrote Augustine, "is divided into two sorts, such as live according to man, and such as live according to God. These we mystically call two cities or societies, the one predestined to reign eternally with God, the other condemned to perpetual torment with the devil" (Book XV, Chapter I).[7]

It is significant that he chose for his image the city. As Hannah Arendt often reminded us, it was Augustine who pointed out that the city is founded on fratricide: Cain killed Abel and founded the city of Enoch; Romulus killed Remus and founded Rome. And it was Augustine who asked that question that echoes down through the ages:

> Justice removed, then, what are kingdoms but great bands of robbers? What are bands of robbers themselves but little kingdoms? The band itself is made up of men; it is governed by the authority of a ruler; it is bound together by a pact of association; and the loot is divided according to an agreed law. If, by the constant addition of desperate men, this scourge grows to such a size that it acquires territory, establishes a seat of government, occupies cities and subjugates peoples, it assumes the name of kingdom more openly. For this name is now manifestly conferred upon it not by the removal of greed, but by the addition of impunity. (Book XV, Chapter I)

"Impunity" is another name for "legitimacy," what rulers gain by being, as Weber repeatedly put it, "believed to be legitimate." And Augustine followed that with this marvelous tale:

> It was a pertinent and true answer which was made to Alexander the Great by a pirate whom he had seized. When the king asked him what he meant by infesting the sea, the pirate defiantly replied "The same as you do when you infest the whole world; but because I do it with a little ship I am called a robber, and because you do it with a great fleet, you are an emperor." (Book IV, Chapter 4)

For Augustine the model for the empire-indistinguishable-from-a-great-robber-band was pagan Rome. But this doesn't mean that pagan Rome itself was the whole of the earthly city, nor that it was transformed into the heavenly city when it became Christian. Things are more complicated; the two cities "are in this present world mixed together and, in a certain sense, entangled with one another" (Book XI, Chapter 1). No institution, not even the church, is entirely within the city of God. It depends on the state of the individual soul. The people, a minority who faithfully follow the word of God and thus constitute the earthly branch of the heavenly city (the other branch being in actually existing heaven), live in the world as pilgrims surrounded by people not destined for salvation who make up the earthly city. This earthly city "is often divided against itself by lawsuits, wars and strife, and by victories which either bring death or are themselves short-lived" (Book XV, Chapter 4). These wars are generated by the sinful nature of the members of the earthly city, and the best they can be expected to achieve is an "earthly peace" (the robber band solution), whose true character Augustine captures brilliantly with the words "divided by victory." However flawed, it's the best one can hope for in the earthly city (Hobbes: "Not so hurtful as the want of it"). So, to achieve this peace, the earthly city wages war. "For, if it conquers, and there is no one left to resist it, there will be peace, which the opposing parties did not have while they strove in their unhappy poverty for the things which they could not both possess at once" (Book XV, Chapter 4).

And this peace is valuable not only to the faithless, for "the Heavenly City—or, rather, that part of it which is a pilgrim in this condition of mortality, and which lives by faith—must of necessity make use of this peace also, until this mortal state, for which such peace is necessary, shall have passed away" (Book XIX, Chapter 17).

Augustine sometimes seems to be saying that the faithful, who live in this faithless world as pilgrims, will not participate in wars, but this is not his message. In his interpretation, the passages in the Gospels that seem to forbid all violence pertain only to the state of one's soul, not to one's actual behavior.

> If it is supposed that God could not enjoin warfare, because in after times it was said by the Lord Jesus Christ, "I say unto you, That ye resist not evil: but if any one strike thee on the right cheek, turn to him the left also," the answer is, that what is here required is not a bodily action, but an inward disposition. The sacred seat of virtue is the heart, and such were the hearts of our fathers, the righteous men of old. . . .
>
> What is the evil in war? Is it the death of some who will soon die in any case, that others may live in peaceful subjection? This is merely cowardly dislike, not any religious feeling. The real evils in war are love of violence, revengeful cruelty, fierce and implacable enmity, wild resistance, and the lust

of power, and such like; and it is generally to punish these things, when force is required to inflict the punishment, that, in obedience to God or some lawful authority, good men undertake wars, when they find themselves in such a position as regards the conduct of human affairs, that right conduct requires them to act, or to make others act, in this way. (*Contra Faustum*, XXII, 74–79)[8]

Augustine is said to be the father of just war theory. He is by no means the first person to argue that some wars may be fought for causes more nearly just than others, or that wars should not be waged out of love of violence or desire for revenge. But it is probably fair to call him the founder of just war theory in the Christian tradition. There is a fine distinction here between Augustine's just war and holy war. For Augustine, war itself is a part of the earthly city and cannot be holy. Yet if it is necessary and therefore just, there is a way that a good Christian can participate in it without sin. But his condition for being both a good Christian and a soldier is severe to the point of seeming impossible. The Christian soldier will hate war and violence, have no spirit of revenge, no enmity toward the enemy. Rather than finding value in just war, the Christian soldier will hate just war more than any other, because this is the kind of war in which he must fight.

"But the wise man, they say, will wage just wars. Surely, however, if he remembers that he is a human being, he will be much readier to deplore the fact that he is under the necessity of waging even just wars. For if they were not just, he would not have to wage them, and so there would then be no wars at all for a wise man to engage in" (*City of God*, Book XIX, Chapter 7). If he joins in only just wars and if he keeps his heart pure, the Christian soldier may do all the things that soldiers do to their enemies and still remain innocent. It is an image that we know well, it having come down to us in song and story and medieval legend. It is the image of the Knights of the Round Table and the crusaders; it is the very person Don Quixote wanted to be. It is easy to make fun of, as Cervantes did, and it is easy to show that such a cavernous gap between state of mind and actual behavior is not likely to be achieved by many people. But no one can say that it is impossible altogether. There is no reason to doubt that Augustine believed the words he was writing, that he truly hated war and loved peace but believed that war was sometimes a tragic necessity. And he gave us yet another adornment for killing, a basis for believing that a killing carried out by someone in a fit of rage and hatred, or possessed by some malevolent intent, will be somehow different from a killing carried out by one innocent of such feelings and intentions. For Max Weber, those who took on the burden of carrying out the state's right of legitimate violence were making a pact with the devil, so if such a person ran a sword or a bullet through your head, that would appear to be a satanic act. But if the person who does this to you is of a gentle and saintly nature, and carries out the act with no malice or self-interest, would that take away the pain?

Augustine did not go to war, but he did leave us with an extraordinary account of what it is like for a well-intentioned human being to be a judge, with the power to exercise the right of legitimate violence in the form of torture and execution, in this world of imperfect knowledge.

> For, indeed, those who give such judgment can never penetrate the consciences of those upon whom they pronounce it. Therefore they are often compelled to seek the truth by torturing innocent people merely because they are witnesses to the crimes of other men. And what of torture applied to a man in his own case? . . . For if . . . the accused now chooses to flee from this life rather than endure those tortures any longer, he will confess to a crime which he has not committed. . . . In this case [the judge] has tortured an innocent man in order to discover the truth, and has killed him while still not knowing it. (*City of God*, Book XIX, Chapter 6)

Given the impossibility of certain knowledge, will the wise man agree to do such work?

"Clearly he will take his seat, for the claims of human society, which he thinks it wicked to abandon, constrain him and draw him to this duty" (*City of God*, Book XIX, Chapter 6). We know that some judges are sadists, and probably many more experience at least a flash of sadistic pleasure at the suffering they bring to suspects and criminals. But I think we can believe Augustine that, when as bishop he served as judge in the episcopal court (which is surely what he is really talking about in the above paragraph), he found it painful to have to torture not only suspects but also witnesses, and sometimes accidentally to kill them, in the absence of perfect knowledge of the state of their souls, which God would have but no human can.

But not only is he telling us that he found it miserable to torture people; he also is telling us that if you torture them with the proper sadness, you are innocent of sin, so it's OK for you to keep on doing it. It seems that many have been persuaded by this argument; after all, Augustine, the torturing judge, was canonized a saint.

While granting sainthood to a person capable of causing violent death is an extreme case, in general the method of using religion to legitimize violence is a method of raising the killer's moral status, adorning his or her action with the sacred or the godlike, making it easier to carry out. Another way to make killing easier uses the directly opposite method, that of disvaluing the persons to be killed. How this works, and why it often doesn't, is the subject of the following chapter.

NOTES

1. Citations are from *The Iliad of Homer*, trans. Richmond Lattimore (Chicago: U. Chicago Press, 1951).
2. Robert Emmet Meagher, *Herakles gone mad: rethinking heroism in an age of endless war* (Northampton, MA: Olive Branch Press, 2006), 35–6.
3. G. Ernest Wright and Reginald H. Fuller, *The Book of the Acts of God* (Garden City: Doubleday, 1957), 104.
4. Wright and Fuller, *Acts*, 108–9.
5. Wright and Fuller, *Acts*, 104.
6. Wright and Fuller, *Acts*, 109.
7. Citations are from Augustine, *The City of God against the Pagans*, ed. and trans. R. W. Dyson (Cambridge: Cambridge University Press, 1998).
8. Citations are from Augustine, *Contra Faustum*, XXII, 74–79, quoted in Henry Paolucci, ed., *The Political Writings of St. Augustine* (Chicago: Henry Regnery, 1967).

Chapter 4

Distance and Distance-Collapse

When the sky is rent asunder; when the stars scatter and the oceans roll together; when the graves are hurled about; each soul shall know what it has done and what it has failed to do.

—Koran 82:1–5

If the doors of perception were cleansed every thing would appear to man as it is, infinite.

—William Blake

THE ART OF DISTANCING

Pronouncing it "legitimate" is not the only way of making killing easier. Establishing greater distance between you and the one you mean to kill can achieve the same result; distance allows you to avoid becoming fully aware of what you have done. In his *On Killing*, Lieutenant Colonel Dave Grossman helpfully breaks down the notion of "distance" into physical distance and emotional distance, and then further breaks down the latter into social distance ("viewing a particular class as less than human"), cultural distance ("racial and ethnic differences"), moral distance ("intense belief in moral superiority"), and mechanical distance ("killing through a TV screen, a thermal sight, a sniper sight, or some other kind of mechanical buffer").[1] One could quibble with this list by adding more items to it (for example, perhaps for a certain type of sociopath, everybody seems distant and unreal, like shadows on a screen), or by pointing out that, in some cases, the absence of distance—intimacy—is one of the conditions for the impulse to kill, as with patricide or the killing of a lover. As for the first quibble, Grossman's point is not weakened by adding items to his list, and as for the second, Grossman's (and my) subject is war, where it would be rare to find two intimate people on opposite sides of a battlefield (rare, but possible, as in civil wars). In particular, unlike the war depicted in *The Iliad*, in which everyone seems to know everyone else by name, the modern battlefield is a place where strangers kill strangers. And while it is easy enough to care nothing one way or another about strangers, it is also difficult personally to hate them enough to want to kill them, though easy enough to hate them as a stereotyped category.

In his circa 1947 book *Men Against Fire*, US Army historian Brigadier General S. L. A. Marshall reported a soon-to-become famous survey of what US soldiers actually did in battle in World War II. He reported that on average, only 15 to 20 percent actually fired their weapons while aiming at people. Marshall concluded that "the average and healthy individual . . . still has such an inner and usually unrealized resistance towards killing a fellow man that he will not of his own volition take life if it is possible to turn away from that responsibility. . . . At the vital point he becomes a conscientious objector, unknowing."[2]

OVERCOMING THE FEAR OF KILLING

Many doubted these results, especially military officers who said it did not match their combat experience. But the US Army and Marines took them seriously enough to change their training methods, for example by replacing the bull's-eye target with the pop-up, human-shaped target on the rifle range, thus changing shooting from a slow and thoughtful process ("squeeze the lemon") to a conditioned response (pop-bang). This is said to have greatly reduced the number of "sudden conscientious objectors" in the infantry.

However, the most recent edition of Marshall's book, republished by the University of Oklahoma Press, includes a new foreword by RAND Senior Defense and Political Analyst Russell W. Glenn that includes persuasive evidence that Marshall made up the fire-ratio statistics. Examination of Marshall's field notes taken during his surveys reveals no statistics on that subject, and the officer who accompanied him later said he had no recollection of any such questions being asked. I suppose the debate will go on, and I am by no means the person to adjudicate it. But what is interesting is that while Glenn, and presumably the University of Oklahoma Press as well, believe that the book's principal assertion of fact is a lie (or, as Glenn puts it more gently, a "fabrication"), they still consider it worth reprinting and recommend that members of the US military officer corps study it.

Glenn's argument is that, statistics aside, Marshall was correct that there were too many troops who failed to fire on the enemy, and that this was a problem. Marshall was vague about where this mental block, as he called it, came from; sometimes he talked about "human nature" and sometimes about "the moral code and ideals of his [i.e., American] society." As to the mental block, he claimed that "studies by Medical Corps psychiatrists of the combat fatigue cases in the European Theater . . . found that fear of killing, rather than fear of being killed, was the most common cause of battle failure in the individual."[3] On the one hand, he wrote, this was "something to the American credit," but on the other hand, it was something that must be "defeated."[4]

Quite possibly, the story of the Medical Corps's finding is yet another of Marshall's exaggerations, but we can still believe him that the fear of killing is a real factor in combat, the natural result of the contradiction between the ethic of legitimate violence and the daily-life ethic of most ordinary people. And it is something that is believed by virtually all military organizations, as can be seen by the great effort that their basic training programs put into overcoming it. It's the very problem that DIs are assigned to solve.

WHAT DIs TEACH

How this is done is well known. Partly it is achieved by teaching new recruits to obey all orders automatically, partly by training them in conditioned-response firing, partly by heaping ridicule and contempt on any hesitation as weak and womanish, partly by destroying the authority of the mother on young recruits, partly by distancing them from the enemy through stereotyping. Of course, mocking mothers and stereotyping enemies are not written into the training manuals; they are part of the informal culture of basic training. Typically the enemy is depicted as one or another animal, or inferior human subtype, or believer in a religion or doctrine unworthy of the human race, or some combination of these. When I went through Marine Corps basic training at Quantico in Virginia, the hypothetical enemy was the Gook. I can remember an instructor with a captain's rank telling us, "You camouflage your position with the branches upside down, the underside of the leaves have a different color, Joe Gook gonna look down from the hilltop and say, 'Ah, soooo.'" Interestingly, in 1958, "Joe Gook" spoke Japanese. "Gook" at that time included Chinese, Koreans, Japanese, and Okinawans; later it came to include Vietnamese and other Southeast Asians. In the Marine Corps culture of that time, the fact that Japan had signed a peace treaty did not mean the Japanese were no longer an enemy; it meant only that they were now a pacified enemy. "Gook" is not heard much anymore, but if you ask a GI what they call Iraqis and Afghans and now Iranians, they can come up with quite a list of terms: Rag Head, Dune Coon, Sand Nigger, Sand Monkey, Camel Fucker, and so on.

Be that as it may, overcoming the inner resistance to killing by means of distancing—persuading the troops that the enemy is a being utterly different from you, whose life has no value—is a method that has its dangers. The problem is that it is based on a falsehood: The truth is that the life of the person you killed, qua life, had as much value as yours or that of any other human being. And the danger is that a soldier may suddenly realize that, and suffer distance-collapse.

TOGETHER IN THE BOMB CRATER

In Remarque's World War I novel *All Quiet on the Western Front*, the German protagonist Paul jumps into a crater to seek protection from bombardment, and a French soldier falls in on top of him. Paul, as he was trained to do, knifes the Frenchman, wounding him mortally. But the bombardment does not let up, so he must stay in the crater facing the dying Frenchman. And the Frenchman doesn't die quickly, but gurgles and bleeds, hour after hour, little by little changing from dangerous enemy into ordinary fellow. Paul attempts to dress the wound, while the Frenchman watches him with terrified eyes. In the process, their eyes meet. After many more hours, the Frenchman dies. One part of Paul is relieved; another part is devastated: This is the first person he has killed personally. He speaks to the dead man:

> "Comrade, I did not want to kill you. . . . But you were only an idea to me before, an abstraction. . . . It was that abstraction I stabbed. But now, for the first time, I see you are a man like me. . . . Why do they never tell us that you are poor devils like us, that your mothers are just as anxious as ours, and that we have the same fear of death, and the same dying and the same agony—Forgive me, comrade; how could you be my enemy?"[5]

Paul searches the Frenchman's pockets and finds a photograph of his wife and little daughter. Then he finds the thing he fears the most: the man's name, Gerard Duval. So, the man he has killed had a wife, a child, a trade (he was a printer), and a name. Paul wildly promises to write to the wife, then thinks better of it; well, he will send her money, he will devote his life to taking care of her. It is not that Paul has undergone a conversion to pacifism or to some other ethical doctrine, or that he has made a decision to desert the war. It only means that the devices that were interfering with his grasp of reality—the distancing devices—have collapsed, and he has suddenly been confronted with what he has done. As for what can be done about that, he has no idea.

Even as he makes promises to the dead man, he understands that he will not keep them; later he puts all these feelings aside, saying to himself, "After all, war is war."

In Bao Ninh's novel *The Sorrow of War*, which is based on the author's experiences as a soldier in the North Vietnamese army and as a veteran struggling to maintain his sanity after the war was over, a similar story is told. The narrator, Phan, is in a battle with South Vietnamese ARVN troops supported by US artillery and bombers. Phan jumps into a crater.

> And then this guy jumped in on me, as heavy as a log. I was so frightened I stabbed him twice in the chest through his camouflage uniform, then once more in the belly, then again in the neck. He cried in pain and writhed around convulsing, his eyes rolling. I realized then he'd already been badly wounded before jumping in. His own artillery had blown his foot off and he was bleeding all over, even from the mouth. His hands were trying to hold in his intestines, which were spilling out of his belly and steaming. . . . I pushed his guts back into his belly and tore my shirt off to bandage him, but it was so hard to stop the bleeding.[6]

Phan is horrified, and feels pity for the man. When the bombardment lifts, he climbs out of the crater, and tells the man to wait while he looks for bandages. He finds some medical equipment, but then can't find the crater among the hundreds on the battlefield. He runs around, calling, "Hey, Saigon, Saigon, hey!" It is raining, and the craters begin to fill with water. When morning comes, he sees that all the craters have water to the brim.

> I pushed off. I was going a little mad. I began to imagine his death, water slowly rising on him. . . . He'd died still hoping desperately that I'd come back and save him, as I promised. . . . Now, even after many years, whenever I see a flood I feel a sharp pang in my heart and think of my cruel stupidity. No human being deserved the torture I left him to suffer.[7]

I would not be surprised to learn that Bao Ninh had read Remarque; his book is fiction after all, and it is an acceptable literary technique to include recognizable literary references to earlier works. The point is that in combat it does sometimes happen that a soldier is paralyzed, at least momentarily, by the sudden insight that the person he is supposed to kill, or has just killed, is just an ordinary folk. And one way that can happen is by being trapped together in a shelter during a bombardment. An unusual version (not fictional) of the tale was told by Vietnam War veteran Allen Nelson.

NATIVITY IN THE JUNGLE

My Marine company was going through a village, when we were attacked by some Vietnamese soldiers. Many Marines were killed and many were wounded. The rest of us just ran around, trying to find a place of safety. I ran behind a Vietnamese house and ran down into their family bunker.

Once I got down inside this bunker, I realized that there was someone there with me. . . . It was a young Vietnamese girl, maybe 15 or 16 years old. [Nelson would have been maybe eighteen or nineteen then.] . . . She was very afraid of me, but for some reason she would not get up and run away. She was breathing very hard, and she was in great pain. So I crawled over to her and realized that she was naked from the waist down. . . . I looked between her legs, and I saw the little head of a baby. . . . I took my hands and put them between her legs. And to my shock and surprise, a baby came out of her body and into my hands. . . . The girl snatched the baby from my hands. She bit the umbilical cord with her teeth. She wrapped her baby in black rags, and crawled out of the bunker and ran away into the jungle. . . .

When I came out of the bunker, I was a different person.[8]

While military training and discipline may succeed in "defeating" the "mental block" against killing sufficiently to get most of the troops actually to fire on the enemy, that doesn't mean that it succeeds equally well in preventing this from causing damage to the human psyche. Post-traumatic stress disorder (PTSD) is a term coined in the US during the Vietnam War, and popularized, it is said, by the Vietnam Veterans Against the War (VVAW). It indicates the various states of mind of people who have not been able to recover from the mental damage done them by some shocking experience, especially war. Before the term "PTSD" was coined, its wartime version was called "battle fatigue" (the term Marshall used), before that "shell shock," and before that it apparently had no name at all. Ninh's novel brilliantly depicts that state of mind; the narration moves jerkily between flashback and the present, through violent mood swings, trying to connect things that do not connect and to find meaning in events that mean nothing, as the author draws a portrait of himself barely hanging on to his sanity by the therapy of writing. Nelson spent his entire life after being discharged from the Marines battling PTSD. (That tale is told in the interview cited in endnote 8.)

POST-TRAUMATIC STRESS DISORDER

As there are many kinds of trauma, there are many kinds of resulting disorder, and PTSD is a catch-all term. Recorded cases include trauma from almost being killed, from having a close friend killed, from witnessing a death, from a bomb exploding nearby, and from the experience of killing someone. As novelist Pat Barker records in her trilogy on World War I, when the British military decided that "shell shock" was an illness that could be cured by the then recently developed methods of psychiatry, it was assumed that "cured" meant being able to go back to the trenches.[9] The person who could bear trench warfare was "normal," and the person who could not was "sick" and needed medical treatment (a version of the "war is the natural condition of man" position). Medical treatment would aim at producing such a "normal" person who, facing extreme personal danger and loss of comrades, witnessing and also causing grotesque and gruesome deaths and mutilations of human bodies, would feel no emotions strong enough to interfere with his efficient functioning as a soldier. For the person whose trauma was caused by the experience of killing, this would mean reestablishing distance from the enemy. For the person whose trauma was the moment the scales fell from his eyes, so that he saw what was being done, therapy would mean reattaching those scales, as it were: finding some way of re-concealing what had been revealed, de-realizing what had been realized.[10]

The problem of "psychiatric casualties" on the battlefield is no minor matter for the military. In World War II, about half a million US troops were discharged for psychiatric disabilities. A 1944 study showed that among troops kept in continuous combat for sixty days, 98 percent will have some kind of psychological breakdown. The 2 percent who do not break down are those with "aggressive psychopathic personalities."[11] Since World War II, wealthy countries, especially when they are fighting wars on other people's turf, have been able to mitigate this problem by rotating their troops out for Rest and Recreation (R&R; this also generally on other people's turf) before the sixty days are up. Poor countries, especially those that are being invaded, don't have that luxury.

"Battle fatigue" and "shell shock" referred to breakdowns in the combat zone; post-traumatic stress disorder, as the name indicates, refers to troubles that occur later, sometimes much later. Just as war offers its participants endless variations on the theme of horror, so PTSD can take many forms. It sometimes happens that a veteran who seems to have recovered will have a sudden relapse taking the form of nightmares, depression, flashbacks, or aberrant behavior. Some of these seem to be caused by, or accompanied by, a failure of distancing. By this, I don't mean only a failure to "put it all behind you," though that is of course a part of it. I mean that suddenly, perhaps in a nightmare or in a flashback, killing loses all its adornments, the distance that separated you from the enemy collapses, the victim is recognized as an ordinary person, and the victim's death becomes "sheer death."

Chapter 4

THE ENEMY MOST DEAR TO YOU

Gary Hulsey joined the US Marines at seventeen and did three tours in the Vietnam War. After he was discharged, he struggled to build a life for himself and suffered from insomnia. Every night he drank himself to unconsciousness to keep away the nightmares. One morning he woke up to find his wife of three weeks dead beside him, with the knife he kept under his pillow buried in her chest. He pled insanity, but he was not medically insane, and the "PTSD defense" was not yet well established. He was sentenced to twenty years, was paroled after eight, and apparently has managed to live quietly since then. In an interview on CNN, the gray-bearded Hulsey said, "War is hell. Hell is defined as being separated from God. God doesn't walk around in the war zone."[12] (To that I would add, that may be true, but often enough God's self-appointed agents do.)

This seems to be a pattern among PTSD victims: The veteran in his confusion sees the person most dear to him as an enemy, and attacks. Allen Nelson also experienced this; he was just about to smash the Viet Cong enemy with a lamp when his little boy cried, "Daddy, daddy, what are you doing?" which saved him from wife murder.[13] Here the person in all the world most alien to you, joined to you only by a kill-or-be-killed relationship, becomes one with the person in all the world most dear to you. And the equation works in both directions. You see the person most dear to you as a mortal enemy; at the same time you see the mortal enemy—the person(s) you killed in the war—as equivalent to the person most dear to you. When you killed that person on the battlefield, you were killing your wife (child, mother, sister, brother).

In Leslie Marmon Silko's magnificent novel about a native American struggling to maintain his sanity after his experiences fighting the Japanese in World War II, she depicts the same experience taking place in reverse, as it were.

> When the sergeant told them to kill all the Japanese soldiers lined up in front of the cave with their hands on their heads, Tayo could not pull the trigger. . . . In that instant he saw Josiah [his beloved uncle] standing there; the face was dark from the sun, and the eyes were squinting as though he were about to smile at Tayo. So Tayo stood there, stiff with nausea, while they fired at the soldiers, and he watched his uncle fall, and he knew it was Josiah; and even after Rocky started shaking him by the shoulders and telling him to stop crying, it was still Josiah lying there. . . . Rocky made him look at the corpse and said, "Tayo, this is a Jap! This is a Jap uniform!" And then he rolled the body over with his boot and said, "Look, Tayo, look at the face," and that was when Tayo started screaming because it wasn't a Jap, it was Josiah.[14]

HERAKLESIAN SYNDROME

Reading accounts of ancient battles such as *The Iliad*, it is hard to imagine those heroes as susceptible to PTSD, at least not the men. In the anti-war Greek tragedies, it is generally the women who go mad. There is at least one remarkable exception, however.

Euripides's *Herakles* has been, among the canon of Greek tragedies, poorly regarded and rarely played. I am no specialist in Greek drama, but according to William Arrowsmith, who was, Swinburne described the play as a "grotesque abortion," Gilbert Murray as "broken backed," and Gilbert Norwood as a tragedy that "falls so clearly into two parts that we cannot view it as a work of art."[15] The problem is the apparent absence of any connection between the first and second parts of the play.

Part one makes perfect sense. While Herakles is away doing heroic deeds, horrible Lycus invades Herakles's country, usurps Herakles's kingship, and decides to kill Herakles's wife and children to prevent them from taking revenge. As Lycus is on the verge of doing this, Herakles returns in the nick of time and destroys Lycus and his supporters. So far, so good.

In part two, everything goes haywire. The goddess Madness (Lyssa) appears with instructions to place her spell on Herakles. She does, and in his madness he sees his wife and children as the wife and children of Eurystheus, his worst enemy, the king who had forced the Twelve Labors on him. Believing this, he shoots arrows into them. This done, he is knocked unconscious and tied down. Later he wakes; sane again, he realizes what he has done, and is condemned to a life of mourning and penance.

One can see why this would be troubling to a drama critic. In the middle of the play, the critic sees what looks like a sudden, violent change of mood, of attitude, almost of world. But this is because the critic fails to notice that the playwright is following a consistent theme: He has presented the legitimate violence and the illegitimate violence as, qua violence, the same. Euripides gives us "the killing of a woman and her children" in three different versions. The first is designed to be satisfying to the audience: The just hero prevents the illegitimate killing of his wife and children by killing the evil tyrant and his supporters. The second is the one that takes place inside Herakles's head: By a logic not much better than that used by Lycus, he "legitimately" kills his enemy Eurystheus's wife and three children. Had the killing as Herakles imagined it been depicted on the stage, the audience might have accepted it, though not so easily; it could be fitted into some category such as "the natural desire for revenge." The third killing is what is depicted on the stage as what actually happened: killing his own wife and children while imagining them to be his enemy. The playwright has forced these three modes of killing on his audience in a torrent of action, the second and third simultaneously, breaking down the walls separating the neat categories of "their unjust killing" and "our just killing." In his consciousness, Herakles has killed Eurystheus's wife and children, this understood to be a permissible—or at least understandable—act. When he wakes up from his madness, those people he killed are his own wife and children—neither permissible nor understandable. The physical actions—the effect his arrows had on his victims' bodies, the blood spilled, the medical causes of their deaths—do not change from the one to the other; they are one. There is but one action, with two meanings. When Herakles was killing Eurystheus's wife and children, he was killing his own wife and children. The play is not "broken backed" at all; the two allegedly contradictory acts are the same act.

Moreover, as Greek classics scholar and translator Robert Emmet Meagher points out, before the goddess Madness puts a spell on him, Herakles himself gives us a preview of what that spellbound behavior is going to look like.

> And I—a task for my one hand alone
> shall go and raze this upstart tyrants house,
> cut off that blaspheming head and give it
> to the dogs to paw. All those men of Thebes
> who took my goodness and returned me ill—
> this bow ... shall slaughter them with rain of winged shafts
> till all Ismenus chokes upon the corpses
> and Dirce's silver waters run with blood. (*Herakles* ll. 565–73)

Meagher argues that this description "closely resembles the descriptions of berserkers in numerous epic traditions, as well as in modern battlefield accounts."[16] Seen in this perspective, Herakles's madness is the continuation of the state of mind he entered in taking vengeance on the usurper Lycus. "In plain words, Herakles can't stop killing; from Lykos (Lycus), he goes on to kill his own children."[17]

It would be a mistake also to suppose that the violent attack of madness depicted here by Euripides is an "isolated" product of the poet's imagination. If Herakles's attack on his family had been behavior utterly unknown to the audience, the play would have made no sense to them. And when, some fifty years after the play was first performed, Plato in the opening scene of *The Republic* has Socrates asking old Cephalus if he really thinks that justice obligates one to return a borrowed sword to its owner who is suffering from madness, this makes it pretty clear that madness and weapons were considered a dangerous combination in the Greece of that time.

Let us propose, then, that there is something we could call the Heraklesian Syndrome. In the play as written, Herakles's actions are caused by a literal deus ex machina: The goddess Hera, who hates Herakles because he was born out of Zeus's infidelity to her, sends Madness to put her spell on Herakles and force him to kill the people he loves best. But if he really had had no idea of what he was doing, that would mean that while he has every reason to feel grief, he would be innocent, and have no need to feel remorse. It would mean also that the critics are right, and the play is not interesting.

If the madness is no more than a means for Hera to control Herakles's action and force him to carry out the murders, then the play is a horror story, not a tragedy. But the madness does not transform Herakles into a robot operated by remote control. Madness, after all, thinks, however confusedly. The madness muddles Herakles's thoughts, but the muddled thoughts are his own. Herakles is depicted in Greek mythology as a great killer not only of monsters but also of human beings, without showing any sign of being troubled by this. What Hera does is force him, in the most violent way imaginable, to become aware of what he has been doing.

The quotation from the Koran that I use as the epigram for this chapter gives a most persuasive image of heaven and hell, from which I have been borrowing the expression "each soul shall know what it has done." It recalls William Blake's famous words in a book that, like this one, is about hell: "Every thing would appear . . . as it is."[18] In this rendering, the day of judgment simply means the day we see reality "as it is," the day we "know." The distance we have established between ourselves and our acts will collapse, and we will meet those acts, face on. Depending on how they appear to us then, we will experience heaven or hell.

"OR HAS THE BLOOD OF THOSE YOU'VE SLAIN MADE YOU MAD?"

To make sure that we understand that Herakles's madness is not just some excitement of the moment but is rooted in his past, the poet has Herakles's father (not Zeus, but the cuckolded man who brought him up) ask, "What do you mean, my son? What is this journey that you make? Or has the blood of those you've slain made you mad?" (*Herakles* ll. 965–7).

What the goddess Madness does to Herakles is give him the same distance from his wife and children as he has had for all his other killings. Then—and this is the cruel thing—instead of allowing him to stay blissfully mad, she takes the madness—and the distance—away again, forcing him to see what he has done. Herakles, the great killer, now knows what killing is.

But there is a weakness in this interpretation. The Greek gods, Hera included, have no particular compunction about killing human beings. It was surely them Shakespeare was thinking about when, in *King Lear*, he had

Gloucester say, "They kill us for their sport" (4.1.37). Sometimes they kill people themselves; sometimes (as in this play) they cause them to kill one another and sit back to watch. Wouldn't the claim that Euripides depicted these gods as arranging a situation to reveal the terrible equivalence of all killing be anachronistically to import an entirely different set of values into the Greek religious system?

But Euripides wrote the play. If there is creeping into it a value system different from that found in Greek mythology, it is he who put it there. If the Greek gods, themselves immune to the fear of death, are depicted as seeing little horror in violent death so long as it is the death of an enemy, that is not so of Euripides, the author of *The Trojan Women* and *Hekuba*. In these plays about the sufferings of women in war, the questions of which side in the war is just or whether the various killings (and the following enslavements) are unethical are not the issue; the suffering is simply what it is. Following this line of thought, *Herakles* can be read as an attempt to force into the awareness of the audience the simple insight that killings as killings are equivalent, no matter who is killed.

But if it is a truth, accessible to our apprehension if only the obstacles are removed, then we don't need a god to show it to us. It is there, to be observed. But tragically, one of the ways it is forced on our consciousness is through Heraklesian Syndrome. Our will to know the truth of the matter, in its confused search, muddles together the persons most hated and most loved, resulting in what the Greeks called "*mania*" and what we, lamely, call PTSD. We need to find better ways to teach ourselves these things.

NOTES

1. Dave Grossman, *On Killing* (Boston: Little, Brown, 1995), 188–9.
2. S. L. A. Marshall, *Men Against Fire: the problem of battle command* (Norman: U. of Oklahoma Press, 2000), originally published in Washington, *Infantry Journal* (New York: William Morrow, c1947), 79.
3. Marshall, *Men Against Fire*, 78.
4. Marshall, *Men Against Fire*, 79.
5. Erich Maria Remarque, *All Quiet on the Western Front*, trans. A. W. Wheen (New York: Ballantine, 1982 [English orig. Little, Brown, 1929]), 223.
6. Bao Ninh, *The Sorrow of War, a Novel of North Vietnam*, ed. Frank Palmos, trans. Phan Than Hao (New York: Anchor Books, 1996 [orig. Hanoi: Writers Association Publishing House, 1991]), 84.
7. Ninh, *The Sorrow*, 84–5.
8. Allen Nelson, "You were never my enemy," interview with Allen Nelson, by Brian Covert, 2009, http://www.indybay.org/newsitems/2009/02/02/18567572.php.

9. See especially the first volume of her trilogy: Pat Barker, *Regeneration* (Plume/Penguin, 1993).

10. In the author's note to *Regeneration*, Barker cites an article by Dr. W. H. R. Rivers, who treated "shell-shocked" British troops during World War I and who plays a role in her novel. Rivers's recollections make clear that being willing and able to return to the trenches were the criteria of a perfect cure, but that this was rarely achieved. W. H. R. Rivers, "The Repression of War Experience," *The Lancet*, February 2, 1918.

11. Roy L. Swank and Walter E. Marchand, "Combat Neuroses: Development of Combat Exhaustion," *Archives of Neurology and Psychology* 55 (March 1944).

12. Gary Hulsey, "Vietnam vet suffers PTSD, murders wife: Gary Hulsey interviewed by CNN's Miguel Marquez," 2012, accessible on YouTube.com.

13. Nelson, "Never My Enemy."

14. Leslie Marmon Silko, *Ceremony* (Penguin, 1977), 7–8.

15. William Arrowsmith, "Introduction to *Herakles*," in *The Complete Greek Tragedies*, vol. 3, *Euripides*, eds. David Grene and Richmond Lattimore (Chicago: U. of Chicago, 1992), 270–1. All citations from *Herakles* are from the translation in this edition.

16. Meagher, *Herakles gone mad*, 147.

17. Meagher, *Herakles gone mad*, 54

18. William Blake, *The Marriage of Heaven and Hell* (New York: Dover, 1994), 36.

Chapter 5

(Just) War Is Hell: Part I

Justice moved my great creator.
—Words inscribed over the gate to Hell, according to Dante

HELL: MORAL/AMORAL

When you say "War is hell," what are you saying? On the one hand, especially when the cliché is used by masters of war like General Sherman, it seems to mean war is an activity that takes place outside the sphere where ethical judgment could apply at all. But look more closely and you see that it is simultaneously a claim that war, like hell, operates under the highest of possible moral authorities.

As I pointed out in the introduction, if you follow the image of those religions that take hell seriously, "war is hell" does not simply mean it's a horror; it also is an attempt to give the horror a moral dimension. Hell, after all, is where we sinners get what we deserve. Among various degrees of legitimate violence, hell would be the limiting case, both in the sense of being as violent as violent gets, and of being as legitimate as legitimate gets. Among humanly enacted violent activities, the one that approaches hell most closely—in scale at least—is war. And among types of war, the one that purports to be closest to hell in its legitimacy is what we call just war.

Michael Walzer, in his modern classic *Just and Unjust Wars*, argues that Sherman's "war is Hell" is "a moral argument, an attempt at self-justification. Sherman was claiming to be innocent of all those actions (though they were his own actions) for which he was so severely attacked."[1] According to Walzer, Sherman's "moral argument" is, ironically, that in war it is impossible to act morally, and so no one can blame him for the things he did.

And indeed, Sherman repeatedly made statements of that type. For example, on the occasion of his ordering the residents of Atlanta to leave the city: "If the people raise a howl against my barbarity and cruelty, I will answer that war is war, and not popularity seeking."[2] Walzer takes Sherman's "war is Hell" to mean that the violence of war cannot be limited. Walzer's aim is to refute that. He argues that moral limits can be placed on the causes for which wars can be fought and, once a war begins, moral limits can still be placed on the tactics and weapons used. Walzer writes, "Even in hell, it is possible to be more or less humane, to fight with or without restraint."[3] In this and the next chapter, I want to consider both of those positions from a variety of angles, and also to suggest a third: that there are times when the influx of moral principles into warfare, far from reducing its brutality, carries its brutality to the furthest limit.

"VIOLENCE PUSHED TO ITS UTMOST BOUNDS"

To make his case, Walzer addresses the arguments made by the great philosopher of war Carl von Clausewitz.

Can the violence of war be limited by moral considerations? Carl von Clausewitz thought not. In his *On War*, he wrote:

> War is an act of violence pushed to its utmost bounds; as one side dictates the law to the other, there arises a sort of reciprocal action which logically must lead to an extreme.
>
> Self-imposed restrictions, almost imperceptible and hardly worth mentioning, termed usages of international law, accompany it without essentially impairing its power.
>
> Violence, that is to say, physical force (for there is no moral force without the conception of States and Law), is therefore the means; the compulsory submission of the enemy to our will is the ultimate object.
>
> Now, philanthropists may easily imagine there is a skillful method of disarming and overcoming an enemy without causing great bloodshed, and that this is the proper tendency of the Art of War. However plausible this may appear, still it is an error which must be extirpated; for in such dangerous things as War, the errors which proceed from a spirit of benevolence are the worst.[4]

For Clausewitz, justice in war is not a big issue. Just or not, war is "violence pushed to its utmost bounds," and it is dangerous foolishness to suppose that this violence could be limited by "a spirit of benevolence." Walzer cites Clausewitz and seeks to refute him by pointing out that his notion of "limitless war" is an abstraction, and that most actual wars are limited, as Clausewitz later admits. "No one," says Walzer, "has ever experienced 'absolute war.'"[5]

Walzer takes Clausewitz, along with Hobbes and Thucydides, as the chief representatives of the kind of thinking he wants to refute in his book. According to this thinking, where war begins, law and morality fall silent. All judgments made in wartime must be made on the basis of militarily realistic reasoning; one must choose a line of action not on the basis of its moral worth but only on the basis of its likely contribution to victory. Against this abstract argument, Walzer points out that in actual warfare, moral judgments are sometimes made both during the action and after. Even in the midst of warfare, human beings continue to be moral agents both in the sense that they continue to be responsible for what they do, and in the sense that they often act on the basis of that responsibility, or when they haven't, at least claim that they have. When Walzer says that Sherman's "war is Hell" is "a moral argument, an attempt at self-justification," that doesn't mean he accepts that argument: "The clearest evidence for the stability of our values over time is the unchanging character of the lies soldiers and statesmen tell. They lie in order to justify themselves, and so they describe for us the lineaments of justice."[6] Just as hypocrisy is the tribute vice pays to virtue, so the lies of soldiers and statesmen prove that actions in wartime are not immune to moral judgment. Walzer calls this "the moral reality of war."[7]

THE DUEL

Interestingly, Clausewitz begins his discussion of the nature of war with a statement that contradicts his later claim that the violence of war is limitless. "War," he says, "is nothing but a duel on an extensive scale."[8] But in a duel the violence is limited by rules. As Walzer points out, "If I wound my opponent, shoot his second, and then beat him to death with a stick, I am not dueling with him, I am murdering him."[9] And in fact, the duel provides an important model in the theory of just war.

A duel can take place only when both parties have agreed to it, and to the rules under which it is to be carried out. A location and time are determined; weapons—the same for both sides—are chosen; in the case of swords, it must be decided whether the duel ends with the first blood drawn or continues further; in the case of pistols, it must be decided how many steps the duelers are to take, and how many shots may be fired (often only one, rarely more than three), and so on. And, with rare exceptions, the duelers may use violence against no one but the other dueler. These conditions account for why dueling was for so long not considered criminal behavior. Each party knows what dueling is and has accepted its conditions. Each party is seeking to kill or wound the other, and has in effect given the other permission to try to do the same; when one is killed or wounded, there are no grounds for complaint, as that is just what the loser had been trying to do to the winner. Though duels are illegal now in most countries, we still accept this principle in contact sports and martial arts. Clausewitz uses the example of wrestling; I think boxing illustrates the situation more clearly. In a boxing match, boxers treat each other in a way that if they did the same to someone outside the ring, they would be arrested for criminal assault. As with a duel, a boxing match takes place at an agreed time and place, under a severe set of rules. The violence of boxing is intense, blood is usually spilled, boxers' bodies—especially their faces—are often permanently deformed by the battering they take, sometimes they suffer brain damage, and occasionally they are killed in the ring. Presumably they know what they are getting into and have agreed to it, and each receives no more than what he (and, in recent times, she) is trying to give out. So long as they follow the Marquis of Queensberry rules (no headbutting, no hitting below the belt, no horseshoes inside the gloves), society does not consider any injustice to have been done.

The same holds true for contact sports played between teams. Sports like soccer, American football, and rugby are played at an agreed-upon location, within agreed-upon boundaries, and for an agreed-upon period of time. The players wear uniforms to distinguish the teams from each other, and to distinguish the players, who can be smashed into and (depending on the sport) tackled, from the referees and spectators, who cannot. There is rarely a game with no injuries, and occasionally a player is crippled or killed. Again, if players were to treat people off the field the way they treat players on the opposing team, this would be considered criminal activity. But on the field and during game time, we call it sport. A kind of reverse golden rule applies: You may treat others in the way you have accepted they may treat you. Players may complain to the referees about how they are treated not when it begins to hurt but only when it breaks the rules.

AGINCOURT: THE DUEL WRIT LARGE

It is possible, as Clausewitz says, to imagine a model of a battle between armies as a kind of duel, and in history there have been battles that approached that model. One of the most famous is the October 1415 Battle of Agincourt, so vividly described in Shakespeare's *Henry V*. This battle was fought on a mostly level field, larger than a soccer field but still a limited space. It was finished between sunup and sundown on a single day. The English and French armies camped at the opposite ends of this field the night before, and made no attempt to harm one another until morning. The warriors were dressed such that they could be identified as on the French or English side. No contact was made between the armies until both had readied themselves for the battle.

No one other than combatants was on the field. Local villagers considered it safe to climb the hill next to the field to watch. But then, famously, some of the French troops committed a foul. Unable to make headway attacking the English soldiers, they circled around the English soldiers and attacked the unarmed boys watching the English baggage. Shakespeare has King Henry, on hearing of this, say, "I was not angry since I came to France / Until this instant" (4.7.58–9). Just prior to this, Shakespeare has the king weeping upon hearing of the deaths of the Duke of York and the Earl of Suffolk. Death in battle merits tears; only a violation of the rules merits anger.

Henry V, like all Shakespeare's plays, can be read in many ways, and one way is from the standpoint of just war theory. In his *Henry's Wars and Shakespeare's Laws*, international lawyer Theodor Meron does just that, comparing the many references to the laws of war in the play with the theories and practices that prevailed when Henry lived. He finds the play to be a remarkably accurate account of the medieval use of international law to try to place limits on war.

International law, then as now, divides just war theory into two aspects, *jus ad bellum*—that the war is fought for a just cause—and *jus in bello*—that the war is fought in a fair manner. As for the first, Meron reminds us that the Hundred Years' War, of which Henry's invasion of France was a part, "was a war of rights."[10] Henry believed that by right of inheritance he was the heir to the throne of France, and the play begins with him asking the archbishop of Canterbury to assure him of the legality of this claim. The archbishop, who, in Shakespeare's telling, has a vested interest in this war (he says out of the king's hearing that he hopes a war with France will prevent Parliament from carrying out its plans to seize church lands), gives a lengthy, complex, and far-from-convincing account of the king's right, assuring him that an invasion of France will be just and legal. Thus, Shakespeare shows us both how law is designed to limit war and how states use the same law to justify going to war.

As for *jus in bello*, the play has the king issuing an order that there shall be no looting and no quarreling with noncombatants. "We give express charge, that in our marches through the country, there be nothing compelled from the villages, nothing taken but paid for, none of the French upbraided or abused in disdainful language; for when lenity and cruelty play for a kingdom, the gentler gamester is the soonest winner" (3.7.114–20). And one English soldier is hanged for looting, an incident that sources say really took place. Moreover, the play makes clear that in the Battle of Agincourt, the French attack on the baggage train was also considered a violation of *jus in bello*. The wonderful character the Welshman Fluellen, who throughout the play gives a running commentary on the rules of war, on hearing of the attack says, "Kill the poys and the luggage! 'tis expressly against the law of arms. 'tis an arrant piece of knavery, mark you now, as can be offer't; in your conscience, now, is it not?" (4.7.1–4).

Then there is Henry's order to kill the French prisoners. In the play, this decision is attributed partly to Henry's anger at the attack on the baggage train but mainly to the fact that the French seemed to be preparing one more charge, which would make it dangerous to have hundreds of lightly guarded French soldiers standing in the English rear. John Keegan was at least partly agreeing with Clausewitz when he called this decision "comprehensible." The incident does seem to be a good illustration of Clausewitz's point: On the battlefield, when you are in a pinch, the logic of war trumps all else, and the claims of benevolence seem "almost imperceptible and hardly worth mentioning." Keegan writes, "If Henry could give the order and, as he did, escape the reproval of his peers, of the church and of the chroniclers, we must presume it was because the battlefield itself was still regarded as a sort of moral no-man's land and the hour of battle as a legal *dies non* [a day on which the law is suspended]."[11]

Thus the Battle of Agincourt, in the telling both of the chroniclers and of the playwright, can serve as a model of a battle carried out under the rules of just war, and of how, when "military necessity" demands it, those rules can be thrown out the window. At the same time, it was a bloody slaughter, mostly of the French. Keegan gives the figure of six thousand French troops killed, all within a few hours.

RAPE AND PILLAGE

The play gives us another image of *dies non*, closer still to what could be called absolute war. Before Agincourt, Henry's army had placed the city of Harfleur under siege. After some days, in the playwright's telling, the governor comes up on the wall to talk. Henry explains to him in detail, and with Shakespearian eloquence, what will happen if the governor refuses to surrender the town. Henry will suspend the laws of war, and allow his soldiers to destroy Harfleur entirely.

> If I begin the battery once again,
> I will not leave the half-achieved Harfleur
> Till in her ashes she lie buried. (3.3.7–9)

Not only will he have his soldiers burn the city, but also he will release them from the other rules of just war. They will be free to rape the women, pike the babies, bash in the heads of the elderly.

> The gates of mercy shall be all shut up,
> And the flesh'd soldier, rough and hard of heart,
> In liberty of bloody hand shall range
> With conscience wide as hell, mowing like grass
> Your fresh-fair virgins and your flowering infants. (3.3.10–14)

In carrying out these acts, Henry says, the soldiers will be doing the work of fiends in hell.

> What is it then to me, if impious war,
> Array'd in flames like to the prince of fiends
> Do, with his smirch'd compulsion, all fell feats
> Enlink'd to waste and desolation? (3.3.15–18)
> No mercy to young or old.
> Your fathers taken by their silver beards,
> And their most reverend heads dash'd to the walls.
> Your naked infants spitted upon pikes. (3.3.37–40)

The situation will resemble hell not only in the limitlessness of the violence but also in the belief that the victims, even the raped women, deserve what they are getting.

> What is't to me, when you yourselves are cause,
> If your pure maidens fall into the hand of forcing violation?
> (3.3.19–21)

Their sin, it seems, is that of refusing to surrender.

> What say you? Will you yield, and this avoid,
> Or, guilty in defence, be thus destroy'd? (3.3.42–3)

This speech is edited out of the Laurence Olivier movie version of *Henry V*, filmed during World War II. In the 1989 Kenneth Branagh version, Branagh's Henry uses body language to show relief after the governor answers that he will surrender the town. Believing that Henry really didn't want all these terrible things to happen makes it easier for movie-viewers to see him as a hero. But it would be wrong to understand this speech as Henry's last-ditch effort to keep his troops under control. Threatening a besieged town with rape and pillage, and carrying out that threat if the town refuses to surrender, is a military tactic. And if the threat is not sometimes carried out, it will no longer be effective as a threat. It even has a name: The OED defines "military execution" as "delivering a country up to be ravaged and destroyed by the soldiers." Whatever we imagine he might have thought about it personally, Henry was using a then well-known tactic and, on that day, it worked. Henry's account of what the tactic of military execution entails is accurate, except that it leaves out the looting, probably the most important part for many of the troops. The rules of just war are nullified. The soldiers may do what they feel like doing to the townspeople (though not to each other; this is no war of each against all). In particular, four actions usually considered crimes are permitted: You may kill noncombatants at random, rape any woman, steal, and destroy property, including by arson. Though these behaviors are permitted, Henry doesn't describe them as just; rather he uses the vocabulary of crime to describe them: "conscience wide as hell"; "licentious wickedness"; "murder"; "villany"; "foul hand"; "bloody-hunting slaughtermen." But while he is describing crime, it is, legally, not-crime: The law has been suspended. As Henry says, if the people of Harfleur continue to resist, they will be "guilty in defence," so it will be their own fault if they are "thus destroy'd." In his view, these lands are rightfully his, and the people there are usurpers. Thus while *jus in bello* is suspended, *jus ad bellum*, far from being suspended, is precisely what decriminalizes the ravaging of the town, the very "legitimacy" of the legitimate violence.

HELL ACCORDING TO THOMAS

In this sense, Henry's references to "Hell" and to "the prince of fiends" should not be taken as hyperbole, or as meaning only "a place of the most extreme suffering imaginable." There is a structural similarity between the tactic of military execution and the way hell is imagined. For this, we have the testimony of no less an authority than Saint Thomas Aquinas. In what might be called a functional analysis of the moral dynamics of hell, Thomas wrote,

> If we consider the ordering of the demons on the part of God who orders them, it is sacred; for He used them for Himself; but on the part of the demons' will it is not a sacred thing, because they abuse their nature for evil.[12]
>
> For punishment is referred to God for its first author. Nevertheless the demons who are sent to punish, do so with an intention other than that for which they were sent; for they punish from hatred or enmity; whereas they are sent by God on account of his justice.[13]

This is a clear and straightforward account of the mechanism by which high justice can metamorphose into the behavior of fiends in hell. Henry, in a position analogous to that of the God in Thomas's account, is the enabler of the massacre, but innocent of its consequences—or at least has plausible deniability. What is puzzling, however, is Henry's assumption that his troops ordinarily refrain from doing these things only insofar as they are "in my command," and if they escape from that, then of course they will be happy to behave like fiends in hell. Thomas imagined fiends and demons as evil by nature, but Henry's troops are ordinary folks. In the history of warfare, military organizations often enough have shifted—and still do shift—to the rape-and-pillage mode. Presumably the explanation for this—unless you believe that human beings are essentially evil—would be the effect on the psyche of prolonged exposure to combat. But still one can't but believe that some of the young soldiers come out from this nightmare weeping, and that many are traumatized for life.

According to the chroniclers, Henry's mercy to the surrendered people of Harfleur was limited. The population was not slaughtered but, with the exception of a few elites and people with enough money to buy their way out, the population was (as was the population of Atlanta) deported. And the town was sacked, "to the great gaine of the Englishmen."[14] This was apparently considered relatively lenient. When on the same expedition Henry's army took the town of Caen, they massacred the residents.[15]

This doesn't mean that Henry was an especially cruel king. On the contrary, during his reign he is reputed to have been unusual in trying, though without much success, to reduce the cruelty of war and military occupation by issuing ordinance after ordinance forbidding (or limiting) massacre, robbery, extortion, arson, and rape.

But from ancient times, rape and pillage had been an important part of military activity—the climax, as it were, of a successful campaign. Soldiers were paid either very little or nothing at all, so the spoils they could get by sacking a city were part or all of their wages. The Roman historians tell how from the days of the Republic, pillaging a city and enslaving captives—especially women, presumably part of the "property" the conquerors had rights to—were the chief compensations for the troops: For many of them, this was what war was all about. For the warriors of medieval Europe, the practice was supported not only by the authority of ancient Rome but also by that of the Bible, as can be seen in the passage I quote earlier, in which Moses gives detailed instructions on the rules for pillage, massacre, and enslavement in a city that has been defeated in war (Deuteronomy 20:10–17). The boundary between a holy army and a robber band has at times been, as they say, fuzzy.

CASTLES OR GIRLS, WE'LL BREACH THEIR DEFENSES!

Rape has been considered a crime in most countries and cultures for centuries, if not in positive law, then in customary law. Since World War II, under the influence of the United Nations, the Nuremberg and Tokyo trials, the

Geneva Conventions, and other international gatherings, it has come to be considered a war crime. A person learning this for the first time might want to ask two contradictory questions: One, why did it take so long? Two, in what sense is rape a *war* crime? Most of the actions we call war crimes are aimed at killing, wounding, or causing physical pain to the enemy. Isn't rape carried out for the (alleged) pleasure of the rapist? Even when it is done in the cruelest manner, doesn't that nonmilitary motivation place it in the category of a personal crime, no less criminal than a war crime, but different?

This misses the degree to which sexuality is intertwined in military action—something we sometimes know and sometimes forget. For example, when we are reading about George Washington's or Dwight Eisenhower's campaigns, we are not likely to think about this aspect of warfare. However, if an invading army is approaching one's town, just about everyone knows that it's wise to hide the women. Depending on the situation and the mood of the invading troops, officers may try to prevent mistreatment of the local women, or to promote it, or, like King Henry, make clear that they will stand out of the way. It is believed by some that the tacit permit to mistreat the women will usefully lower the morale of the enemy (though it risks enraging them and causing them to fight harder) and raise the morale of your troops (though it risks disillusioning at least some of them). Even if permission is rarely given, the fact that the invading army is carrying this capability adds to the terror it inspires. In this way, rape, in addition to being a personal crime, can serve as a military tactic.

But there is something in the phenomenon of military action not captured by this sort of rational choice analysis, well expressed in the soldier's ditty in Goethe's *Faust*:

> Show us a fortress
> Proudly defended,
> Give me a mistress
> Haughty and splendid
> . . . .
> This is the life for us,
> This is the strife for us
> Castles or girls, we'll
> Breach their defenses
> War-spoil and love-spoil
> Are ours to be won.[16]

The key word here is "spoil." In this bit of brilliant doggerel, the "love-spoil" is not a means/tactic by which to achieve the end/conquest. It is one aspect of the end itself, a concrete, tactile way the individual soldier can personally experience the conquest. "War-spoil" refers to the things the army acquires by right of conquest—or did in Goethe's era: the right to rule the land and dominate its people. "Love-spoil" refers to what the individual warriors (believe they) have acquired through the right of conquest from time immemorial: the rape right.

I have never read or heard a persuasive analysis of how this reasoning works, nor am I going to attempt one here. To the poet, however, it seems to be obvious (which is not to say he is persuaded by it). And interestingly, the other poet, Will Shakespeare, wrote the same reasoning into his *Henry V.* As he ends the play, it is Henry who "gets the girl" not by rape but as a kind of war-spoil and love-spoil mixed together. When his love-spoil, Princess Katherine, asks him how she could possibly love the enemy of France, Henry gives a wonderfully garbled answer:

> No; it is not possible you should love the enemy of France, Kate; but, in loving me, you should love the friend of France; for I love France so well that I will not part with a village of it; I will have it all mine; and, Kate, when France is mine and I am yours, then yours is France and you are mine. (5.2.180–6)

And in the negotiations between Henry and the French king, the same theme continues:

> KING HENRY. You may, some of you, thank love for my blindness, who cannot see many a fair French city for one fair French maid that stands in my way.
>
> FRENCH KING. Yes, my lord, you see them perspectively, the cities turned into a maid; for they are girdled with maiden walls that war hath never entered.
>
> KING HENRY. Shall Kate be my wife?
>
> FRENCH KING. So please you. (5.2.443–51)

It seems it makes sense to talk about the conquest of France and the conquest of Katherine all in the same sentence. The cities they take are said to have been "raped"; presumably the word will not be used with regard to the princess.

In modern times, rape has been outlawed in the military regulations of most countries, so it may seem inappropriate to include this illegal behavior in a discussion of just war. After all, it is precisely this kind of behavior that the laws of just war are aimed to eliminate. But the notion that the conquering (and sometimes also the losing) soldier has a right to the women is ancient and continues to run deep. As Shakespeare and Goethe discerned, it seems to be an integral component of the warrior mentality, not easy to separate out from the strictly military components. The massive rapes carried out by the

Russian troops in eastern Europe and Germany, by the Japanese troops in China and south Asia, by the Serbian troops (allegedly under orders) in the former Yugoslavia, and the US troops in Vietnam are famous, but rapes have been carried out, individually and in gangs, by all armies everywhere. And we hear that even when United Nations peacekeepers enter a country, brothels pop up around their camps, presumably permitted in hopes of reducing the rape rate.

This aspect of traditional military culture may be part of the reason why it is so difficult for women to achieve equality in the military. Much of the debate on this issue misses the point, because it falsely assumes that only legal warfare will be fought. Certainly women can do all the things that legal warfare requires. Women are even capable of long-distance war crimes, such as are carried out by aircraft. The military Old Guard, who argue that women can never be soldiers in the way men can, can't publicly state the real reason. They know that there is more to warfare than legal operations. They know that an army that does not carry with it at least the tacit threat of rape and pillage is no army at all in the traditional sense. "Yes," they want to say, "you can fire a machine gun and drive a tank, but how good are you at the rape and pillage?"

The question is probably unanswerable, but it is also unaskable.

NOTES

1. Michael Walzer, *Just and Unjust Wars: A Moral Argument with Historical Illustrations* (New York: Basic Books, 1977), 32.
2. William T. Sherman, *Memoirs of General W. T. Sherman* (Renaissance Classics, 2012), 257.
3. Walzer, *Just and Unjust Wars*, 33.
4. W. Carl von Clausewitz, *On War*, ed. Anatol Rapoport, trans. J. J. Graham (Penguin Books, 1968 [English orig. Routledge and Kegan Paul, 1908]), 103, 101, 102.
5. Walzer, *Just and Unjust Wars*, 24.
6. Walzer, *Just and Unjust Wars*, 19.
7. Walzer, *Just and Unjust Wars*, 15.
8. Clausewitz, *On War*, 101.
9. Walzer, *Just and Unjust Wars*, 25n.
10. Theodor Meron, *Henry's Wars and Shakespeare's Laws: Perspectives on the Law of War in the Later Middle Ages* (Oxford: Oxford University Press, 1993), 17.
11. John Keegan, *The Face of Battle* (UK: Penguin Books, 1978), 109.
12. Thomas Aquinas, *Summa Theologia*, part 1, question 109, article 2, trans. Fathers of the English Dominican Province (New York: Christian Classics, 1948 [English orig. 1911]).

13. Thomas Aquinas, *Summa Theologia*, part 1, question 114, article 1.
14. Holingshed, quoted in Meron, *Henry's Wars*, 85.
15. Quoted in Meron, *Henry's Wars*, 87.
16. Goethe, *Faust*, part 1, trans. David Luke (Oxford: Oxford University Press/ Meron, 1987), 29–30.

Chapter 6

A Container for a Universal Solvent: (Just) War Is Hell: Part II

> The commander will not wish to take precautions to such an extent as to reduce his chances of military success.
>
> —Major General A. P. V. Rogers

THE SEARCH FOR HUMANITARIAN KILLING

How is it possible, the old riddle goes, to make both a universal solvent and a container that can hold it? Clausewitz sees a successful army as like a universal solvent. The whole point is to build an organization that will penetrate all possible obstacles. It may be stopped by a yet stronger war machine, but that means that it has failed. The logic of war itself, Clausewitz teaches, carries its violence to the extreme limit, and efforts to limit this process through international law are inconsequential. On the other hand, virtually all societies have ethical systems that condemn violence, and seek if not to ban it, at least to place limits on it. In the days of Henry V, the laws of war were a combination of canon law, the remains of medieval chivalry, and customary law developed for practical reasons on the battlefield. The attempt to secularize the laws of war and to organize them into a system based on rational principles is said to have begun with Hugo Grotius. In the prolegomena to his 1625 "The Rights of War and Peace," Grotius explains his reasons for doing this work. On the one hand, he was horrified at the brutalities of the Thirty Years' War.

> Throughout the Christian world I observed a lack of restraint in relation to war, such as even barbarous races should be ashamed of; I observed that men rush to arms for slight cause, or no cause at all, and that when arms have once been

taken up there is no longer any respect for law, divine or human; it is as if, in accordance with a general decree, frenzy had openly been let loose for the committing of all crimes.[1]

On the other hand, he saw danger at the other extreme.

> Confronted with such utter ruthlessness many men, who are the very furthest from being bad men, have come to the point of forbidding all use of arms to the Christian, whose rule of conduct above everything else comprises the duty of loving all men. . . . But the very effort of pressing too hard in the opposite direction is often so far from being helpful that it does harm. . . . For both extremes a remedy must be found, that men may not believe either that nothing is allowable or that everything is.[2]

With admirable clarity, Grotius here defines the awkwardly ambiguous position of just war theory. It seeks to prohibit some of the cruel practices of war and to permit others. It aims to reduce the effects of war as far as is possible, and at the same time to rescue war from those who seek to abolish it. The same ambiguity characterizes the efforts of the lawyers and activists who seek to strengthen the laws of war today. By clarifying what counts as a war crime, they also, intentionally or unintentionally, clarify what kind of war is not a crime. One can imagine three sorts of motivation for this kind of work: (1) to reduce the scope of legal military activity little by little in the hope of abolishing it altogether; (2) persuaded by those who believe that the abolition of war is probably not achievable, to use international law to reduce the suffering caused by war as much as possible; and (3) to make war seem a clean and honorable activity (closer to the way it is portrayed in romantic fiction) and thus protect it from its enemies. There is something to be said for each of the first two positions, and perhaps even for the third. If we must enter hell, it is probably better if the fiends and devils there are required to obey at least some rules.

RULES FOR JUSTLY INITIATING HELL: *JUS AD BELLUM*

First of all, a just war must be fought for a just cause. But notions of what counts as a just cause have changed over the years. From ancient times, many people have believed that the most just of all possible wars were those fought in the name of one's religion, either to defend it or to extend it. The Old Testament and the Koran are filled with tales of wars against infidels; Catholic Europe sent crusade after crusade to try to win Jerusalem back from what they then called the Turk; the Reformation gave birth to an era during which Christians fought each other. Today, though international law does not recognize religion as a just cause for war, we have seen a resurgence of the jihad, and while few others than then US president George W. Bush have publicly called the War on Terror a crusade, for many of those involved in that war, that is what it is.

Just cause has, at different times, meant vengeance for wrongs done, punishments for insults (to a country's flag, for example, or to one of its ambassadors), pursuit of a country's or its sovereign's rights (as with Henry V), mistreatment of a country's nationals living or traveling abroad—the ingenuity of kings and queens and their advisors has produced a very long list. In modern times, wars—notably World War I—have been fought in the belief that they would establish a lasting peace. The reason for going to war that in terms of cost-benefit analysis might be the most "rational"—namely, to steal a country's wealth—is no longer recognized as a just cause, which is probably why so many other causes have been invented.

In the past, if the cause was just, it was considered permissible for a country to begin hostilities against another, but in 1945 it was written into the Charter of the United Nations that henceforth only defensive wars would be considered legal (article 51). In the principles set out for the Nuremberg war-crimes trials, the primal war crime—the unmoved mover of belligerency, as it were—was what they called "the crime against peace," that is, making war where there had been no war: aggression. But when a country is attacked, military resistance is allowed.

Of course it was hoped that by outlawing aggressive war, the world would become a more peaceful place: With no aggressive war, there should be no occasion for defensive war either. But this hope could be entertained only by ignoring a principle believed to be basic by military strategists, which was pounded into our heads when I was at US Marine Corps Basic School: The best defense is a good offense. When you are facing an enemy, or a potential enemy, you do not sit and wait for the other to start killing you. A far better way to protect your turf is to make the first move, and fight the war on their turf. Using this principle, even when a country is the first to take action, it can claim that the action is defensive. Thus, since the UN charter was adopted, there has been war after war in which both sides insist they are on the defense. Another way to get around this rule is not to call your action "war," but rather "police action," "collective defense," "military operation," "humanitarian intervention"—again, the list is long, as is the list of the wars fought under these various excuses since 1945. (As commentators can't agree as to what counts as a "war" or a "military action," estimates of the number of wars since 1945 range from several score to over one hundred.)

RULES FOR KEEPING HELL JUST AND ORDERLY: *JUS IN BELLO*

If the international laws pertaining to war are intended to bring order into that activity, it is a problem that they themselves are not that orderly. This body of law has been built up over centuries, is grounded in a variety of different principles and motivations, and is riddled with loopholes. Some is customary, some based on treaties. Some of the treaties are codifications of customary law; others are responses to modern conditions, in particular to technological advances in weaponry. Some are motivated by an ethical intention to reduce suffering; some seem to be rooted in the spirit of chivalry; some are designed, like the rules of football, to make it possible for the game to proceed in an orderly manner; still others, like the rules against poison gas, are grounded in the mutual interest of both sides and depend on reciprocity. This last sort follows yet another variation of the golden rule: "We won't do xxx to you (only) so long as you don't do xxx to us." And as the only international organization with the authority to enforce these laws—the United Nations—doesn't have the power to enforce them more than sporadically, they are enforced—if at all—mainly by individual states. Sometimes states do prosecute some of their own soldiers for war crimes but generally only those in the lower ranks. High-ranking war criminals on the losing side—generals or politicians—are sometimes punished by the winners or their allies. I have heard of no case of a high official on the winning side being tried for a war crime.

Thus, a survey of the rules pertaining to *jus in bello* comes up with a motley collection of good intentions (remembering always where the road paved with such materials will get you to). One of the first modern attempts to codify the laws of war was the Declaration of Saint Petersburg of 1868, which sought to counter the effects of advances in the technology of weaponry, and whose authors seem to have been motivated by the belief that it is possible, by regulating the bullets, to make the experience of being shot down on the battlefield a little less painful. In prefacing this declaration, however, they set down with admirable clarity one of the basic principles of *jus in bello*. The declaration states that the legitimate object of war (which is to win) "would be exceeded by the employment of arms which uselessly aggravate the sufferings of disabled men, or render their death inevitable."[3] The key term here is "uselessly," a word well fitted to the nineteenth-century drive for rationalization of means in all possible fields; it would not be stretching things to replace it with "inefficiently." This is the principle that ties together about all the just war treaties listed below: If this offensive behavior is not going to have an appreciable effect on your chances of winning anyway, then don't do it.

In the 1868 treaty, the contracting parties agree not to use "any projectile of less weight than four hundred grammes, which is explosive, or is charged with fulminating or inflammable substances." In 1899, this was amended to include "bullets which expand or flatten easily in the human body," that is, dumdum bullets.[4] Since then, high-explosive bombs that send out shrapnel that wreaks havoc inside the body, high-velocity bullets that make a small hole going in and a huge hole coming out, and napalm (jellied gasoline) and white phosphorus, which stick to the body or clothing while they burn at ultra-high temperatures, have all been developed and are not prohibited.

In the Hague Convention of 1907, the first two prohibitions listed in article 23 are the use of poison and "to kill or wound treacherously individuals belonging to the hostile nation or army."[5] These seem to be based more on rules of chivalry than on a modern notion of minimizing suffering. It is not obvious that dying from poison entails more suffering than dying from a bullet or a sword; it would depend on the poison and the nature of the wound. Perhaps the point is that using poison doesn't give the victim an opportunity to fight back, which violates the rules of dueling (but neither does bombing nor sniper fire). Poison has the reputation of being a "dirty trick" more fitting for a Lucrezia Borgia than a Sir Lancelot. In World War I, poison gas, despite article 23, was used by both sides. Today, its use, along with that of biological weapons, is outlawed, but its possession is not. Many military organizations possess these weapons and train their troops in their use. (When I was in the Marines, training included taking off and putting on gas masks in tear-gas chambers.) The point is, if the enemy begins to gas you, it becomes legal to gas them back: again, the reverse golden rule.

As for treachery, what could it mean? Does it mean not giving the other a fighting chance? Is it treachery to shoot a person who doesn't know you're there? or from an airplane so high the victims can't shoot back? or from a robot aircraft? In the context of modern warfare (and perhaps in any warfare), the word "treachery" or its equivalent can be regularly heard in speeches criticizing the enemy, but it is not useful as a term of law.

"Were the Hague peace conferences," Adam Roberts asks, "just an excessively optimistic attempt to make provision for the ultimate oxymoron, a humane war?"[6] Roberts argues that this conclusion would be too simple. He begins the essay from which this quotation was taken with the statement "This is an account of a failure," reminding us that those conferences were followed by World Wars I and II, which were characterized by "hideous excesses in the manner of their conduct." At the same time, he argues, "the Hague Conventions were to have a significant impact on events."[7] At the time this was written—1994—I might not have agreed with that assessment. After the US began its War on Terror and what remained of the structure of international law (prohibition of aggression, rights of POWs, ban on torture, equality under the law) started to come crashing down around us, the value of what we were losing—however evasive, hypocritical, or beside the point it had often seemed—became painfully obvious. It would be wrong to attempt an overall judgment; cases must be looked at separately. Here I will take up a few examples.

RAT-A-TAT-TAT

Consider again the problem of bullets. It was after the Hague Convention outlawing dumdum bullets that the machine gun became operational, giving birth both to the expression "the industrialization of warfare" and to the gangster slang "I'll fill you full of lead." The machine gun does have the capacity to fill (or "pump") a person full of lead, causing more damage to the internal organs, and presumably more pain, than a single dumdum bullet. But why the term "industrialization"? I suppose part of the reason was that the machine gun, the weapon the most responsible for making defense stronger than offense, thus bringing about the trench warfare of World War I, is in fact a machine. So, the symbol of the most feared warrior was no longer the charging infantryman with fixed bayonet or the mounted cavalry officer with sword drawn, but a machine operator. Moreover, the Maxim, perhaps the most effective of the various types in use at that time, uses a conveyor belt to bring the bullets up promptly and line them up with the gun barrel. That is, it introduces the principle of the factory assembly line into warfare. From the standpoint of the workers/soldiers, it amounted to a kind of speedup on the line. It may seem a terrible irony that a technology designed for mass production would be turned to the purpose of mass destruction. But the matter may be less ironic than it seems. According to Sigfried Giedion, the first operational factory "assembly line" was actually a disassembly line, used for disemboweling and dismembering pigs in the slaughterhouses of Cincinnati in the nineteenth century.[8] The situations are entirely different, but in both cases the conveyer belt is what brought modern efficiency to the mass production of death. Regarding the Battle of the Somme July 1, 1916, a failed British attempt to advance against machine-gun fire and break through the German lines, John Keegan writes, "In all the British . . . lost about 60,000, of whom 21,000 had been killed, most in the first hour of the attack, perhaps in the first minutes."[9] From the standpoint of the Germans, that's a well-run slaughterhouse.

BOMBS AWAY

In the late nineteenth century, when many teams around the world were trying to build an airplane that would really fly but none had succeeded, there were three sorts of people who had a special interest in this project. These were the science-fiction writers, the military strategists, and the international lawyers. It was obvious before any airplane ever got off the ground that one of its principal uses would be to drop bombs on people and buildings from the air. Jules Verne's *The Flight of Engineer Robur*, published in 1886, contains a drawing of a fantastical aircraft hovering over Africa and bombing terrified Africans. H. G. Wells's *The War in the Air*, published in 1908, just five years after the Wright brothers' plane wobbled up off the ground, contains a picture of New York City bombed into what looks like a firestorm. It seems that it was evident to the science-fiction imagination that bombing colonies and great cities was built into the nature of the airplane.[10]

Military people, for their part, saw a number of possible uses for the airplane. Some argued that it should be used only against uniformed enemy troops—what they call close air support. Others argued that given that airplanes can fly behind enemy lines, it is only natural that they should be used to attack not only uniformed enemy but also the trucks and trains bringing supplies, the roads and rails on which those trucks and trains move, and, by the same logic, the factories where the supplies are manufactured and the power plants and oil refineries that keep those factories running. Some argued that the factories should be bombed only at night when the workers are at home (assuming the factories aren't running twenty-four-hour shifts); others took the opposite position that the workers should be bombed even in their homes, which, from the standpoint of military strategy, makes sense. But if so, then doesn't it make even more sense, if you have enough airplanes and bombs, to bomb everybody? In this manner, the logic of war, as Clausewitz said, once you enter into it, moves to its extreme conclusion.

One of the most influential advocates of the "bomb everybody" position was Italian Brigadier General Giulio Douhet. In his *Lufterrshaft* (1921, published in English as *Command of the Air* in 1942), he argued that bombing the enemy's civilian population was the best way to bring a quick end to a war. "A people who are bombed today as they were yesterday, and who know they will be bombed again tomorrow and see no end to their martyrdom, are bound to call for peace at length."[11] Thus, indiscriminate bombing will turn out to be the most humane way of making war. This argument was later used to justify the firebombings and atomic bombings in World War II.

In the Western world, it is popularly believed that the first case of indiscriminate bombing was the 1937 German attack on the city of Guernica during the Spanish Civil War, but this is not so. The first indiscriminate bombings were carried out by the European colonials in their colonies. Sven Lindqvist gives a long list, which he does not claim to be complete: France in Morocco in 1912; Spain in Morocco in 1913; Britain in Somaliland and northeast India in 1915, in Egypt in 1916, on the India-Afghanistan border in 1917, in Afghanistan in 1919, in Ethiopia in 1919, in Iran, Trans Jordan, and Iraq in 1920, and in Iraq again in 1923; France in Syria in 1925; Britain again in Burma and India in 1935; Italy in Ethiopia from 1935; and Japan in Shanghai in 1932.[12] These bombings seem to have had little influence on international law. It was Europeans bombing one another that triggered demands for regulation.

During World War I, strategic bombing attacks by both sides were initially directed at military targets (aside from enemy lines, also factories, railways, warehouses, etc.), but the bombs were so inaccurate they landed pretty much anywhere, leading each side to believe that the other side was carrying out intentional indiscriminate bombing. This would give each side the right, according to the laws of war, to respond in kind. But Major General Hugh Trenchard, the first head of the British Royal Air Force, used a different logic to defend indiscriminate bombing. "The moral effect of bombing," he argued, "stands undoubtedly to the material effect in a proportion of 20 to 1."[13] He has been mocked for pulling numbers out of the air, but by "in a proportion of 20 to 1," he probably meant only "a lot more." What is important, first of all, is that he had expressed another aspect of the World War I "industrialization of warfare." To expand productivity—in the case of war, destructivity—by a factor of twenty is to apply the principle of efficiency: increasing the desired effect by a factor larger than the increase in the expenditure of effort required to achieve it: a kind of reverse Taylorism. At the same time, though he did not use the word, Trenchard had grasped that indiscriminate bombing is a strategy of terrorism. "Moral effect" is an euphemism for terror, and terrorism is the strategy of expanding the fear effect of violence by using it indiscriminately. With his "20 to 1," Trenchard was one of the first to express clearly the strategic argument for terror bombing.

RULES FOR JUST BOMBING

The international lawyers also began thinking about the question of bombing before the airplane was invented. The 1899 Hague Convention placed a five-year moratorium on the dropping of explosives from the air. The reasoning behind the five years was that at the time the only aircraft available for dropping explosives was the balloon, which goes only where the wind takes it and therefore has no means to obey any regulations as to where bombs should be dropped. Thus balloon bombing was to be banned, but the committee anticipated that within five years, a more accurate bomb carrier would be invented, capable of following the rules. (They were close: The Wright brothers' plane got off the ground just four years later.) At the same time, they included in the Hague Treaty the following:

> Article 25: The attack or bombardment of towns, villages, habitations or buildings which are not defended is prohibited. Article 26: The commander of an attacking force, before commencing a bombardment, except in the case of an assault, should do all he can to warn the authorities. Article 27: In sieges and bombardments, all necessary steps should be taken to spare as far as possible edifices devoted to religion, art, science and charity, hospitals, and places where the sick and wounded are collected, provided they are not used at the same time for military purposes. The besieged should indicate these buildings or places by some particular and visible signs, which should previously be notified to the assailants.[14]

"Bombardments" include, of course, bombing from the air. These articles bring into marvelously clear focus the conflict between Clausewitz's principle that the logic of war brushes aside humanitarian attempts to limit it and moves inexorably to the extreme, and the natural human desire to use the law to arrest the slide toward total destruction. As such, the articles bequeathed to later generations of warriors a number of puzzles. What does "not defended" mean? If a town tries to defend itself by bringing in some antiaircraft guns, does that mean they are giving the enemy permission to bomb it? Must an air force commander tell the enemy in advance where he is going to strike next, like a boxer saying, "Now I'll do a right cross, next comes a left hook"? Are people who are being destroyed by bombardment, and who try to save themselves by painting a red cross on top of their building, to be considered war criminals? Looking at the matter from the perspective of the military commander, British military lawyer A. P. V. Rogers captures the nature of these regulations with fine clarity: "The commander will not wish to take precautions to such an extent as to reduce the chances of military success."[15] This is Clausewitz's principle in a nutshell: What is outlawed on the battlefield by these laws are cruel and destructive actions *that do not contribute to military success*. But cruel and destructive actions that do not contribute to military success are not, strictly speaking, military actions. They are not, in Clausewitz's definition, acts of war. They are inefficiencies, a waste of time, men and matériel, motivated perhaps by desire for vengeance, explosive hatred, or some pathological state of mind created by the war situation, but not in accord with the cool logic of military strategy. From the standpoint of that logic, these actions can be dispensed with. Eliminating them amounts to a rationalization of means. "Military necessity" applies where victory hangs in the balance, and it is there that the rules of international law come to be perceived as "almost imperceptible and hardly worth mentioning."

In late 1922, another conference, this time under the League of Nations, opened at the Hague in the hope of negotiating a more specific set of rules for aerial bombardment. What they agreed upon included the following:

> Article 22: Aerial bombardment for the purpose of terrorizing the civilian population, of destroying or damaging private property not of a military character, or of injuring non-combatants is prohibited. . . . Article 24: Aerial bombardment is legitimate only when directed at a military objective, that is to say, an object of which the destruction or injury would constitute a distinct military advantage to the belligerent.[16]

The Hague Rules of Aerial Warfare, of which these two articles are part, were never ratified by any country, though some jurists consider them to have become part of international customary law. But concerning these two articles, once again one must ask, If the destruction or injury of an object does not constitute a distinct military advantage, then why do it? Such actions may satisfy the passions of war, but they violate the logic of war. It may be that the destructiveness of war can, at least in some cases, be reduced if the warriors control their rage and stick to business. This seems to be what the above-quoted articles are aiming at. But they in no way contradict Clausewitz's dictum. According to him, it is the logic of efficient, strictly-business war-making that generates the "military necessity" that leads inexorably to the extreme. Of course, in real war, cool reasoning cannot be easily separated from the effects of emotion. "Morale," which is essential to victory, is largely emotion, as is terror, which contributes to defeat. If the theories of Trenchard and Douhet are to be believed, the use of indiscriminate bombing to improve morale on your side and to incite terror on the other is a matter to be included in the cool calculations of warriors. The experience of World War II terror bombings indicates that Douhet was wrong to believe that bombed civilians would rush to their leaders and demand that they capitulate; it seems that, on the contrary, it often had the opposite effect of hardening their determination to fight on. On the other hand, it may be true that it has a positive effect on the morale of your own troops and citizenry.

ABSOLUTE JUST WAR

In refutation of Clausewitz, Walzer wrote, "No one has ever experienced 'absolute war.'" But that depends on how you understand the word "absolute."

If, as Hannah Arendt argued, birth is what gives human beings the concept of a new beginning, death is what gives us the concept of an absolute ending. In that sense, everyone who has been killed in a war has "experienced absolute war" (assuming it's OK to describe dying as an "experience"). Just war theory, like the logic of war itself, seeks to relativize death by judging, say, five hundred dead to be only half as bad as one thousand dead, and in a sense this is certainly true. But from the standpoint of the five hundred dead, it is as bad as it gets. To paraphrase Walzer, no one has ever experienced relative death.

But this way of thinking takes us away from the logic of war. By "absolute war," I presume both Walzer and Clausewitz mean a war that, taken as a whole, has moved to its most extreme form. But Clausewitz understands as well as Walzer that his "absolute war" is the end point of a process of reasoning, an abstraction. "Reasoning in the abstract, the mind cannot stop short of the extreme because it has to deal with the extreme, with a conflict of forces left to themselves, and obeying no other but their inner laws. . . . But everything takes a different shape when we pass from abstractions to reality."[17]

In reality, with boots on the ground in an actually existing terrain, there are many factors that inhibit a war from going to the extreme. For example, as Clausewitz himself admitted, it is physically impossible to concentrate all of one's forces in a single location for a single battle. If one side judges that the military strength of the other is not so strong, it may judge that a limited effort will be sufficient. And it often happens that wars are fought over issues that aren't worth a supreme effort. "The smaller the sacrifice we demand from our opponent, the smaller, it may be expected, will be the means of resistance which he will employ; but the smaller his preparation, the smaller ours will require to be. Further, the smaller our political object, the less value shall we set upon it, and the more easily shall we be induced to give it up altogether."[18]

But this reasoning works the other way: The greater our political object, the greater the value we set upon it, the more we will be drawn toward the use of absolute means to obtain it, and the less inclined we will be to risk failure by allowing the laws of war to restrict our efforts. What, then, if we consider the value of our political object to be absolute?

With this in mind, I want to take up what I consider to be the decisive case study in Walzer's *Just and Unjust Wars*, the British decision to use terror bombing against Germany at the beginning of World War II.

One of the virtues of Walzer's book is that he tests his ideas against actual situations (unlike Clausewitz, who, even when he does discuss real situations, does so abstractly). And these situations are not made up simply of forces, tendencies, logics, and possibilities; they are crowded with human beings. In discussing Britain's terror-bombing campaign, Walzer does not flinch.

As a direct result of the adoption of a policy of terror bombing by the leaders of Britain, some 300,000 Germans, most of them civilians, were killed and another 780,000 seriously injured. . . . And the British policy had further consequences: it was the crucial precedent for the fire-bombing of Tokyo and other Japanese cities and then for Harry Truman's decision to drop atomic bombs on Hiroshima and Nagasaki. The civilian death toll from Allied terrorism in World War II must have exceeded half a million men, women and children. How could the initial choice of this ultimate weapon ever have been defended?[19]

Walzer recounts the various justifications offered at the time—reprisal, revenge, damaging German morale, boosting Allied and especially British morale, reduction of casualties in the long run—and one by one finds them wanting. But he finds one simple argument worth taking seriously, that of Sir Arthur Harris, the head of Bomber Command: "It was the only force in the West which could take offensive action . . . against Germany, our only means of getting at the enemy in a way that would hurt at all."[20] Walzer quotes Churchill saying essentially the same thing: "The bombers alone provide the means of victory."[21] Here, Walzer, instead of making a criticism with the benefit of hindsight, imagines himself as the one who had to make the decision, given the situation and the state of knowledge in Britain at the time: "Suppose that I sat in the seat of power and had to decide whether to use Bomber Command . . . against cities?"[22] He vividly describes the situation. Now, we know that Germany eventually lost the war, but in 1941 that was not at all obvious. France was defeated, British forces were driven off the continent, Germany was winning everywhere—not only winning, but practically unopposed. And Germany was clearly preparing to invade the British Isles. If Britain was to respond at all, Bomber Command was all there was. But the bombers could get through the antiaircraft fire (and then only some of them) only if they flew at night. And especially at night, their accuracy was terrible. "A study made in 1941 indicated that of those planes that actually succeeded in attacking their target (about two-thirds of the attacking force), only one-third dropped their bombs within five miles of the point aimed at."[23] So if the bombers were to be used at all, they had to be used to attack targets too big to miss: cities. The other possibility was not to use them: "Offensive action could have been postponed until (or in the hope of) some more favorable time."[24] The British could have built up their defenses and prepared for an eventual return to the continent (in fact, they were doing that already). Walzer does not claim certainty here. In his role as the person charged with making the decision, he cannot know absolutely that bombing will lead to victory, or that a policy of Fortress Britain will not. It is, he says, a wager. But there is one more factor that, for Walzer, is decisive. Nazism is absolute evil. On this, he is eloquent.

Nazism was an ultimate threat to everything decent in our lives, an ideology and a practice of domination so murderous, so degrading even to those who might survive, that the consequences of its final victory were literally beyond calculation, immeasurably awful. We see it—and I don't use the phrase lightly—as evil objectified in the world, and in a form so potent and apparent that there could never have been anything to do but fight against it. . . . Here was a threat to human values so radical that its imminence would surely constitute a supreme emergency.[25]

Thus, he says, "Surely I must wager. There is no option; the risk otherwise is too great."[26]

We can believe Walzer that he is not making this point lightly. For example, he does not claim, as others might, that because the necessity for bombing was so great, it can be considered to have been legal. He calls the decision "overriding the rules of war"; the rules remain intact, and the acts that violate them remain illegal. When in his imagined role as decision-maker he chooses to send in the bombers, he says, "I accept the burden of criminality."[27] (In contrast, in his Harfleur speech, Shakespeare's Henry V sees the burden of criminality as falling on his troops, not on himself.) He also argues that by 1942, the supreme emergency was over, and the terror bombing should have been stopped then, which would have saved Dresden and many other cities.

I have set down Walzer's argument here neither to oppose nor to support his conclusion, but because it is a clear and persuasive example of Clausewitz's dictum: The logic of war, pushed to the extreme, will override humanitarian law. Of course, Walzer raises the bar higher than does Clausewitz: The law for him is hardly "imperceptible." But, as Clausewitz argued, the value we set on the political object of the war will determine the importance we ascribe to victory. As the value of the political aim increases, the closer we approach absolute war, and the more we are inclined to choose "military necessity" over humanitarian law. For Walzer, Nazism was "immeasurably awful," "evil objectified in the world." If so, then the necessity to defeat it becomes absolute. Against absolute necessity, the laws of war are blown away. Given the premises, the logic works and the conclusion follows. Here I only wish to point out that this is Clausewitz's logic.

Thus we see how an absolute *jus ad bellum*, passed through the mechanism of war, can produce a city under firestorm, a situation that very closely resembles the image we come up with when we try to imagine the extreme of human suffering: hell. Does this mean that absolutely just war is the most hellish of all?

WAR AND HELL

To return again to Sherman's words, when one says "war is Hell," what is one saying? One is saying first of all that war is suffering carried to the extreme limit. But, as we have seen, Sherman's statement has a deeper level. Rarely, I think, has so much been said in three one-syllable words. To say that war is hell may give the impression that war is where all ethics have been abandoned and chaos reigns, but that is not what hell is all about. Hell, as we saw in Saint Thomas's authoritative account, is the realm of evil, and at the same time the very place where evildoers meet their ultimate enemy. The punishers may be devils and fiends, beings of an evil nature, but the ghostly, sadistic tortures are all (so the story goes) deserved, and authorized by God's will: the most legitimate of all instances of legitimate violence. Hell, as we understand it, would not be made more bearable by subjecting it to just rules. Hell is just.

When Sherman said war is hell (remembering that Sherman, like Thomas and Henry V, was a Catholic at least in his upbringing), we can be sure that he did not picture himself as one of the sinners cast into that place to receive his deserved punishment. Quite the contrary; in his autobiography, he repeatedly makes clear that he sees himself as avenger.

"I can make this march, and make Georgia howl!"

"[We] were perfectly justified in stripping the inhabitants of all they had."

"I propose to abandon Atlanta . . . to sally forth and ruin Georgia."

"Let it be known that if a farmer wishes to burn his cotton, his house, his family and himself, he may do so. But not his corn. We want that."

"We can punish South Carolina as she deserves."

"My aim was to whip the rebels, to humble their pride, to follow them to their inmost recesses, and make them fear and dread us. 'Fear of the Lord is the beginning of wisdom.'"[28]

To summarize: Hell is worse than war in at least three respects. First, the sinners have no opportunity to fight back. In fact, while fighting is the essence of war, in hell there is no fighting at all, unless perhaps among demons. Second, as the sufferers are being punished under the authority of God, they cannot comfort themselves by believing that they are in the right, and that their punishment is unjust. And third, they cannot find peace by dying. Thus it is, as Dante wrote, a place where all hope is abandoned.

On the other hand, there are at least three ways in which war is worse than hell. First, it victimizes innocents, which hell, ruled by divine justice, presumably never does. Second, as war is carried out under the guidance not of an infallible intelligence but of fallible human beings, it often produces suffering far out of proportion to the necessity (assuming for the moment the validity of the notion of "military necessity") of the case. From this standpoint, just war theory can be seen as an attempt to provide rules by which the cruelty of war can be brought closer to the standard of a well-run hell. Third, while war and hell share the ability to do the magic trick of transforming the highest claims of justice into the cruelest form of behavior, they differ as to who is to carry out those cruelties. In hell, this is done by fiends, beings who have been created for that work. Remembering this can help us see an essential aspect of war: It is an activity organized so as to require human beings to do the work of fiends.

NOTES

1. Grotius, "Prolegomena, 28, The Rights of War and Peace," in *The Theory of International Relations*, eds. M. G. Forsyth, H. N. A. Keens-Soper, and P. Savigear (London: George Allen and Unwin, 1970), 54.
2. Grotius, "Prolegomena," 54–5.
3. The Declaration of Saint Petersburg, signed November 29, 1868, I A.J.I.L. (Supp.) 95–6 (1907).
4. Hague Declaration (IV, 3), Concerning Expanding Bullets, I A.J.I.I. (Supp.).
5. Hague Convention (IV), Respecting the Laws and Customs of War on Land, Annex to the Convention (I Bevans 631, signed October 18, 1907).
6. Adam Roberts, "Land Warfare," in *The Laws of War: Constraints on Warfare in the Western World*, eds. Michael Howard, George J. Andreopoulos, and Mark R. Shulman (New Haven, CT: Yale University Press, 1994), 122.
7. Roberts, "Land Warfare," 116, 122–3.
8. Sigfried Giedion, *Mechanization Takes Command: A Contribution to Anonymous History* (Oxford: Oxford Clarendon Press, 1970), 217.
9. Keegan, *The Face of Battle*, 260.
10. Sven Lindqvist, *A History of Bombing*, trans. Linda Haverty Rugg (New York: The New Press, 2003), 4, 29.
11. Quoted in Lindqvist, *A History of Bombing*, 60.
12. Lindqvist, *A History of Bombing*, 31–71.
13. Quoted in Tami Davis Biddle, "Air Power," in *The Laws of War*.
14. Hague Convention (IV), Respecting the Laws.
15. A. P. V. Rogers, *Law on the Battlefield* (Manchester: Manchester U. Press, 1996), 58.

16. Hague Rules of Aerial Warfare, 32 A.J.I.L. (Supp.) 12 (1938), signed February 19, 1923, not in force.
17. Clausewitz, *On War*, 105, 106.
18. Clausewitz, *On War*, 109.
19. Walzer, *Just and Unjust Wars*, 255.
20. Arthur Harris, quoted in Walzer, *Just and Unjust Wars*, 258.
21. Walzer, *Just and Unjust Wars*, 260.
22. Walzer, *Just and Unjust Wars*, 259.
23. Walzer, *Just and Unjust Wars*, 258.
24. Walzer, *Just and Unjust Wars*, 258.
25. Walzer, *Just and Unjust Wars*, 255.
26. Walzer, *Just and Unjust Wars*, 260.
27. Walzer, *Just and Unjust Wars*, 260.
28. Sherman, *Memoirs*, 277, 279, 280, 305.

Chapter 7

The Ecstasy of War?

> *Doll Felt Guilty. He couldn't help it. He had killed a human being, a man. He had done the most horrible thing a human could do, worse than rape even. And nobody in the whole world could say anything to him about it. That was where the pleasure came. Nobody could do anything to him for it. He had gotten away with murder.*
>
> —James Jones, *The Thin Red Line*

SO WHY DO IT?

In war, soldiers are trained to do, and in fact do, "the most horrible thing a human could do," the work of fiends. And they must face other soldiers who are prepared to do "the most horrible thing a human could do" to them. If war is hell, it's the behavior of the soldiers that makes it so. If that's all there is to it, why don't they all simply walk away? Of course, some do. But most stay on. Why? There are many answers. Deserters can be arrested and given death sentences, or simply shot. The ancient *Shang-chun-shu* put it with classic Chinese conciseness: The secret is to "bring about a condition where people find it . . . dangerous not to fight."[1] Certainly that fear is part of it. Then there is, also from ancient times, the belief that soldiers are motivated by patriotic love of the motherland. Since World War II (as shooting deserters came under disapproval, looting became more difficult and patriotism more dubious), military analysts have argued that soldiers stay in battle because they can't bear the idea of betraying their comrades—the members of their squads.

All these are surely factors, but they serve to divert attention from one more possibility. Might it be, as some claim, that war, not as a means to an end but the activity in itself—at least sometimes, for some soldiers—gives pleasure? More specifically, that war's quintessential act—that of killing a human being under the state's license to do so—is the key to war's attraction? This seems to be what James Jones is saying about his fictional character Private First Class Donald Doll. Interestingly, Doll thinks of—savors, you might say—his killing of a Japanese soldier as "murder," though under military law it is not. Why does he continue to think of it as a crime? In Jones's account, if it is not murder, then Doll will not have "gotten away" with anything. For Doll, "where the pleasure came" is not only the circumstance that no one could punish him, but also that the thing no one could punish him for, despite its being declared legal by the state, was still "the most horrible thing a human could do": murder. Is this embodiment of good and evil in a single act—the exercise of "legitimate violence" itself—war's special characteristic and, at least for some, its pleasure?

THE PLEASURE OF FACING DANGER

James Jones is unusual in confronting this possibility directly; writers about military matters often shift the focus to other aspects of the war experience. Military historian S. L. A. Marshall wrote, "The so-called 'realists' of war fiction such as Eric [sic] Remarque view through a glass darkly every last motion of the combat soldier. But what normal man would deny that some of the fullest and fairest days of his life have been spent at the front or that the sky ever [never?] seems more blue or the air more bracing than when there is just a hint of danger in the air?"[2]

Certainly pleasure can be derived from danger, especially if one feels one has been brave in the face of it. As an example of such "fullest and fairest days," Marshall offers a tale of how an American unit, receiving heavy bombardment in Holland during World War II, tied a heifer where it would be hit—and cooked—by an artillery shell, providing them with a steak dinner.[3]

Remarque's *All Quiet on the Western Front*, far from ignoring this aspect of combat, contains a similar episode. The protagonist Paul and his unit enter a farmhouse under withering bombardment and find there two suckling pigs, which they slaughter and cook, along with potato pancakes, on the farmhouse stove, and give themselves a banquet.[4] But the thrill of *facing* danger must be distinguished from the thrill of *posing* a threat. What these stories have in common is, first of all, a victory over fear—possibly short lived. They show the wonderful ingenuity of young people to invent a way, smack in the middle of a fierce war situation, of doing not-war, of refusing to act out their assigned roles as "victims of bombardment" by asserting its very opposite: "party time!"

THE PLEASURE OF LOOTING

But while enjoying a banquet is certainly not military action, looting is. For presumably both the heifer and the suckling pigs were the property of a farm family who had either fled or been killed. In both stories, the troops assume that the war situation and their status as soldiers have placed them outside the law, giving them the right to appropriate these farm animals without being accused of burglary . . . as the stories are told, without even noticing that it is burglary. To the extent that this is condoned—openly or tacitly—by the military authorities, it is transformed from looting to "appropriation," and falls within the general category of legitimate violence. It amounts to using state power to obtain a free lunch.

In these stories, the pleasure of wielding a tiny fragment of state power is mixed with the pleasure of eating when you are hungry—hardly a military action in itself. The question is whether there is a special pleasure in military action itself. Before dismissing this idea as beneath contempt, we would do well to remember that almost all of us know the vicarious pleasure of war that we experience from dramatically written history books, fiction, and especially film.

VICARIOUS PLEASURE

War movies fall into several categories. There are the comic or semi-comic films, in which large numbers of clown-like enemies die humorously. There are the ninety-minutes-of-hate films, in which in the first part, the enemies do things so despicable that when in the second part the tables are turned and the enemies are cruelly killed, the audience feels free to indulge in the pleasure of vicarious sadism without guilt. Then there are the anti-war films. These are written and directed in such a way as to persuade the audience that war is a cruel and ugly business. In the first and second sorts of films, those who die on our side never have limbs or half the skull blown away, but suffer a small bullet hole near the heart (which doesn't bleed), lie down, say something wise, and close their eyes to die. In the anti-war films, they scream and curse and bleed, and die with their eyes open. This certainly comes closer to the reality of war, but for that very reason these films come closest to what is sometimes called, evocatively, the pornography of violence. Is it really true that people flock to movie theaters to see these films in order to confirm their anti-war sentiments? We learn where they are being shown by looking at the entertainment pages of the newspapers, where they are listed alongside comedies, romances, and science fiction thrillers, and we munch popcorn while watching them. Can we do this and claim that the vicarious attraction of war is something unknown to us?

But vicarious war and real war are worlds apart. This is surely one of the reasons veterans often feel alienated and alone when they return home and find themselves among people who have never been to the front. Anti-war films are not romances, but still the theaters don't stink of death, and there is dramatic background music, which seems to bring coherence to the incoherent; on the actual battlefield, there is no music, and no audience to weep or gasp at what is happening to the troops.

WAR AS ROMANCE

In his 1910 "The Moral Equivalent of War," William James never wrote that war might be a pleasure, but he argued that it provides society with something so precious that if we are to rid the world of it, we will need to find an alternative that offers equivalent value. But what that precious thing is is not so clear. After writing eloquently about the bestialities of war and identifying himself as a pacifist, James goes on to describe "the higher aspects of militaristic sentiment." War, he says, "is the romance of history," and "the possibility of violent death the soul of all romance. . . . Militarism is the great preserver of our ideals of hardihood, and human life with no use for hardihood would be contemptible." War is "human nature at its highest dynamic"; it is "the supreme theatre of human strenuousness."[5]

This language is familiar to me. I heard similar things many times from my father, who would have been six when James wrote this essay and who, like James, never went to war. Indeed, most of this talk is about the charm of war to the observer, the reader of romantic history, not about how it is to the foot soldier. If the assertion is that the value of war is that it gives authors interesting material to write about, that would not be a persuasive reason to start one. I agree with James that a life devoid of the need for courage and hardihood would be an insipid affair, but I see little danger of that coming to pass. As for strenuousness and danger, an alternative to the military life can be found, for example, in the life of a firefighter, which requires at least as much bravery and dedication as the life of a soldier, with none of the bestiality. But no one ever used the virtues of the fire department to argue "the higher aspects of arson."

WAR AS PROVIDER OF "MEANING"

Chris Hedges, who spent some years as a combat reporter, wrote a best-selling book about that experience with a remarkable title that somewhat echoes James's, *War Is a Force That Gives Us Meaning*, and which is helpful in understanding the complexity of the question. On the one hand, the book, like James's essay, eloquently and passionately depicts war as an unspeakable horror. On the other hand, Hedges raises the question, If it was that bad, why did he keep going back? He compares it to a drug addiction.

> And like every recovering addict there is a part of me that remains nostalgic for war's simplicity and high, even as I cope with the scars it has left behind, mourn the deaths of those I worked with and struggle with the bestiality I would have been better off not witnessing.[6]

I think I can understand, at least partly, what he means by "high"; I am less sure about "simplicity" and "meaning." As for the high, war takes you to the very edge of human experience, that is, to the edge of death ("edge" if you are a survivor), after which routine, daily life may seem tawdry. In his very useful *What Every Person Should Know about War* (2003), Hedges offers a physiological explanation, pointing out that in a combat situation, the body produces massive amounts of adrenaline, which may mean that the experience not only resembles a drug high but actually is one, which can lead to addiction, an urgent desire to get back into a situation in which your body provides you again with that fix, and a crash into depression when the adrenaline runs out.[7] As for simplicity, I suppose that refers to the fact that a combat situation focuses one's attention on a very few matters. But again, in extreme sports like rock climbing or boxing, the mind stays pretty well focused on what you are doing, though perhaps not so focused as when you are walking through a minefield.

What puzzles me is the word "meaning." In the title of his book and again in the text, Hedges asserts that war "gives us meaning," but I am unable to find where he tells us what that meaning is. While on page 10, he writes that "tragically war is sometimes the most powerful way in human society to achieve meaning," on page 11 he asserts that "the myths are lies." Is there a difference between the meaning and the myths? "Meaning," it seems, does not point to an object. War does not mean *something*, it just *means*. For a soldier, the possibility, discovered after the war, that this "meaning" may *mean* nothing might be hard to bear.

WAR AS HISTORIC SPECTACLE

James never went to war; Hedges did but not as a soldier. J. Glen Gray, author of the valuable *The Warriors*, in World War II was with the infantry in Italy, participated in the Normandy invasion, and then served in France, not in a combat unit but in intelligence. While he confesses that he was sometimes excessively harsh with the prisoners he interrogated, he does not tell us if he ever fired a gun at anyone.

Like James and Hedges, Gray pulls no punches in his description of the horrors he witnessed, while at the same time seeking to understand the nature of the charm war seems to have, at least for some. He lists three "secret attractions of war": the spectacle it presents, the comradeship it offers, and the destruction it permits.[8]

Regarding the first attraction on Gray's list, it is certainly true that not only does war produce a spectacle to be seen, and to be passed down through the generations in song and story (as the saying goes), but also it organizes vast numbers of people as participants in this story. In fact, it is hard to see how, without war, what we call "history," whether European, Egyptian, Chinese, Indian, Japanese, or any other, could have taken the "story" form that it has. (Hard, but possible. There are alternative ways of understanding the meaning of events by arranging them over time, notably the history of class struggle, history of ideas, history of technology, women's history, history of [you name it]—the list is long. All of these are in some way connected to war but need not be centered on it.) Concerning the history shaped by war, Gray writes, "There was also the intense nervous excitement of great moments, in which even the dullest of us were conscious of participating in historical events of overawing importance."[9]

Perhaps this is what Hedges was trying to express with the vague word "meaning." Certainly it is an awesome experience to be joined together with a multitude of other people in a collective effort to bring about changes in the world on such a scale as to be called "historic." And perhaps the "tawdriness" and "uneventfulness" of civilian life of which veterans often complain is the sense of no longer being part of any such story, the sense that the story is being acted out elsewhere, by the rich and powerful.

This sounds remarkably like the phenomenon written about so eloquently by Hannah Arendt in her analysis of the happiness that can accompany participation in collective political action. According to Arendt (who valued Gray's book enough to write a foreword to it), when large numbers of people act together, they can generate a power great enough to give birth to new beginnings in history, and this can give the participants a kind of happiness unlike that which accompanies any other human activity.[10] Is Gray saying that the same can be true of the collective action of warriors?

It's true that there are few human enterprises that involve so many people in coordinated action as does war. It's tempting to say "modern war" until you remember the names Xerxes, Alexander, Hannibal, Caesar—no sense going on. And just because many of these "new beginnings" exacted a horrific price in death and suffering doesn't mean they weren't new, or that they didn't affect the course of history. It's easy to understand Gray, engaged in the collective project of putting the French Republic back on the map, being awed at the scale of the events going on around him. But it's also important to remember that Arendt herself argued that war and collective political action are not variations of the same phenomenon. "Politically speaking, it is insufficient to say that power"—for her, the power generated by collective political action—"and violence are not the same. Power and violence are opposites; where the one rules absolutely, the other is absent."[11] Perhaps we can say that Gray and Arendt give us a clearer picture of that to which we need, in James's words, a moral equivalent.

As for the comradeship, Gray admits that this is less a reason to praise military life than a criticism of modern society in which a sense of community is so hard to attain. Probably that is why the military comradeship, achieved in the context of the artificial and scientifically constructed military organization and in a situation of temporary danger, is so often, after the danger has passed, the object mainly of nostalgia, the emotion one feels when something has been lost.

And as for destruction, I have no doubt that this can give great pleasure. However, if that's all there is to it, then one should be able to find happiness by seeking employment in a wrecking company or a company carrying out strip mining. But Gray's "destruction" doesn't mean just blowing up buildings, burning orchards, and driving tanks over rice fields; it is a euphemism for killing people. Is that not the essence of war? If there is a pleasure *specific* to war, must it not be sought in the act of killing?

Gray wrote, "The deepest fear of my war years, one still with me, is that these happenings had no real purpose."[12] Like Hedges, his experiences of war led him on the whole to take a stand against it, but still he clings to the idea that it all had some kind of purpose or, as Hedges put it, "meaning."

THE PLEASURE OF MEANINGLESSNESS

I want to consider the opposite possibility, that the specific attraction of war—the one that it does not share with any other group activity—may be its offer of *a release from meaning*—its *meaninglessness*. (Gray writes that war offers a "feeling of liberation," but he does not say from what.[13]) Consider again James Jones's eerily named infantryman Donald Doll, who has been brought by the war to something close to a psychopathic state. He is elated to realize that war has released him from ordinary morality. Or rather, he is elated not by the realization but by the experience of acting on that realization. He has done the worst thing a human being can do, and no one can criticize him for it: "That was where the pleasure came." One is reminded of Thucydides's cryptic comment at the end of his description of how the rebellion in the city of Corcyra disintegrated into a war of each against all: "Human nature, always rebelling against the law and now its master, gladly showed itself ungoverned in passion."[14] Human beings, he seems to be saying, are not developed and fulfilled by the law but rather are oppressed, diminished, and made unhappy by it, so that release from its restrictions produces a state of excitement—passion, as he says. The state of war—and especially a war of each against all—is accompanied by fear, misery, horror, and nausea, all of which Thucydides describes brilliantly. But behind all that, the passage seems to say there is something else powerful enough to keep the warriors going at it: a feeling of release, a sense that one is now master of the law or at least is in a space where the law has been silenced. If, as Hobbes wrote, "freedom is the silence of the law," then its radical silence in wartime would be freedom indeed. Nevertheless, Hobbes, who was the first to translate Thucydides's writings into English and who quite possibly got his insight for the state of nature from these passages, never described that state as one in which people would be able to act "gladly."

WAR AS A STATE OF EXCEPTION

There is a crucial difference between Hobbes's state of war and Thucydides's Corcyra. For the Corcyrans, rule of law is the normal state, and in the process of their revolt, they have found themselves liberated from it, a state of exception. The state of nature as described by Hobbes has no past, so there is nothing for its absence of law to be an exception to. (That is, assuming the state of nature is as Hobbes described it. I have argued above that for his description to make sense, one must assume that it did have a past. See chapter 1.)

Is the alleged attraction of war not simply the absence of law, a situation *prior to* established law, but rather the *liberation* from law, that is, a state of exception?

For Carl Schmitt, the premier theorist of the state of exception, the important question is Who has the authority to declare such a state? Important, he says, because that is the moment when the sovereign is revealed: "Sovereign is he who decides the exception."[15] In fact, there are many lesser personages who decide exceptions: judges or juries who choose mercy over the letter of the law, soldiers who end a war by voting with their feet or start one by firing the first shot, civil disobedients who establish themselves as "sovereign individuals" by choosing conscience over law. For Schmitt, being a statist and, for a time at least, a Nazi, such cases do not hold his attention. What interests him is a general state of emergency, "a case of extreme peril, a danger to the existence of the state, or the like."[16] This is not surprising, given that he published *Political Theology* only two years after the failed Kapp Putsch in Germany. He writes, "The exception appears in its absolute form when a situation in which legal prescriptions can be valid must first be brought about."[17]

Such a situation, he argues, can be met only by suspending the law. But this is inaccurate. Under martial law or a state of siege, "the law" is not suspended; only certain laws are, mainly those (human rights laws, etc.) that restrict state power. Moreover, laws are suspended not for everyone but only for the one he calls the sovereign, and this is what excites Schmitt.

Under a state of siege or martial-law regime, traffic law is not suspended (though it is in war zones: Tanks don't stop for red lights); laws against theft are not suspended (though the laws forbidding police from shooting looters on sight may be). If law means rules under which, if you do not obey them, you can be punished, for ordinary citizens the burden of the law is increased. Curfews are imposed, speech and publication are censored, public meetings are forbidden, and the jails overflow. Of course, this may be not "law" strictly speaking but simply command. Still, except for the sovereign, the "suspension of law" in a state of exception does not mean "all is permitted."

Is the declaration of a state of exception a declaration of war by a government against its people? Or to put the question the other way, is war a state of exception carried out against an enemy people? There are similarities. Both are "exceptions," suspensions of what we consider the ordinary rule of law; both are "declared" by the person or body considered to be the sovereign. This is based on the belief that law can be suspended only by a power prior to the law: Law cannot suspend itself. Of course, there are international and national laws of war, and some countries have written bodies of law that specify what can and what cannot be done in a state of exception. But there is a puzzle here. "Exception" *means* not being decisively bound by law. Sovereignty—if Schmitt's view is correct—*means* the prelegal power to declare war or other states of exception. So, whatever restrictions the law places on the actions a government may take in a state of war or martial law, the sovereign can erase with a further declaration of exception.

This is the stuff out of which Nazi and other absolutist political philosophy is constructed. But it also is woven into the political philosophy of states committed to the rule of law. The exception is at the heart of their "right of legitimate violence." If we ask in what exactly that right consists, we find that it is the right that the state, as sovereign, has (claims to have) to declare exceptions.

The death penalty, which some states have abolished, is the most extreme form that the exception takes in peacetime ("peacetime" meaning neither at war nor under martial law).[18] It is carried out in situations in which it is not needed for self-defense, against individuals who perhaps once were, but no longer are, a danger to society. It is justified by a variety of rational-choice-type arguments, which we all know, and, as we also know, it is given emotional support by the desire for vengeance, or, more politely, "closure." But the *right* to treat a person in this exceptional way belongs to the sovereign state.

Under governments that follow the rule of law, the death penalty is carried out against people who have been convicted of crimes according to a legal procedure, not always but (we hope) usually correctly. In war, the situation is different: The people we kill have, so far as we know, not been convicted, accused, or even suspected of any crimes. We can give no explanation of why we have killed this, that, or the other particular person, except that the person was on the other side. Like the domestic state of exception (a state of siege or martial law), the state of war suspends not all laws but only some. The soldiers are not supposed to kill one another (though they sometimes do), and they are supposed to obey the international laws of war where possible. Shifting to the state of war, even where international law is followed, entirely changes the way foreign people, property, and territory may be treated. You may enter foreign territory without a passport, destroy property there, and kill people there, including civilians if they get in the way. You may, "if necessary," occupy people's property, including their homes, and steal their food, fuel, blankets, whatever you need. You may force people out of their towns and villages and put them in internment camps. You may declare martial law in the territory under your control.

Giorgio Agamben, in his detailed study of the state of exception, argues that the suspension of law does not result in law vanishing from existence. Rather it is a situation where on the one hand there are commands that don't have the ethical value of law but can force obedience as if they did, and on the other hand there is law that, while having no force, is not altogether gone but remains as law-that-has-been-suspended and as such defines the situation: It is that to which the state of exception has been excepted. "The state of exception is an anomic space in which what is at stake is force of law without law (which therefore should be written: force-of-law)."[19]

In its simplest sense, for there to be a state of exception, there must be something for it to be excepted from, and that something is the law, which is, one might say, "conspicuously absent." This description closely resembles the war situation as understood by Private Doll: The norm forbidding killing is "in force" (the act amounts to murder) but is "not applied" (it's OK to do it), whereas the killing itself, while not having "the full value of law" (it leaves Doll feeling the bloodguilt), retains its "force" (the killed person is indeed dead). The forceless law "floats as an indeterminate element," "a mystical element, a sort of legal mana."[20]

For a vivid image of the operation of this mystical "legal mana," consider again the speech Shakespeare has Henry V give before the walls of Harfleur. Henry is threatening to declare the state of exception in its most extreme form, as even the laws of war are to be suspended. He will release the troops from under his command; they can enter the city and do "anything." In releasing them, he will make his power over the city not lesser but greater. When they enter the city released from his authority, the troops will be acting on his authority: It is on his authority that they are released from his authority. What they do will not be legal, neither will it be punishable. In Agamben's telling, acts that have lost their authority continue to have their power to coerce. All this is quite mysterious.

In ordinary wartime, this mystical "legal mana," in the form of the right of belligerency, is delegated by the state to the troops on the ground, on and under the sea, and in the air. The troops can feel it flowing through them—state power itself—most intensely in the act of killing an enemy with impunity. It is easy to imagine how this feeling of state power—*the right legitimately to use state violence*—flowing through your body could produce a state of ecstasy not likely to be experienced in civilian life. And it is easy to imagine how it could produce an intense patriotism in the troops, in the form of gratitude to the state for this seemingly mystical empowerment. But it is easy also to see how the discovery that it was all, as Agamben also writes, a "fiction" (cf. Hedges: "the myths are lies") could bring about the spiritual collapse that we call PTSD.

THE THREE PHASES OF WAR

War as exception can be divided into three phases. As models, these can be described as follows.

The first phase begins with the declaration of war itself. A declaration of war establishes a state of exception and sets (attempts to set) limits to that state: the laws of war seek to prohibit acts of violence that are not really war but that use war as an excuse. For it is not surprising that some soldiers will feel that if some acts previously considered crimes are now permitted, then why not all? In this first phase, the laws of war are obeyed, and the limits they set are maintained. As it was for Private Doll, the law is simultaneously there and not there, and the acts of war are simultaneously criminal and commendable.

The second phase begins when it turns out that the prohibited acts are, or might be, militarily effective, so a wider range of exception is permitted. That is, in phase one the laws of war permit exceptions to the laws of peacetime; in phase two "military necessity" permits exceptions to the laws of war. After all, torture might actually get you useful information at least sometimes (the argument that it never can is guesswork); massacre and rape might effectively demoralize the enemy; terror might usefully spread panic; looting can get food and other necessities for the troops and also raise the morale of the looters. (Avoiding these things because they might have a negative effect, so-called blowback, for example by strengthening the enemy's will to resist, is also an argument from military necessity; it means avoiding them when their military cost is greater than their benefit. The corollary to the blowback argument is that if it turns out that the military benefit is greater than the cost, the action in question may be taken.)

As the logic of war moves forward, and especially if you begin to lose, and if losing seems to you catastrophic, then more and more exceptions are made until you approach the third phase, not "anything that works" but just "anything." Thus, the logic of war carried to its extreme can bring you not only, as Clausewitz argued, to absolute war but even beyond "war" properly speaking. For somewhere along the line, the logic changes from the logic of military necessity to the much simpler logic embedded in the deep structure of the logic of military necessity: the logic of the progressive decrease—at the furthest extremity, the entire disappearance—of things forbidden.

The link between phase two and phase three is found in the massacre. Massacre, rape, and pillage have long been used as a rational military tactic: military execution, as described above. It is madness rationally chosen. Rationally considered, if a town that has refused to surrender is subjected to rape, pillage, and massacre, other towns will be more likely to surrender to avoid that fate—a useful consequence. However, for the troops who engage in this massacre, the experience is not that of carrying out a rational military operation but rather the experience of "all is permitted." A massacre itself, the *activity* of a massacre, is not military action, properly speaking. It is not "fighting," as it takes place after the fight is over. It is not coordinated action, but rather wildly chaotic. It does not aim to take territory, as the town is already taken. It does not aim for victory, as the enemy in that town is already defeated. It does not take place under the order of the commander, but rather results from the suspension of his command.

This limiting case, the endpoint of the unfolding of violent behavior, violence that has broken free from the restrictions laid upon it by the logic of war, can appropriately be called: thanatopia.

THANATOPIA

The logic of war simultaneously places limits on the violence that is permitted and, when "necessary," breaks through those limits. According to this logic, acts forbidden in peacetime are permitted in wartime only insofar as they can reasonably be expected to contribute to victory. The knowledge that these acts ought to be forbidden, and usually are, hovers in the atmosphere like *mana*, and the people who carry them out are seen as doing so out of duty only: The acts are "necessary," a painful, even agonizing obligation. In this sense, continuing presence of the law is most poignantly seen in the divided soul of the soldier.

But to Private Doll, "that was where the pleasure came." And here we come to thanatopia, or what has otherwise been called the pornography of violence. To label it as pornography is apt, as it does share some characteristics with that genre. The most obvious is that it is experienced more often vicariously than directly, more often by the voyeur than by the actor. And the pleasures of both largely derive from the fact that both are understood to be forbidden, the simultaneity of "thou shalt not" and "but go ahead." It is when the desire for that pleasure breaks free from the restrictions set on it by "military necessity" and independently motivates action that the state of thanatopia—the Paradise of Death—begins to show its face.

Descriptions of the state of thanatopia are rare, but they exist. A veteran of the Russian army's brutal battles in Afghanistan wrote this:

> The thirst for blood . . . is a terrible desire. It is so strong that you cannot resist it. I saw for myself how the battalion opened a hail of fire on a group that was descending towards our column. And they were OUR soldiers, a detachment from the reconnaissance company who had been guarding us on the flank. They were only 200 metres away and we were 90% sure they were our people. Nevertheless—the thirst for blood, the desire to kill at all costs.[21]

It's not clear whether the storyteller here is speaking as a participant or as an observer. His "you cannot resist it" suggests the former, while his "I saw" suggests the latter. "Not everyone," he writes, "can master this feeling, this instinct, and stifle the monster in his soul."[22] Which leaves open the possibility that perhaps he was one who could. We need not accept his conclusion that this is an "instinct." Rather, it is best understood as a feeling produced by war: the military discipline (all is forbidden but what we tell you), the state of exception on the battlefield (some of the forbidden is permitted because we tell you—but, frustratingly, not all), and the behavior of the enemy (who do the forbidden to us—seemingly without limit). As the war passes through stages of permissiveness, it seems that some troops (again, not all) carry it out to the end.

Actions such as those described by the Russian veteran, in which one unit knowingly fires on another unit of the same army, are rare but not unknown in any army. When I was in the US Marines, I was several times wryly informed that in real war, the young, inexperienced lieutenants (of which I was one) often get shot from behind on the battlefield (in case the reader misses the point, this doesn't mean they are running away). Norman Mailer's classic *The Naked and the Dead* describes what amounts to the murder of a lieutenant by his troops. In the last days of the Vietnam War, the fragging of officers in the US Army became so rampant that it could no longer be kept secret, got into the mainstream news, and affected the outcome of the war.

War is hell, the lowest depth of horror authorized by the highest moral source. In his moral passion, Saint Thomas Aquinas believed that the horrific punishments of hell were necessary but was unable to believe that gentle-hearted avenging angels would be able to carry them out. It was for him a matter of simple logic that the work of hell, being in its enactment essentially evil, could be done only by beings evil by nature, those we imagine as devils, demons, and fiends. But in the case of war, we have only human beings, few of whom can approach the moral character of fiends, and those who do come close, though they may experience some moments of ecstasy, in the end will pay a price.

Some, in the heat of battle, slip from "much is permitted" to "all is permitted." Some break down on the battlefield, some later. Some recover, some only partially, some never. Human beings are not cut out to do the work of fiends, as Dr. Jonathan Shay's PTSD patients testify.

> "Got worse as time went by. I really loved fucking killing, couldn't get enough. For every one that I killed I felt better. Made some of the hurt went away."

> "When I look back at that stuff, I say, 'That was somebody else that did that. Wasn't me.' . . . Y'know, at the time it didn't mean nothing."

> "War changes you. Strips you. Strips you of all your beliefs, your religion, takes your dignity away, you become an animal. I know animals don't."

> "I became a fucking animal. I started putting fucking heads on fucking poles. Leaving fucking notes for the motherfuckers. Digging up fucking graves. . . . They wanted a fucking hero, so I gave it to them. They wanted a fucking body count, so I gave them body count. I hope they're fucking happy. But they don't have to live with it. I do."[23]

NOTES

1. J. J. L. Duyvendak, *The Book of Lord Shang* (London: Probsthain, 1928), 224.
2. Marshall, *Men Against Fire*, 79.
3. Marshall, *Men Against Fire*, 184–5.
4. Remarque, *All Quiet*, 233–6.
5. William James, "The Moral Equivalent of War," in *Pragmatism and other Essays* (New York: Washington Square Press, 1963), 292–5.
6. Chris Hedges, *War Is a Force That Gives Us Meaning* (New York: Random House, 2002), ff.
7. Chris Hedges, *War is a Force*, ff.
8. J. Glen Gray, *The Warriors: Reflections on Men in Battle* (Lincoln: U. of Nebraska, 1959), 28.
9. Gray, *The Warriors*, 10.
10. Hannah Arendt, *The Human Condition*, 2nd ed. (Chicago: U. of Chicago, 1958), chapter 5, ff.
11. Hannah Arendt, "On Violence," in *Crises in the Republic* (San Diego: Harvest, 1972), 155.
12. Gray, *The Warriors*, 24.
13. Gray, *The Warriors*, 44.
14. Thucydides. *The Complete Writings of Thucydides: The Peloponnesian War*, Crowley translation (New York: Modern Library, 1954), book 3, 84.
15. Carl Schmitt, *Political Theology: Four Chapters on the Concept of Sovereignty*, trans. George Schwab (Chicago: U. of Chicago, 2006), 5.
16. Schmitt, *Political Theology*, 6. I understand that taking a Nazi theorist seriously is a risky business. It feels a bit like carrying a bomb. His attraction for extreme situations, including violent ones, often proves illuminating, but there's always the danger the words may blow up in your hands. I hope my use of Schmitt in this and the next chapter helps draw attention to aspects of the war situation that have been missed by other theorists. But while reading them, don't light any matches.
17. Schmitt, *Political Theology*, 13.
18. Jacques Derrida, *The Death Penalty*, trans. Peggy Kamuf (Chicago: U. of Chicago, 2013), 129.
19. Giorgio Agamben, *The State of Exception*, trans. Kevin Attell (Chicago: U. of Chicago, 2005), 38.
20. Agamben, *Exception*, 39, 51.
21. Quoted anonymously in Rodric Braithwaite, *Afgansty: The Russians in Afghanistan, 1979–89* (Oxford: Oxford University Press, 2013), 228.
22. Braithwaite, *Afgansty*, 228.
23. Jonathan Shay, *Achilles in Vietnam: Combat Trauma and the Undoing of Character* (New York: Atheneum, 1994), 78, 83.

Chapter 8

SuperLeviathan: A Peaceful Use of Hell?

What will they do to oppose it? What they have always done: they will turn it into ridicule.

—Rousseau

THE ARTICLES-OF-CONFEDERATION ANALOGY

When I was a senior in high school in San Francisco, I entered a speech contest sponsored, if I remember correctly, by the local branch of the Rotary Club. In the speech, I argued for what I proudly and ignorantly thought was my original idea, that the way to achieve world peace was to think of the United Nations as analogous to the Articles of Confederation, call a continental congress writ large, and produce a constitution for the world, one that would create (to use the phrase I had learned in my civics classes) a strong central government.

I didn't win a prize; it was naive of me to think, in the 1950s, that Rotary Club members might be impressed by, let alone attracted to, the idea of setting up a political authority higher than the US government. The US Congress had been arguing the subject since the debates over the Kellogg-Briand Pact and the League of Nations, some still favoring one or another version of the proposal, others, I suppose, sick of hearing about it. In 1954, the year I gave this talk, Congress was debating the Bricker Amendment, proposed by Senator John Bricker of Ohio, which would have made it unconstitutional for the president to enter into such a treaty without the full approval of both houses of Congress. (The Bricker Amendment failed to pass the Senate by one vote but is said to have been an important factor damping the enthusiasm of the world-government proponents.) The supporters of the Bricker Amendment are remembered as conservative patriots who saw world government as overruling national sovereignty and leading to despotism. Looking back on it now, though, it seems to me that for many of its supporters, the world-federalist proposal was (and to the extent that it's still around, still is) an outrageously America-centric proposal: Far from setting up a power over America, it dreamed of absorbing the world's peoples into a Greater America: American exceptionalism with nothing left for it to be the exception to.

What I also didn't know then was that my talk was only repeating an expanded version of the dumbed-down Hobbesism that the American educational system was injecting in those days into the country's common sense via the tale of the Continental Congress and the strong central government. And I had no clear notion of what this Hobbesist solution entailed.

Hobbes himself acknowledged the concept of world government, not by proposing it but by registering its absence. Immediately following his depiction of the state of nature, which, having over it no "common power to keep them all in awe," is a state of war of each against all, he goes on to say, "It may peradventure be thought, that there was never such a time, nor condition of war as this." To this doubt, he responds first that such a condition exists among native people of America (here he was simply misinformed) and second that it exists among sovereign powers (a more persuasive example): "[Yet] in all times, kings, and persons of sovereign authority, because of their independency, are in continual jealousies, and in the state and posture of gladiators; having their weapons pointing, and their eyes fixed on one another . . . which is a posture of war."[1]

In context, it is clear what is the thing the absence of which allows this situation.

PLANNING PERPETUAL PEACE

But Hobbes did not propose a world state to transcend and pacify the sovereign states. The credit for this is generally given to the Abbé de Saint-Pierre, who called for a confederation, not of all the peoples of the world but of all the states of Europe. Rousseau's discourse on this proposal (through which the proposal mainly came to be known) begins with elaborate praise for its author: "Never did the mind of man conceive a scheme nobler, more beautiful, or more useful than that of a lasting peace between all the peoples of Europe. Never did a writer better deserve a respectful hearing than he who suggests means for putting that scheme into practice. What man, if he has a spark of goodness, but must feel his heart glow within him at so fair a prospect?"[2]

In Rousseau's account, the Abbé's proposed confederation is not exactly a SuperLeviathan. It does have the ability to call down violence against any state that breaks its rules, but not with its own troops; like the United Nations today, it depends on the military forces of the member states. A rebellious state shall first "be put to the ban," and then "all the Confederates shall arm and take the offensive, conjointly and at the common expense," against that state.[3]

In Rousseau's estimation, the Abbé's proposal is both possible and impossible. "Realize his Commonwealth of Europe for a single day, and you may be sure it will last forever; so fully would experience convince men that their own gain is to be found in the good of all. For all that, the very Princes who would defend it with all their might, if it once existed, would resist with all their might any proposal for its creation."[4] Why would princes—or, as we would say today, the people who "hold the reins of government"—oppose this proposal? According to Rousseau, "The whole life of Kings, or of those on whom they shuffle off their duties, is devoted solely to two objects: to extend their rule beyond their frontiers and to make it more absolute within them. Any other purpose they may have is either subservient to one of these aims, or merely a pretext for attaining them."[5]

Moreover, these two projects are intertwined: "War and conquest without and the encroachments of despotism within give each other mutual support." "War furnishes a pretext for exactions of money and another, no less plausible, for keeping large armies constantly on foot, to hold the people in awe. In a word, anyone can see that aggressive Princes wage war at least as much on their subjects as on their enemies."[6]

This hypothesis is worth careful consideration: Take away the possibility of international war, and you take away from a government much of its ability "to hold the people in awe," an ability Hobbes considered essential for domestic peace.

The situation is made worse still, Rousseau continues, by the fact that the political calculations are made by the Prince's ministers. "Ministers are in perpetual need of war, as a means of making themselves indispensable to their master, of throwing him into difficulties from which he cannot escape without their aid. . . . They are in need of it, as a means of oppressing the people on the plea of national necessity, of finding places for their creatures, of rigging the market and setting up a thousand odious monopolies. . . . With a lasting peace, all these resources would be gone."[7]

The plan itself, says Rousseau, is perfectly practicable: "What will they do to oppose it? What they have always done: they will turn it into ridicule."[8] Which is what, one might add, they still do.

Moreover, Rousseau is not above indulging in a bit of ridicule himself. While he praises the Abbé for authoring the plan itself, for his failure to see the impossibility of having it enacted, Rousseau accuses him of "simplicity" and of judging "like a child."⁹

Rousseau's conclusion is that, as the peaceful commonwealth cannot be established by persuading those who hold state power, the only practical alternative would be to establish it by revolution. And so, "while we admire so fair a project, let us console ourselves for its failure by the thought that it only could have been carried out by violent means from which humanity must needs shrink."¹⁰

PEACEFUL REPUBLICS?

Immanuel Kant introduces his proposal for perpetual peace—the formation of a "great International Federation"—by noting that the idea "has been ridiculed in the way in which it has been presented by an Abbe de Saint-Pierre or Rousseau (perhaps because they believed its realization to be so near)"; on this point he seems to have misread Rousseau. In any case, he insists the idea should be taken seriously.¹¹

He begins by accepting Hobbes's essential worldview. "A State of Peace among men who live side by side with each other, is not the natural state. The state of Nature is rather a state of War; for although it may not always present the outbreak of hostilities, it is nevertheless continually threatened with them. The State of Peace must, therefore, be *established*" (italics in original).¹²

But while he accepts Hobbes's statement of the problem, he differs with Hobbes on what to do about it. He argues, first of all, that international peace will be possible only if every state becomes republican. Here he is offering a solution to the problem posed by Rousseau, that however much peace may be in the interests of a people, war will always be in the interest of princes and their ministers. In a republic, Kant believes, the decision to go to war will be made by the citizens and this is a decision the citizens will be unlikely to make, "for in decreeing it they would necessarily be resolving to bring upon themselves all the horrors of War. And, in their case, this implies such consequences as these: to have to fight in their own persons; to supply the costs of the war out of their own property; to have sorrowfully to repair the devastation which it leaves behind; and, as a crowning evil, to have to take upon themselves at the end a burden of debt which will go on embittering peace itself."¹³

This hypothesis of Kant's is sometimes said to be the source of the contemporary theory that "democracies don't make war against each other." But whatever else may be said in favor of that idea, it is different from Kant's. Kant's hypothesis is that citizens of republics who have the power to refuse consent will not want to go to war with anyone, not so much out of humanitarian or brotherly feelings toward peoples of other countries as from a rational understanding of their own interest. And as to that, the experiences of the twentieth century and the first decades of the twenty-first century have not been encouraging. Citizens of what we now call "democracies" have been quite capable of waging total war against countries with other forms of government, sustaining massive casualties, and carrying out fire- and atomic bombings. In some cases, citizens were wildly enthusiastic about going to war, at least at the beginning (as with World War I), and when they were not, governments have still been able to make war without the citizens' consent (as with US involvement in the war in Vietnam). Moreover, today the rich countries are seeking to develop ways to fight wars by sending robots (drones, etc.) into combat rather than people, which if successful will greatly reduce the amount of horror the citizens on the rich side will have to face (though it will in equal measure increase the horror on the other side).

WHO WILL WATCH THE WATCHERS?

The hypothesis that rights-bearing citizens are likely to be relatively peaceful is only one of the two main pillars of Kant's argument; the other is that these relatively peaceful republics should be joined in an international federation. But here again Kant resembles the Abbé rather than he does Hobbes. To follow Hobbes's model on an international scale, member states would have to hand over their sovereignty to the entity that would stand above them and keep them all "in awe": SuperLeviathan. In Kant's formulation, the member states maintain their independence. "This Federation will not aim at the acquisition of any of the political powers of a State, but merely at the preservation and guarantee for itself, and likewise for the other confederated States, the liberty that is proper to a State, and this would not require these States to subject themselves for this purpose—as is the case with men in the state of nature—to public laws and to coercion under them."[14]

On the surface, Kant's proposals seem to be contradictory. Here he writes that in his proposed federation, states will not be subjected to coercion under the law; elsewhere he describes his proposal as "a FEDERATION regulated by law" (caps in original).[15] Sometimes he argues that human beings will be driven to the establishment of such a federation as the only means to escape the suffering of war, which means they will, like the people in Hobbes's natural condition, be acting in their self-interest, illustrated in his famous "The problem of the institution of a State, however hard it may appear, would not be insoluble even for a race of devils, assuming only that they have intelligence."[16] But in the main, his argument is a moral one, and the progress toward a peaceful world federation is seen as an advance in human morality.

These are not, I believe, contradictions in Kant's reasoning so much as they are contradictions in the situation to which he is struggling to find a solution. Kant follows Hobbes in saying that the state of war is so intolerable that self-interest will drive people to take whatever steps are necessary to get out of it. Yet he stops short of proposing a world-scale Leviathan, which, as he says, would be likely to become a "soulless despotism."[17] But if the laws of the federation are not coercive, Hobbes would ask, how can you be sure either states or individuals will obey them? Again, Kant accepts Hobbes's statement of the problem but balks at his solution.

> The difficulty which the mere thought of this problem puts before our eyes is this. Man is an animal which, if it lives among others of its kind, requires a master. For he certainly abuses his freedom with respect to other men, and although as a reasonable being he wishes to have a law which limits the freedom of all, his selfish animal impulses tempt him, where possible, to exempt himself from them. He thus requires a master, who will break his will and force him to obey a will that is universally valid, under which he can be free. But whence does he get his master? Only from the human race. But then the master is himself an animal, and needs a master. . . . This task is therefore the hardest of all; indeed, its complete solution is impossible.[18]

Here Kant has identified one of the central dilemmas of politics: Who will watch the watchers?

There are a number of ways of dealing with this dilemma: One can escape into cynicism, or into hopeless resignation, or into that peculiar mix of cynicism and state-romanticism that declares that, even though it has seldom, if ever, happened before, surely *this time* the watcher will be wise and benevolent. Kant does none of these, neither forgetting what realism teaches nor abandoning the ideal. If a "complete solution is impossible," how then can we approach a partial solution?

Three conditions, he argues, are necessary: "a correct conception of a possible constitution, great experience gained in many paths of life, and—far beyond these—a good will ready to accept such a constitution. Three such things are very hard, and if they are even [ever?] to be found together, it will be very late and after many vain attempts."[19]

The first of these—a correct conception of a possible constitution—is what Kant is attempting to produce in these writings: a workable model to strive for. By "great experience," Kant is referring, I believe, to the experience of the horrors of war after war. If human beings can be brought to accept a world federation only by force, and if SuperLeviathan is ruled out because the unwatched watcher will surely turn into a soulless despotism, then the "force" that will compel us to accept this federation can only be the force of the wars that we ourselves make, and then suffer under. "The barbaric freedom of established states ... through wasting the powers of the commonwealths in armaments to be used against each other, through devastation brought on by war ... they stunt the full development of human nature. ... Thus [our race] is *forced* to institute a cosmopolitan condition to secure the external safety of each state" (italics added).[20] Here Kant is ready to use the "realist" argument—self-interest. But with the third condition, "good will," he introduces a moral argument.

AS THOUGH

As can be seen from the above quotations, for Kant, the world federation is to be achieved not through a sudden convulsion of history but rather through a long process. There is an obvious objection to this way of thinking, expressed in the question: Are you telling us to wait? In particular, since Kant argues that the progress toward peace is progress to becoming fully human, does this mean that in our lifetimes, we have no choice but to live out our lives half developed? Kant has an answer for this too, one that has not satisfied everyone.

Moral-practical reason presents us with an "irresistible veto: There shall be no war." Search as we will through history, search as we will through the world at present, search honestly as we will the depths of our own hearts, we will find considerable resistance to this "irresistible." "We must, however, act *as though* perpetual peace were a reality, which perhaps it is not, by working for its establishment and for the kind of constitution that seems best adapted for bringing it about" (italics Kant's).[21]

Kant famously—for some, notoriously—is a believer in progress: History is moving us toward a final goal, the fully developed human. Among the many problems with this, one of the greatest is that it always leaves us behind. In whatever age we live, all we can hope for is to be half-baked specimens of this fully formed true human. Kant's "as though" is a kind of metaphorical time machine with which we can leap forward along the imaginary timeline of progress. If we can't create the state of peace itself, at least we can work to create in ourselves the state of human development that would accompany the state of peace. This needs to be distinguished from the mystical notion that if you achieve peace in your heart, then "peace on earth" is achieved. Peace on earth is not achieved: We remain in the present, where, as usual, "everywhere is war." To imagine otherwise is self-deception. What is not self-deceiving is "adopting the maxim of working for [peace] with unrelenting perseverance." It is a matter of acting not as though peace has been achieved, but as though its achievement is possible. Kant's as-though doesn't release us from the need to struggle, but it gives us the heart to keep at it.

PEACE PROPOSALS AFTER WORLD WAR I

Certainly Kant was right in predicting that as war got worse, more and more people would set themselves to the task of trying to get rid of it. And indeed, during Kant's lifetime, war got worse. Revolutionary fervor and Napoleonic charisma not only resulted in horrific casualty rates but also brought about, however briefly, a model of unified Europe not as a state of peace but rather as one of extreme domination: Pax Napoleana. According to Mark Mazower, the modern European search for a way to organize a power that would stand above the states and promote peace without crushing them began with the Concert of Europe, comprised of Austria, Russia, Britain, and Prussia, and including, after Napoleon was defeated, France.[22] But while from the standpoint of the twentieth century, the nineteenth may have looked like a century of peace, to those who lived through it the era of the Concert of Europe was "a symbol of the very problems—autocratic leadership, bellicosity, an incomprehension of the value of freedom and social change—that a true internationalism was needed to solve."[23]

The outbreak of World War I marked the collapse of the Concert of Europe style of diplomacy. The horror of industrialized war itself, with its Gatling guns and gas, persuaded people of the need to establish some kind of international organization capable of preventing war altogether.

The resulting League of Nations would not have satisfied Hobbes. Its Charter did not require its founding member states to abrogate their "right to all things"—that is, the right of legitimate violence—or to hand it over to the League so as to make it "a common power to keep them all in awe." Rather, as articles 10 and 16 make clear, the Charter, while agreeing with Hobbes that violence can be put down only by greater violence, yet leaves the right to violence with the member states, so that when the League moves to put down a dispute it does so with military forces borrowed from those states. This means that for the League to be successful putting down disputes, the number and power of the states uninvolved in the dispute will have to be far greater than those of the states involved in it. In the 1920s, the League was able to help settle some small disputes (the Yugoslav invasion of Albania [1922], the Greek invasion of Bulgaria [1925], and the war between Bolivia and Paraguay [1928]). But in the 1930s, the League was unable to deal with the wars that were leading up to World War II—the Japanese invasion of Manchuria, the Italian invasion of Abyssinia—that involved fascist belligerents.

In the US, the League was criticized from a number of angles. There was the neo-Hobbesian (we can call it) criticism that the League had not been given enough clout—the SuperLeviathan position. There was the opposite criticism from nationalists that it took away too much sovereignty from the state. A third criticism, more interesting in the present context, was that the League was built on a contradiction, in that it sought to abolish war by means of war. According to this view, the only way to abolish war is to outlaw it altogether.

PEACE THROUGH THE PLIGHTED WORD

In 1927, Charles Clayton Morrison, editor of *The Christian Century*, published a book titled *The Outlawry of War*, with an afterword by John Dewey, in which this position is set out with a wonderful combination of clarity and muddlement. Morrison's critique of the thinking of the League supporters is powerful.

> [The] dominating purpose [of the orthodox peace movement] has been to contrive such an organization of the nations that they could bring the overwhelming force of their united military strength against a nation that violated the common covenant to keep the peace. Force has been the real god of the peace movement. Peace must be compelled, and the war system is the agent of its compulsion. The task of peace, therefore, according to the orthodox view, is to lift the war system out of its exclusively nationalistic status, and universalize it, center its control at a world capital, from which it may be deployed hither and yon against a threatening or overt offender.[24]

Morrison argues that all attempts to make a legal distinction between aggressive and defensive war, or between just and unjust war, are bound to fail. "Any project," he writes, "which undertakes to retain the categories of 'defensive' and 'aggressive' wars, 'righteous' and 'unrighteous' wars, 'permissible' and 'non-permissible' wars, is doomed to failure."[25] In modern warfare, all belligerent nations insist that they are fighting on the defensive, and that their cause is just. The only way to rid the world of war is to outlaw it entirely.

Morrison's critique of the superstate argument is persuasive; his alternative makes clear why the book is no longer in print. The peace should not be backed by sanctions but should be based entirely on "the plighted word." Simply declare in an international treaty that war is illegal, persuade all the nations to ratify the treaty, and war will disappear. There is no need to make a theoretical argument against this notion: It was tried, with results we all remember. Morrison's book was part of the movement that led to the Kellogg-Briand Pact outlawing war "as an instrument of national policy," which was signed in 1929, just two years after *The Outlawry of War* was published. As is well known, Kellogg-Briand was a dead letter from the beginning, as all the signatories understood it to mean that they retained the right of self-defense.

Interestingly, Morrison's book prepares the ground for this interpretation. In a chapter titled "Self-Defense and the Outlawry of War," he argues that "self-defense is neither involved in nor affected by the outlawry of war. Outlawry absolutely has no point of contact with the question of self-defense."[26] "Suppose a state is attacked, and refuses to meet the attack with military weapons. If any state wishes to choose that course, it is its right to do so. But you cannot legislate that it must do so.... Law cannot reach that far. The question of the right of national self-defense is purely ethical, and cannot be involved in or affected by any juridical standard or process. It is in that sense an inalienable right—law cannot 'alienate' or destroy it."[27] Morrison has tossed "war" out the front door but left the back door open.

Why concentrate on Morrison's book when it might be kinder to allow it to fade from memory? The Kellogg-Briand Pact is not just another glorious failure in international relations' history of glorious failures; it also accurately symbolizes the dilemma encountered in attempts to build a system that abolishes war—and Morrison's book faithfully reflects that dilemma. Surely most people in the world would prefer to live their lives without becoming involved in war. The problem is, if you are attacked, is there any conceivable way of responding to that except by war—or, of course, submission? Most people believe there is not. Morrison argues that we must outlaw all war, making no distinction between aggressive and defensive war. So far, so good. But then he asks, as he must, suppose "a 'bandit' nation breaks its international agreement and wantonly violates the law of nations by suddenly attacking a neighboring state."[28] With this, we see that aggressive war is identifiable after all. And we learn that the attacked country has the right of self-defense, which it can carry out with military weapons. Morrison doesn't call this defensive war; it is "defensive (something nameless)." In Morrison, we see the beginnings of the trend to "abolish" war by calling it something else.

THE FIFTEEN DEMOCRACIES AS SUPERLEVIATHAN

What is striking about the various peace proposals of this period is how persuasive each is in showing why the others won't work. Clarence K. Streit's *Union Now* doesn't mention Morrison's work but dismisses the Kellogg-Briand Pact with the comment that its achievement was not to eliminate war but only to eliminate declarations of war, "greatly increas[ing] the danger that the aggressor will attempt swift and overwhelming surprise attack." Streit's argument is that "the best way to prevent war is to make attack hopeless," and that the way to do this is not to attempt to unite the whole world under a single government but to unite what he identifies as "the 15 democracies."[29] This, he is confident, will produce enough power to dominate the rest.

> They have more than 50 per cent control of nearly every essential material. They have more than 60 per cent of such war essentials as oil, copper, lead, steel, iron, coal, tin, cotton, wool, wood pulp, shipping tonnage. They have almost complete control of such keys as nickel, rubber and automobile production. They possess practically all of the world's gold and banked wealth. Their existing armed strength is such that, once they united it, they could reduce their armaments and yet gain a two-power standard of security.[30]

Streit's "Alliance of the Free," looked at from a different angle, could also be called an "Alliance of the Rich." They "controlled" this wealth mainly because of their domination of what we now call the Global South: Streit has inadvertently given us a portrait of the colonialism of the time. The book fairly trembles with power-lust: His "the democracies can secure world control overnight" makes the project sound positively sinister.[31] But as the book was published in 1940, its proposal overlapped with what was about to happen anyway, not to enforce peace but to fight World War II. The "democracies" Streit listed, with the addition of a few more countries, became the Allied side in that war. Not only was Streit's book a bestseller in both the US and Britain, but also after the war was over it was to have considerable influence on the various proposals for establishing international organizations for enforcing peace.

"LET US PRECIPITATE UNIFICATION BY CONQUEST"

Streit published his book just before Pearl Harbor; Emery Reves published *The Anatomy of Peace* (1945) just before Hiroshima and Nagasaki. That is, he wrote it as the war was going on, and his argument against war concerns not so much what it does to the losers as what it does to the belligerent peoples, win or lose. Those who argue that communism is the next historical stage after capitalism are, he says, mistaken: So long as the world remains in the state of war or threat of war, all political systems will lead to fascism. Especially this is true in the age when technology has made war into total war. Fascism is simply the shape that a nation naturally assumes when it fights total war after total war. The argument is persuasive.

Like Streit, he believes that war can be abolished only by force; unlike Streit, he wants to include not just part of the world under the new unified state but all of it. Thus, while for Streit order is enforced on the insiders by law and on the outsiders by war or threat thereof, for Reves order will be established entirely by law enforcement: "Human nature is such that man does not accept rules unless they are imposed upon him by constituted authority."[32] "Thus the world state is to be established on the model of the nation state. In the nation state, we have not been able to abolish crime. But what we have been able to achieve is to define quite clearly what we mean by crime, to establish a certain system of laws with coercive force; to establish independent courts to apply these laws and to establish police, prisons and punitive measures to give effect to the decisions of courts of law."[33] This is to be applied on a world scale as Global Leviathan.

In response to the instinctive fear people (I included) have of the superstate, Reves says that this is misplaced. The superstate, he argues, is what we are living in now: the state in the midst of World War II. The world state will not be at war and so will not need the coercion, the secrecy, the deception, the periodic states of emergency that war calls for. Come to think of it, it should have no particular need for patriotism. The idea is tempting. Carl Schmitt argued that the state takes on its character from the fact that it has enemies. In the absence of those enemies (shall we say having eliminated those enemies?), will the state become an unprecedentedly benevolent force? Or will we then learn what the dictum "absolute power corrupts absolutely" really means?

Reves's book wavers between overwhelming pessimism and barely possible hope. The first three chapters are titled "The Failure of Capitalism," "The Failure of Socialism," and "The Failure of Religion." Nothing works. Later we learn that internationalism is a failure, self-determination of nations is a failure (the self-determination movement led to only an increase in the number of nation-states, making the situation worse), collective defense is a failure, both disarmament and rearmament are failures. None of these puts an end to the war of each against all among the nation-states. Only the Hobbesian solution will save us. And as it is the only possible solution, it is bound to happen one way or another. If we do not achieve the world state by common consent, then the great powers will continue to struggle until one wins it all. "As in an elimination contest, one of these or a combination will achieve by force that unified control made mandatory by the times we live in. Of course it will be a strictly anti-imperialist imperialism, a kind of very anti-fascist fascism." Reves follows this dark prediction with a statement darker still. "If we cannot attain to universalism and create union by common consent and democratic methods as a result of rational thinking—then rather than retard the process, let us precipitate unification by conquest. It serves no reasonable purpose to prolong the death throes."[34]

If one thinks very roughly and sets aside a number of details, it is possible to see the present world through Reves's categories, with two processes being carried out side by side, the United Nations representing his "union by common consent" and the United States representing his "anti-imperialist imperialism." Neither of these, however, is anywhere near the goal of world unity, and what the newspaper shows us every day is continuing war.

MUDDLING WAR AND POLICE ACTION

There is another peculiarity of Reves's book that seems to presage the present situation. That is his muddling of the distinction between police work and war. He writes, "Whether the application of force is an act of war or a police action depends upon one single criterion: whether or not the force is being used to execute the judgment of a court, applying established law to a concrete case. If force is used without previously enacted law, defining clearly the principles of human conduct and the norms determining such conduct, then the use of force is arbitrary, an act of violence—war."[35]

Of course, not all police work is based on the specific judgment of a court: A police agent who sees a bank being robbed does not need a judge's permission to interfere. More importantly, the absence of a legal basis is not the defining characteristic of war. On the contrary, the key element in the definition of war is its legality. Renaming military action "police action" simply because laws have been made that permit it serves no purpose other than to conceal what is going on. Reves proposes we establish world peace by giving to the world state the exclusive right of belligerency—the right to make war against people who themselves have no such right. This means that if they forcibly resist, they will become what we today call "illegal combatants."

THE UNITED NATIONS AND THE RETURN OF THE FIFTEEN DEMOCRACIES

Against this background, the special character of the United Nations becomes visible. Unlike Streit's proposal, it doesn't limit itself to "the democracies" but is open to the countries of Asia, Africa, Latin America, and the island sovereignties. Unlike Reves's proposal, it does not claim the right of legitimate violence. Unlike Morrison's proposal, it does not require of its member states that they pledge never to fight any wars. At the same time, it has, in the form of the permanent members of the Security Council, a kind of vestige of the Concert of Europe—plus the US and China. But unlike the Concert of Europe, it has a permanent organization—actually a massive bureaucracy—and also a General Assembly in which non-Europe is powerfully represented.

The UN is generally understood as a far-from-perfect organization, and from the time of its founding, various proposals have been made for its improvement. One of these has been to form, within the UN framework, the union of democracies as had been proposed by Clarence K. Streit—led, both as principal theorist and principal activist, by Streit himself. The idea was not to replace the UN with this body but rather that this body be a UN member, essentially the European Community with the US added, or perhaps NATO upgraded. This has taken the form of the World Federalist Movement and also of Atlantic Union. Like the League of Nations, and for much the same reasons, these proposals met with fierce resistance in the US Congress, but at the same time were endorsed at different times by an extraordinary collection of luminaries: Presidents Truman, Eisenhower, Kennedy, and Nixon; Albert Einstein; Henry Kissinger; Hans Morgenthau; Donald Rumsfeld; Barry Goldwater; George H. W. Bush; and Eugene McCarthy, to mention only a few among hundreds. At the height of this movement, Clarence K. Streit's picture was displayed on the cover of *TIME* magazine. But from the late 1950s, interest began to fade, and by 1986, when Streit passed away, the movement had pretty much ended.[36] But while union never happened, it would be hard to deny Streit's influence, formally and informally, on the North Atlantic Alliance.

PEACE WITH A NUCLEAR ARSENAL

An alternative proposal was, instead of unifying some of the states within the United Nations, to strengthen the UN itself. In 1958, at the height of the Cold War, Grenville Clark, former consultant to Secretary of War Stimson, and Harvard law professor Louis Sohn published an ambitious proposal for the radical revision of the United Nations Charter, titled *World Peace Through World Law*. According to the publisher's note on the dust cover, this book took seven years to compose, and is "the first attempt to spell out in explicit detail, rather than in the usual generalities, all the world institutions and basic rules which are required for the effective prevention of war." It is indeed the work not of dreamers or generalists but of two trained experts. The present and the proposed Charters are set down chapter by chapter, interspersed with commentary explaining each of the suggested changes. Reading it, one is persuaded that this is probably very close to what a fully empowered United Nations would need to look like if it were militarily to enforce peace. In the introduction, Clark writes, what is required first of all is a body of world law that would "forbid the use of force by any nation against any other. . . . This world law must also be law in the true sense of law which is capable of enforcement, as distinguished from a mere set of exhortations or injunctions which it is desirable to observe but for the enforcement of which there is no effective machinery."[37]

This "effective machinery" is what Clark first calls a "permanent world police force"; its official name will be the "United Nations Peace Force." This police/peace force will have, in addition to ground forces, a navy and an air force. It will be divided into standing and reserve forces: The standing force would be distributed throughout the world in its own bases and would include highly trained mobile units ready to move at short notice.[38] Its weapons and other equipment will be developed and manufactured by the United Nations Military Supply and Research Agency. The force will not be armed with nuclear weapons, but "such weapons shall be held in reserve in the custody of the Nuclear Energy Authority," just in case.[39] In short, it will be a military organized, equipped, and trained not for police work but for war.

There will still be nation-states, but "no *national* military forces whatever would exist; and the only military force in the entire world (as distinguished from limited and lightly armed internal police forces) would be [the] world police force" (italics in original).[40] To this end, world law must "forbid the use of force by any nation against any other for any cause whatever, save only for self-defense."[41] Here we have the "except for self-defense" escape clause again, the very same that voided the Kellogg-Briand Pact. But there is a difference. Under the Clark-Sohn United Nations regime, the states will have no means of putting this escape clause to effective use: States are to be genuinely disarmed by a "combination of a comprehensive and highly organized inspection system with a coercive force of overwhelming power."[42] This disarmament is expected to take around ten years, and phrases like "a coercive force of overwhelming power" make clear that Clark and Sohn expected it to be a pretty bloody decade.

It is remarkable that these two Harvard-trained legal experts should have, like Reves before them, muddled together the two very different activities, police action and military action. Perhaps the labeling of the US/UN war in Korea a "police action" had contributed to this muddling. Calling the Korean War a "police action" was only a euphemism of the post–Kellogg-Briand, post–UN Charter era, when to carry out a war, it became necessary to call it something else. But far from limiting the soldiers' actions to the things that police officers are permitted to do, calling them "police actions" rather strengthens the soldiers' position by implying that only this side has legitimacy, and that the troops on the other side are not soldiers but criminals. Despite this label, during the Korean "police action," captured Korean and Chinese soldiers were given prisoner-of-war status. Under the Clark-Sohn United Nations regime, it is not clear whether rebels will be so treated. Given that world law will have transferred the right of belligerency from the states to the United Nations, it is hard to see how rebels could. In Clark and Sohn's Bill of Rights to be attached to the new UN Charter, the right to prisoner-of-war status is not mentioned.[43]

"THERE WILL NO LONGER BE ANY WARS. THEN, ONLY EXECUTIONS WILL EXIST."

In 1937, Carl Schmitt took up the question of world government in his essay "The Turn to the Discriminating Concept of War." In that essay, Schmitt, at that time defending Germany's withdrawal from the League of Nations, makes a powerful critique of the theory that world peace can be achieved by world government. By "discriminating concept of war," he means not simply discriminating between just and unjust war, a distinction that had existed in international law since Grotius, but "a system that monopolizes judgment on just war." "According to Grotius, the unjust war is of course still a war, and something different from . . . murder, robbery, or piracy."[44] The difference has concrete consequences: Captured murderers, robbers, and pirates do not have the rights of prisoners of war, and in cases of murder, robbery, and piracy, the law does not recognize the right of third parties to remain neutral. To Schmitt, it was to these distinctions in the "now obsolete international law [that] war owed its justice, honor and worth."[45] Leaving aside the question of whether traditional war had been as noble an enterprise as Schmitt wanted to believe, what matters here is his view of what the world would look like should a fully empowered world government come into being.

According to Schmitt, if "war" is understood in the traditional way, as something like a duel between states in which either side has a "right" to win, then under world government there would no longer be such a thing as war. This does not mean that there will be no "bloody struggles." But in these struggles, the "dignity" of being a combatant fighting under the authority of the right of belligerency will not be awarded to both sides. The judgment of justice or injustice will have been monopolized by the world state; it will be universal and have no legitimate rivals. If the "bloody struggles" that may arise under this regime still look like war, they will no longer be "war between states" but "international civil war."[46] Schmitt wavers between calling this war and not-war. The "bloody struggles" will look like what we call war, but legally they will be something else. The first stage, during which the world state establishes its hegemony with what Clark and Sohn called "coercive force of overwhelming power," Schmitt describes as the "decisively final war of humanity."[47] But from a legal standpoint, as only one side has the right of legitimate violence, it is not war at all, but police action against criminals. "One will no longer decide between just and unjust wars; rather there will no longer be any wars. Then, only executions will exist."[48]

With legitimacy monopolized by just one side, "not taking a position [that is, neutrality] . . . would be seen as impossible for any morally conscious person."[49] This, Schmitt predicts, will lead not to peace but to "an intensification of war and enmity," "a deeper and more intense distinction between friend and enemy," or, using an expression new at the time, Schmitt writes, "'total' war."[50]

Schmitt quotes, among other works promoting this new form of international law, an essay by British legal scholar Sir John Fischer Williams, who argued that as international law becomes increasingly moral, neutrality fades as an option. At the close of his essay, Fischer Williams approvingly reminds his readers that "Dante . . . bequeathed a unique contempt and punishment on the angels who remained neutral in the great struggle between God and the Devil."[51] Rather than bringing peace, Schmitt implies, world government will only add a new dimension to the expression "War is hell."

The above chapter introduces various people's notions of what ought, or ought not, to happen. The following chapter focuses mainly on what is happening.

NOTES

1. Thomas Hobbes, *Leviathan*, 100.
2. Jean-Jacques Rousseau, "Abstract of the Abbe de St Pierre's Project for Perpetual Peace," in *The Theory of International Relations*, eds. M. G. Forsyth, H. N. A. Keens-Soper, and P. Savigear (London: George Allen and Unwin, 1970), 131.
3. Jean-Jacques Rousseau, "Judgment on Saint Pierre's Project for Perpetual Peace," in *The Theory of International Relations*, eds. M. G. Forsyth, H. N. A. Keens-Soper, and P. Savigear (London: George Allen and Unwin, 1970), 143.
4. Rousseau, "Judgment," 157.
5. Rousseau, "Judgment," 158.
6. Rousseau, "Judgment," 159.
7. Rousseau, "Judgment," 160–1.
8. Rousseau, "Judgment," 160–1.
9. Rousseau, "Judgment," 161.
10. Rousseau, "Judgment," 166.
11. Immanuel Kant, "Idea for a Universal History from a Cosmo-political Point of View," in *The Theory of International Relations*, eds. M. G. Forsyth, H. N. A. Keens-Soper, and P. Savigear (London: George Allen and Unwin, 1970), 184.
12. Immanuel Kant, "Perpetual Peace: a Philosophical Essay," in *The Theory of International Relations*, eds. M. G. Forsyth, H. N. A. Keens-Soper, and P. Savigear (London: George Allen and Unwin, 1970), 205–6.
13. Kant, "Perpetual Peace," 208.
14. Kant, "Perpetual Peace," 213.
15. Immanuel Kant, "On the Commonplace: That May Be Correct in Theory but Is Useless in Practice," in *The Theory of International Relations*, eds. M. G. Forsyth, H. N. A. Keens-Soper, and P. Savigear (London: George Allen and Unwin, 1970), 196.

16. Kant, "Perpetual Peace," 222.
17. Kant, "Perpetual Peace," 223.
18. Immanuel Kant, "Idea for a Universal History from a Cosmopolitan Point of View," in *Kant on History*, ed. Lewis White Beck (Upper Saddle River: Prentice Hall, 2001), 6th thesis, 17.
19. Kant, "Universal History," 6th thesis, 18.
20. Kant, "Universal History," 7th thesis, 20.
21. Kant, "The Metaphysical Elements," 257.
22. Mark Mazower, *Governing the World: The History of an Idea, 1815 to the Present* (Penguin Books, 2012), prologue, ff.
23. Mazower, *Governing the World*, 12.
24. Charles Clayton Morrison, *The Outlawry of War: A Constructive Policy for World Peace* (Chicago: Willett, Clark and Colby, 1927), 179.
25. Morrison, *Outlawry*, 206.
26. Morrison, *Outlawry*, 209.
27. Morrison, *Outlawry*, 211.
28. Morrison, *Outlawry*, 211.
29. Clarence K. Streit, *Union Now: The Proposal for Inter-democracy Federal Union* (New York: Harper and Brothers, 1940), 55, 18.
30. Streit, *Union Now*, 10.
31. Streit, *Union Now*, 23.
32. Emery Reves, *The Anatomy of Peace* (New York: The Viking Press, 1963 [orig. Harper and Row, 1945]), 129.
33. Reves, *Anatomy*, 155.
34. Reves, *Anatomy*, 266, 267–70.
35. Reves, *Anatomy*, 216.
36. Rick Biondi and Alex Newman, *World Federalism 101* (self-pub., 2014), part III, ff.
37. Grenville Clark and Louis B. Sohn, *World Peace Through World Law* (Cambridge, MA: Harvard U. Press, 1958), xi.
38. Clark and Sohn, *World Peace*, 300.
39. Clark and Sohn, *World Peace*, 305.
40. Clark and Sohn, *World Peace*, xx.
41. Grenville Clark and Louis B. Sohn, *World Peace Through World Law* (Cambridge: Harvard U. Press, 1958), xi.
42. Clark and Sohn, *World Peace*, 300.
43. Clark and Sohn, *World Peace,* 350–51.
44. Carl Schmitt, "The Turn to the Discriminating Concept of War" in Carl Schmitt, *Writings on War*, Timothy Nunan tr. and ed. (Cambridge, MA: Polity Press, 2011), 31, 64
45. Schmitt, "Discriminating Concept," 71.
46. Schmitt, "Discriminating Concept," 30–31, 71.
47. Schmitt, "Discriminating Concept," 72.
48. Schmitt, "Discriminating Concept," 70.

49. Schmitt, "Discriminating Concept," 58.
50. Schmitt, "Discriminating Concept," 71.
51. Schmitt, "Discriminating Concept," 58.

Chapter 9

SuperLeviathan Now

THE UNITED NATIONS AS SHERIFF'S POSSE

Emery Reves's account of the two ways the world can achieve peace was given its original formulation by Hobbes, who wrote that Leviathan can be established either by acquisition (forcible conquest) or by institution (contractual agreement).[1]

At the time of this writing, neither plan has been realized, nor does it seem likely that either will be soon. Nevertheless, the two models are useful in understanding the situation we are in. Two massive, intermingled projects are at work today in the sphere of international relations. Each claims to aim at establishing some kind of peace in our world, but neither is doing well. One is the movement to strengthen the United Nations by giving it, little by little, coercive powers (Hobbes's "commonwealth by institution"). The other is the movement to transform the domination that the United States enjoys over some parts of the world into something approaching real governance (Hobbes's "commonwealth by acquisition"). It is not the aim of this book to attempt a full telling of these two immensely complex tales. I shall only mention a few things that pertain to the question at hand.

For Hobbes, the commonwealth enjoys a monopoly of legitimate violence within its own territory, though not in the world. Emery Reves and Grenville Clark believed that the way to achieve world peace is to give that monopoly of legitimate violence to the United Nations, or to some other international organization that stands above the state. As I point out earlier, the right of legitimate violence can be divided into three phases: police action, punitive action, and military action—the right of belligerency. The member nations have fully granted none of these to the UN.

As for the right of belligerency, when the UN Security Council judges that military force is necessary, it calls in the "air, sea, or land forces of Members of the United Nations" (UN Charter, article 42). That is, it borrows the right of belligerency of its member states. The closest the charter comes to giving the UN military authority is in article 43, which authorizes a military staff committee and requires all states to make an arrangement with it to depute some of its military force to the UN. But no such deputation has ever been made. Without a firm organizational backing, the UN has used what Thomas G. Weiss and his coauthors of *The United Nations and Changing World Politics* call the "sheriff's posse" approach to breaches of the peace.[2] The UN and the member states pool their differing authorities. The national armies, though on a UN project, use their own right of belligerency, which the UN does not have; on the other hand, the UN delegates to them the right to intervene in sovereign states, which the national armies do not have. Weiss and his colleagues write, "It is hard to believe that large-scale UN peace operations, which after all started in 1956, remain on such shaky and ad hoc organizational ground."[3]

One can sympathize with the frustration of the authors of this book (described on the back cover as "the standard text on the UN for courses in international organization"), who are dedicated supporters of the UN. It is by no means easy to imitate the state in coercing people into keeping the peace when you haven't been given the means the state has to carry out that coercion. The same is true when it comes to police action and punitive action.

The practice of setting up an international tribunal with the jurisdiction to punish individuals for violations of international law began in earnest with the Nuremberg trials. But while the UN can use the Nuremberg judgments as legal precedent, it cannot use the tribunal as a model. For the legal basis of the Nuremberg tribunal was clearly attained, in Hobbes's terms, "by acquisition." Germany's instrument of surrender, the Berlin Declaration of June 5, 1945, states, "The Governments of the United States of America, the Union of Soviet Socialist Republics, The United Kingdom and the Provisional Government of the French Republic, hereby assume supreme authority with respect to Germany, including all the powers possessed by the German Government, the High Command and any state, municipal or local government or authority."

The tribunal's judicial authority was derived not from the newly established United Nations but from the occupying Big Four, who had taken into themselves the sovereignty of the German state.

The judicial power that was initially given to the UN, on the other hand, was that of the International Court of Justice (ICJ). This court has only a small piece of what is normally thought of as judicial power. As its name implies, it has the authority to make decisions as to what is just, but to declare something unjust is not the same as to declare it a crime. Thus, the ICJ does not make findings of criminality or declare parties guilty of criminal behavior, much less deliver punitive sentences. Nor does it have the authority to order anyone arrested and brought before the court. Cases of noncompliance can be referred to the Security Council.

The first step toward increasing the UN's judicial power was the establishment of the International Criminal Tribunal for Yugoslavia (ICTY) in 1993. Again, the character of this body is reflected in the name: It is a criminal tribunal. The people brought before it spend their nights not in hotel rooms but in jail, or—as the UN prefers to call it—the Detention Unit. The ICTY home page describes at length the good treatment the detainees are given, which is commendable, but it also says they are let out of their rooms for an hour at a time and the doors are locked at night. Of course there will be guards; who they work for and what weapons they carry is not mentioned in the home-page information. In fact, the facility is located inside a Dutch prison complex, and the guards are working under the authority of the Dutch government. Similarly, the police officials who originally detained the prisoners and brought them to the tribunal chambers in the Hague also worked under the authority of one or another state.

Unlike the ICJ, the ICTY tribunal can make judgments not only of legality but also of guilt and can pass sentence. Again, there is a division of labor. The tribunal can authorize arrest and detention, but only officials of a state can enforce this. Similarly, the tribunal can find persons guilty and sentence them to imprisonment, but to serve their time, they are shipped to a prison somewhere outside the Netherlands.

In addition to in the former Yugoslavia, the Security Council has established courts in Rwanda, Sierra Leone, East Timor, Lebanon, and Cambodia, each, like the ICTY, on an ad hoc basis in response to an immediate situation. But just as the UN's borrowed military powers are shaky, so are its borrowed law-enforcement powers. For example, the Extraordinary Chambers in the Courts of Cambodia (ECCC) were established by an agreement between the UN and the Cambodian government. Under the agreement, judicial powers were shared by the two, but the power to arrest and imprison was held by the Cambodian police. At one point, one of the foreign judges ordered the arrest of someone the government did not want arrested, and the police refused to do it, resulting in resignations, mutual accusations, and other matters damaging to the dignity of an international court of law.

In 1998, the Rome Statute was signed, establishing the first permanent international tribunal, the International Criminal Court (ICC). The Rome Statute being a separate international treaty, the ICC is not an organ of the United Nations but an independent body, founded through the consent of the signatories and thus, in Hobbes's terms, established "by institution." Article 12.1 reads, "A State which becomes a Party to this Statute thereby accepts the jurisdiction of the Court with respect to the crimes referred to in Article 5."

However, acceptance by the member states of the "jurisdiction" of the court does not mean that the member states have handed over to the court the right of coercion. On the contrary, the Statute is carefully designed to make sure that does not happen. Article 58 of the Statute gives the Pre-Trial Chamber of the Court the authority to issue a warrant of arrest, but article 59 reads, "A State Party which has received a request for provisional arrest or for arrest and surrender shall immediately take steps to arrest the person in question in accordance with its laws and the provisions of Part 9." Article 76 gives the court the authority to declare the suspect guilty or innocent, and article 77 empowers the court to determine, if the finding is guilty, the appropriate penalty. But again, it is the state that enforces this. Article 103.1.a reads, "A sentence of imprisonment shall be served in a State designated by the Court from a list of States which have indicated to the Court their willingness to accept sentenced persons."

Moreover, article 93 lists various other activities connected with a criminal investigation that may entail varying degrees of coercion—locating persons, questioning witnesses, examining sites, excavating graves, carrying out searches and seizures, freezing assets, and so on—and stipulates that these will be carried out with the cooperation of the member states.

The difference is subtle but clear. The state signatories have handed over to the court the power to decide what coercive measures—arrest, detention, fines—are appropriate in these cases. In signing the statute, they have promised to do as the court requests. But the actual coercion is carried out by the state. The statute contains no provision empowering the court to punish a state that refuses its request. Max Weber's definition of the state as the social organization (successfully) claiming a monopoly of legitimate violence still holds.

At least, it holds for some states.

One of the most visible facts about the various criminal courts is that they "thus far have dealt almost always with situations in powerless countries."[4] In particular, all eight of the investigations so far carried out by the ICC have been in African countries. The point is not that the ICC has been too harsh on African human-rights violators; I have no reason to doubt that the people convicted and sentenced by that court got what they deserved. Rather, the point is that the more powerful governments are able to protect themselves from ICC "intervention." They can do this either by not signing the Statute (China, India, Indonesia, Iraq, and Turkey, for example) or by signing but not ratifying it (United States, Thailand, and Israel). The NATO countries have signed, but so far no one from any of those countries has been brought before the ICC. Hopefully the human-rights work done in the less powerful countries by these tribunals is doing some good. The problem is the human-rights work needed in the powerful countries is not getting done.

RESPONSIBILITY TO PROTECT (R2P)

The movement to transform the UN gradually into a world government "by institution" has not been limited to strengthening its judicial powers. It also includes the strengthening of its military powers, in particular its right to intervene in the affairs of sovereign nations. The most recent form this movement has taken gets its name from a report produced in 2001 by the International Commission on Intervention and State Sovereignty (ICISS) titled "The Responsibility to Protect" and abbreviated "R2P." The argument, briefly, was that when people are being subjected to such horrors as genocide or ethnic cleansing, the obligation to give them some protection should take precedence over the taboo against "interference in the internal affairs of sovereign states." The dilemma is real, because the horrors are real. In the post–World War II world, new countries whose boundaries had been carved out by the big powers, and in particular by the colonial powers, threw together peoples, many of whom had never had much to do with one another, often resulting in ethnic hatreds and ghastly civil wars. When real massacres are taking place, it can seem like an evasion of responsibility for those who might have the power to put a stop to them to refuse to try because there is a rule against violating a country's sovereignty. This position was taken by then UN Secretary-General Kofi Annan, who later was awarded the Nobel Peace Prize. The argument is, "sovereignty was not a license to do as state authorities wished but was contingent on respecting minimal human rights standards."[5] When those minimal standards are not met, intervention is justified.

There are many arguments against this notion. To people in formerly colonized regions, it looks like a disguise for neocolonialism. To anti-war people, it looks like a way of keeping the military industrial complex in business after the end of the Cold War. It's argued that it's quite likely that intervening troops will do more harm than good, or will be seen by local people as doing more harm than good. It's pointed out that sending a large military unit into a country and carrying out military action will have huge consequences and reverberations impossible to predict, so there's no way to know for certain that the intervention will do more good than harm. And it's pointed out that after the intervention is over, the claim that it did more good than harm can never be proved as it has to be based on a counterfact, that is, speculation as to what would have happened had there been no intervention. It's argued that soldiers can't be expected to risk their lives to rescue people in distant countries for altruistic reasons but can be expected to only if their own country's national interest is somehow involved, which means that an intervention will be effective only to the extent that its *jus ad bellum* is supplemented by other, not-necessarily-just, motives.[6] All of these arguments are persuasive.

For pure pacifists, of course, that military action is never justified is a categorical principle, and R2P military action is no exception. As I wrote in its introduction, this book does not take the position of pure pacifism, and the same applies here. It seems to me that it is futile to claim that there is no possible case in which intervention will do more good than harm, as one cannot know all possible cases. In the real world, of which we have imperfect knowledge, it's risky to say "never." R2P is the most recent manifestation of just war theory; its ethic of "more good than harm" is what Weber called the ethic of consequences. To borrow Hobbes's expression, R2P seeks to be "not so hurtful as the want of it." There is no logical proof or philosophical formula that can demonstrate with certainty that benefit A justifies hurt B. The choice between benefit A and hurt B is often agonizing. However, this book is not a treatise on ethics but rather an analysis of some aspects of the nature of war and peace. In this context, I want to ask, What is the nature of the action taken in the name of Responsibility to Protect? What rules of logic does it follow, and by what name should we call it? I can at least hope that taking up the question in this manner may, for someone getting involved in such an operation, be helpful in understanding what he or she is getting into.

R2P defenders, or at least some of them, argue that R2P is different from war properly so called. In what sense is it different? To qualify as R2P, its *jus ad bellum* must not be the national interest of the home country of the troops carrying it out, except in the sense that it is in everyone's interest that the world be a place where such things as massacres don't happen. The action is not R2P if the intervening countries are also interested in the country's oil resources or diamond mines. Also, the intervening military is not technically "at war" with the country's government: War has not been declared, and the military's mission is not, or should not be, to defeat the local army or to cause the local government to surrender, but to prevent it from carrying out certain acts considered criminal.

In his 2014 article based largely on the 2011 Libya intervention, the first intervention intended to be carried out on the R2P model, Roland Paris makes some interesting observations. Among other things, he points out that the motives of the intervening powers were not all that pure; national interest was also a factor. "In the absence of altruism," he writes, "it is simply 'war.'"[7] But this is a strange assertion. Altruistic *jus ad bellum* does not transform military action into something other than war. As I argue above, following Clausewitz, altruism (of course differently defined in different ages and by different peoples) is usually—and often persuasively—claimed as the motive for making war. And the higher the level of altruism, the stronger the motivation to carry war to its ultimate conclusion. More ominously, the more altruistic the self-image of the interveners, the more the opposing combatants appear as criminals, deserving death.

More interesting is Paris's analysis of what he calls the "strategic logic" of R2P. In addition to studying whether R2P is ethical or legal, he says, we need to ask how exactly it proposes to get its way in the intervened country. Looked at in this way, we can see that the strategic logic of R2P is in no significant way different from what Clausewitz called the logic of war. There may be many minor ways by which R2P actions are different from ordinary war, but in the aspect that matters, they are the same. To achieve your mission, you need to win. Or if winning doesn't matter that much, you anyway need to prevail. If the other side fights back, you need to do whatever it takes to "impose your will on the other"; otherwise, your mission is a failure. The 1973 UN Security Council resolution authorizing intervention in Syria contains the phrase "all necessary measures." Of course. This is the phrase regularly inserted into treaties seeking to establish laws limiting war: "except when necessary." In this respect, R2P is no different. Paris wrote that the Libya intervention was not supposed to have regime change as its goal, only the protection of protesters. But it turned out that the only way to protect the protesters was through regime change. In contemporary United Nations lingo, R2P units must be "robust," an Orwellian term that means "able and willing to kill people who don't do what you tell them to." Cities were bombed, Gaddafi was murdered, and whether the intervention was "less hurtful than the want of it" remains arguable. Paris's paradoxical conclusion is "R2P failed because it worked."[8]

Put differently, you could say, that's the way R2P works. It works according to the simple logic discerned by Clausewitz, the logic of war. It can't be elevated to not-war by improving the altruism of the interveners. On the contrary, the greater the altruism, the more splendid the *jus ad bellum* and the greater the justification and motivation for doing "what it takes" to achieve victory. R2P is war. To which the epithet "war is Hell" applies as aptly as to any other war. The dead are as dead, the wounded as wounded, the survivors as devastated, and the PTSD victims as tortured as with any war.

And most importantly, what is achieved by it is not radical peace, not the villagers' peace, but robber-band peace, Leviathan peace, (hopefully) not so hurtful as the want of it but hurtful nonetheless. Radical peace cannot be achieved by this method. You can't get there from here.

In addition to the (gradual) expansion of the powers of the UN and its affiliated international organizations, there has been a radical expansion of the international powers of the United States. While it would be wild exaggeration to say that the US has achieved Hobbes's "commonwealth by acquisition," it has moved lurchingly in that direction. The most recent phase of this process begins with the "War on Terror."

THE WAR ON TERROR

Many people believe that on September 11, 2001, the day of the terrorist attacks on New York City and Washington, D.C., the world changed. They've got it wrong by two days. It was September 13, the day President George W. Bush declared a "war against terror," when the shape of the world changed. The expression "war on terror" is a stunning example of the power that a performative utterance can have when performed by the US president—even when its words are garbled. As many have pointed out, terror, being neither a country nor an organization but a tactic, is not something against which it makes sense to wage war. Still, those words resulted in, if not war properly so called, much bloody struggle and violent treatment of human beings, under a different set of rules. And as the new rules, confused as they are, were decided in a speech by a person who, at least in his own estimation, was sovereign, we can call what followed in much of the world a state of exception. The "war against terror" and the actions carried out in its name changed international law, changed the laws of warfare, and changed the status of the United States in the world community. Now the expression is somewhat out of fashion—"terrorists" have been renamed "illegal combatants"—but its effects on the structure of international politics have not gone away.

MILITARY ACTION AND POLICE ACTION: MUDDLED AGAIN

War is traditionally carried out between sovereign states, or between a state and a rebel group that either wants to take control of the state or separate itself from it. War is (supposed to be) carried out according to certain rules, and it (hopefully) follows a logic that leads in the end to the reestablishment of peace either by the victory of one side or by the negotiation of a peace treaty. But "terrorism" is neither a state nor a group. It is a tactic that can be and is used by loner individuals, rebel groups, and states (as by bombing cities). As a tactic, it has no location, no organization, no collective identity, no fixed battleground. It has no central command headquarters whose overrunning would mean victory. What can you do to bring such a war to an end? With whom do you negotiate terms or sign a peace treaty?

As these questions are unanswerable, some have concluded that the US made a colossal blunder when it declared this "war." It did, but at the same time, it gained for itself real advantages. In the past, terrorism, at least non-state terrorism, had been treated as criminal activity, to be dealt with through the methods of law enforcement. Investigators would gather evidence and seek out suspects, have them arrested, and turn them over to the judicial system for trial. If the evidence warranted, those suspects would be convicted and punished. This can be a tedious and frustrating process, at the end of which the court might find the evidence insufficient and set the suspects free. To mention just one especially frustrating example, on December 21, 2020, it was announced by the US government that a suspect in the Lockerbie bombing case had been arrested in Lybia, just thirty-two years after the crime had been committed. Whether the suspect will be convicted remains to be seen. In war, things are simpler. Soldiers need not collect evidence or single out suspects from the general population. All they need to ascertain is that a person wears the enemy uniform. They don't need to prove that he or she has actually "done" anything hostile. It is perfectly permissible under the laws of war to shoot down a raw recruit who has been brought up to the line only a few minutes before. Law enforcement officers are not supposed to shoot suspects. Soldiers are.

During the Vietnam War, US radio news gave the daily body count in a characteristic fashion: "Today nn Communists were killed." The power of the evil ideology was reduced by this amount. With the Afghan and Iraqi wars, it changed: "Today nn suspected terrorists were killed." The enemy are identified not as soldiers but as suspected lawbreakers. But there is no necessity to arrest them and investigate whether they have in fact violated any law. By muddling war and law enforcement together, the US has given itself a clear advantage. Insofar as the enemies are understood as criminals, they have no right to be treated as prisoners of war if they surrender; insofar as they are understood as fighting a war, US troops may shoot them down on sight. Insofar as other countries' troops are fighting alongside the US, they may do the same.

A further advantage war has over law enforcement is that in the case of law enforcement, it is not enough for a person simply to "be" of a criminal nature. To be arrested and punished, a person must have actually carried out an act prohibited by law. In the war on terror, people are killed or imprisoned for "being" terrorists; whether they have carried out any terrorist acts is not an issue.

The situation bears an uncomfortable resemblance to Carl Schmitt's image of what the world might look like if "war," which takes place between two sovereign entities that both have the right of belligerency, is replaced by "bloody struggles" (no proper legal term has yet been coined) in which only one side has the right of belligerency. This similarity was noted by Timothy Nunan in his introduction to Schmitt's *Writings on War*: "In our time, we find both states and international organizations, themselves both subjects of international law, waging something—but not formal war—against organizations and individuals such as al-Qaida and the Taliban that do not themselves appear as subjects of any international law. On a conceptual plane, this amounts to a creep toward what Schmitt called the denationalization of war—doing away with the war of states in order to transform war into an 'international civil war.'"[9]

Readers of this book will understand that I do not share Schmitt's romantic view of war, but that does not mean that he could not have been able to imagine an alternative that is worse, or in any case terrible in a different way. In his view, establishing a world government as the only entity with the right of legitimate violence drains all opponents of this government not only of their dignity but also of their rights as human beings, defining them as *hostis generis humanis* (enemy of the human race), the legal category, in which pirates, who act outside all law and who can call on no law in their defense, have traditionally been placed. Schmitt's conclusion is worth repeating: "One will no longer decide between just and unjust wars; rather there will no longer be any wars. Then, only executions will exist."

THE TERRORIST AS A NEW LEGAL CATEGORY

Especially in the first phase of this new War on Terror, prisoners captured (or in some cases, as we hear, purchased from their captors) in Afghanistan and Iraq by the US were not granted prisoner-of-war status. If they had the status of POWs, they would have had the rights guaranteed under the Geneva Conventions of 1949 and by the customary laws of war based on centuries of precedent. In particular, it would be illegal to put them on trial simply for making war; it would be legal only if there was evidence that they had committed specific violations of the laws of war. However, the US government insisted that the Geneva Conventions did not apply to them. But if the prisoners were not POWs, then they should have been criminal suspects, which would have given them another elaborate set of rights under US law. However, it turned out that they were not to have these either. They were originally placed in this new legal category by President Bush's executive order of November 13, 2001, under which they were to be tried by military tribunal. (I find nothing in the US Constitution that authorizes the president to establish such tribunals. It seems that the "sovereign" president simply pulled the authority out of the air.) The order states, "It is not practicable to apply in military commissions under this order the principles of law and the rules of evidence generally recognized in the trial of criminal cases in the United States district courts" (Section 1f). Among the rights they are denied are the right to be informed what they are being detained for, the right of habeas corpus (under which if the prosecutor is unable within a reasonable period to show evidence that they have committed a crime, they must be released), the right to confront and question witnesses (for government witnesses may be spies, and if they show their faces in court, they can't be used again), the right to see the evidence being used against them (some of it may be state secrets), the right freely to consult a lawyer, the right to a trial by jury of their peers, the right to appeal to a higher court, the right to an open trial, and (as all these rights are taken away before any judicial determination of guilt or innocence has been made) the right to be presumed innocent until proven guilty. This last is especially stunning. The prisoners are trapped in a kind of vicious tautology, which can be illustrated by the following imaginary conversation:

Prisoner: Why am I being confined here?

Guard: Because you are a terrorist.

Prisoner: By what judicial procedure, and on the basis of what evidence, was it determined that I am a terrorist?

Guard: In your case, no such procedure or evidence is necessary.

Prisoner: Why is that?

Guard: Because you are a terrorist.

What seems to have been forgotten is that the main intention of all these rights of accused persons is not to be lenient to criminals but to make sure the people you are punishing really have committed crimes. Punishment is permitted, but only after it has been determined beyond a reasonable doubt that the suspects have committed crimes. Until that determination has been made, suspects are to be treated not as criminals but as suspects. But these people had been designated, and treated as, "illegal combatants" from the moments of their captures (or purchases). In effect, they were told, like a character in a Kafka novel, "You are accused of being guilty. We are not in a position to tell you of what act you are guilty, or who your accusers are, or what the evidence is, or when, if ever, your trial will take place. Defend yourself as best you can."

When human-rights lawyers argued that the right of habeas corpus should apply to these prisoners, the US government position was that this argument should be rejected, as US criminal law doesn't apply in Cuba, where the prisoners were being held. With this, we could understand why the Guantanamo Bay facility had been selected for this prison camp. US law doesn't apply there, Cuban law doesn't apply there, the law of the prisoners' countries doesn't apply there, and (as the prisoners were not granted the status of POWs) international law doesn't apply there. They had been brought into a space where no law exists for them at all. Occasionally, we read in the papers that other prisoners were being held in undisclosed locations, perhaps on

US warships at sea where they would also be beyond the reach of any law, or in countries whose laws permit interrogation and punishment techniques forbidden in the US. But if neither US nor international law applied to these prisoners, under what legal authority were they being held?

Human-rights advocates and lawyers, to their credit, have challenged this understanding of the terrorist or illegal combatant, with some success. It is not my intention here to attempt to detail the complexities of the various litigations that have been and are going on. Rather, I want to examine the nature of the new world order that has been unfolding in the era of the War on Terror, and to point out the connection between what Nunan called the "creep" toward that model and the situation Schmitt predicted would result from SuperLeviathan coming into existence.

Consider this: After 9/11, the United States granted to itself four special rights hitherto prohibited under international law:

1. The right to invade countries that have no plan or intention of invading the United States.
2. The right to "arrest," for violation of US law, foreign nationals in foreign countries, including people who have never been inside the United States.
3. The right forcibly to bring about regime change in foreign countries.
4. As none of these rights is granted any other country unless it is acting under United States leadership, the right of the US to exempt itself from the principle of equality under the law.

These new rights were not simply announced in the abstract; each has been acted upon. And as international law, like all law, is partly built on precedent, it is not enough to say that the US is simply violating international law; it is changing it. When the world's most powerful country takes these actions repeatedly and with impunity, at some point must one not say that these actions are permitted?

It was after these changes were acted upon that supporters of US foreign policy began to change their use of the word "empire." In the past, when critics accused the US of imperialism, supporters of US policies would deny that the word applied; after the invasions of Afghanistan and Iraq, they began to say, "Yes, and what of it?" Of course, whether considered as empire or as SuperLeviathan, United States hegemony is far from complete. It is effective only in relatively powerless states. The United States is in no position to arrest people, or carry out regime change, inside the territories of China, Russia, or Iran, for example. But, vis-à-vis certain areas of the world, the US is striving to achieve a monopoly of legitimate violence. And as Schmitt pointed out, establishing a monopoly of legitimate violence means delegitimizing the violence of your opponents. By labeling the opponents terrorists or illegal combatants, you are placing them one category down from gangsters (who still have the right to trial if arrested) to an existence that needs to be exterminated—liquidated on sight. If one such being comes within the sights of a drone aircraft, the proper thing to do is to fire the rocket and rid the earth of that being. Thus "war" is replaced by serial executions.

Rousseau wrote, "While we admire so fair a project, let us console ourselves for its failure by the thought that it only could have been carried out by violent means from which humanity must needs shrink."[10] His words no longer serve as a consolation.

CREEPING INTERNATIONALISM?

In the *Oxford International Encyclopedia of Peace*, the entry for "World Governance," after describing the rise and decline of various proposals for achieving peace through world government, concludes with a brief subsection titled by a question: "World Governance by Default?" While theorists such as those discussed in this chapter have sought to come up with a plan by which a Leviathan-scale governing system could be established, the author, Thomas Weber, suggests that "we are, perhaps without even noticing it, moving incrementally toward a form of world governance or world polity that does not require us to take any active steps."[11] He points out that "proposals for a world government with coercive power and a centralized but checked authority seem to have given way to the newer imaginative noncoercive pluralist and decentralized visions of global governance."[12] The one concrete example he gives, the International Criminal Court, is not very persuasive as an example of "noncoercive" governance given that the ICC borrows state power to have people incarcerated, but there are other examples that fit this model better. In his *Governing the World*, Mark Mazower notes the same trend and divides it into two types. One is the internationalizing of government bureaucracies, "a world in which formal supranational orgnizations [play] a relatively minor role and loose but businesslike networks of middle-level officials from different countries, often mingling with regulator and industry experts [get] things done. In this world, there [seems] to be no evident conflict, and rather little formality. Most of what [goes on is] behind closed doors, humdrum, and technical but ultimately of real consequence."[13] Indeed, if the world of nation-states cannot be governed, perhaps it can be managed. But there is no reason to expect that a society organized under the managerial mentality will be democratic.

Where, then, might a force to democratize this largely bureaucratic world be found? "Perhaps," says Mazower, carefully choosing his words, "in that civil society whose magical effects are widely credited with the dissolution of communism and the injection of ethics into international life."[14] The NGO is a new phenomenon; 90 percent of those existing now have been formed since 1970. There are the giant NGOs that have annual budgets larger than some UN agencies and there are the shoestring NGOs that barely survive, but within both, mostly young people from the northern and the southern countries carry on discourses and generate ethics and sensibilities that were unthinkable before World War II. These discourses are far from equal—the money comes from the north—but now the difference is that there are thousands of people from the south involved in these NGOs and struggling against that inequality. Perhaps, tentatively, we can take this as evidence supporting Gandhi's notion that when left to their own devices, people can generally figure out how to get along peacefully.

The forces that are seeking to create, or to become, SuperLeviathan still exist, but if that beast cannot be subdued by main force, there's still a chance it might become entangled in a net.

NOTES

1. Hobbes, *Leviathan*, 133.
2. Thomas G. Weiss, David P. Forsyth, Roger A. Coate, and Kelly-Kate Pease, *The United Nations and Changing World Politics* (Boulder, CO: Westview Press, 2014), 38.
3. Weiss et al., *United Nations*, 38.
4. Weiss et al., *United Nations*, 198.
5. Weiss et al., *United Nations*, 93.
6. Roland Paris, "The 'Responsibility to Protect' and the Structural Problems of Humanitarian Intervention," *International Peacekeeping*, vol. 21, no. 5 (2014): ff. In the online version of this article, page numbers are not indicated.
7. Paris, "Responsibility."
8. Paris, "Responsibility."
9. Timothy Nunan, "Introduction," in Schmitt, *Writings on War*, 23.
10. Rousseau, "Judgment," 166.
11. Thomas Weber, "World Governance," in *The Oxford International Encyclopedia of Peace*, vol. 4 (Oxford: Oxford University Press, 2010), 443.
12. Weber, "World Governance," 443.
13. Mazower, *Governing the World*, 415.
14. Mazower, *Governing the World*, 417.

Chapter 10

Japan's Impossible Constitution

> The right of belligerency of the state will not be recognized.
>
> —The Constitution of Japan, Article 9

THE 1960 AMPO GENERATION

My first encounter with the postwar Constitution of Japan took place in 1961. Just out of the Marine Corps and assiduously working to shift over to a different way of living, I was studying at the Osaka University of Foreign Studies, which had a special nondegree Japanese-language program for foreign students. After class, we had opportunities to talk with the regular students at the university. This was the first generation of students educated entirely under the postwar educational system, making use of their new freedom to study foreign languages (the university itself was founded in only 1949) and eager to discuss everything. As I was at that time the only male American in the Japanese-language program (and, what is worse, white, middle-class, and ex-Marine), they had a lot to say to me. I spent hours in the coffee shop near the campus, listening as they explained to me their ways of thinking, and in particular their differences with America. But whatever their ideologies, which were various, there was one thing all were anxious to persuade me of: the value of Japan's Peace Constitution. Interestingly, they all used about the same manner of explaining this. The explanation resembled a syllogism, with three parts:

> We know what war is. We have experienced it.
> We are not going to go to war again, nor will we send our children.
> And that is written into Article 9 of the Constitution.

Because I was a fairly typical arrogant American, it took me time to accept that these Japanese young people (only slightly younger than I was) might know something that I did not. But they did. Only sixteen years had passed since the firebombing of Osaka, which means that as children they would have experienced if not the bombing then life in the ruins—if not of Osaka, then of one of the other fifty-plus cities that were firebombed. In my three years in the Marines, we had talked about war, but we had not seen it.

Especially notable is the sequence in which they ordered their thoughts. First, what they knew: We have seen war. Next, resolution: We will not go to war. Then, the constitutional prohibition: And so it is written in Article 9. These young people were members of what came to be known as the 1960 AMPO generation. How many of them had actually joined the hundreds of thousands who had taken to the streets the year before to oppose the extension of the Japan-US Security Treaty (AMPO), which they saw as violating Article 9, I do not know, but whether they had or not, this was the generation that embraced their Constitution as a good constitution should be embraced: first as commitment, and second as written law. They did not reject war because the Constitution instructed them to do so. They valued the Constitution because it fit with what they had experienced about war. Only later did I begin fully to realize what good fortune it was to be able to meet young people being educated at that extraordinary moment in their country's history.

In the 1970s, after some more schooling at UC Berkeley (both inside and outside the school buildings), I began teaching in Tokyo, and I noticed a change. College students still mainly supported the Constitution, but their reasoning was different. They would say:

> The Constitution forbids war.
> Therefore, we cannot go to war.

The actors were being replaced by the acted-upon. The renunciation of war was changing from a power (a commitment) to a power taken away ("it is forbidden"). In retrospect one can see that, however subtly, the process leading to the Japan of today had already begun.

1982: CONSTITUTION AS TRAVELOGUE

In 1982, a popular publishing house put out a book consisting of the text of the Japanese Constitution interspersed with color photographs, in travelogue style, of beautiful Japan; somehow the combination made the book a big bestseller.[1] The journal *Shiso no Kagaku* (*Science of Thought*, now defunct) asked me to write on this. At first I refused, explaining that I am not an expert on constitutional law, much less on the Japanese Constitution. The editor (cleverly) said not to worry; they wanted not a scholarly piece on constitutional law but a review of this particular book, whose contents happened to be the Constitution (plus photographs). For better or for worse, I was persuaded by this.

As I began to write, I found that, on the "for better" side, not being a legal expert could be an advantage. Having been trained in political theory, I found myself looking at the Constitution not only as law but also as a political act, making it possible to express its special character in the form of a story. From this standpoint, I wrote an essay that was published in *Shiso no Kagaku* in January 1983.[2] The following is based on that essay, many times retold to include later insights and to reflect changing times. It can be seen as a case study, the story of a remarkable attempt to do what most political scientists and politicians believe impossible in principle: take away from a sovereign state a piece of its right of legitimate violence, the right of belligerency. It was the experience of writing this essay that placed "legitimate violence" at the top of my list of political puzzles that needed to be wrestled with.

THE JAPANESE CONSTITUTION AS A SEIZURE OF POWER

A constitution can be defined as the basic law of a country, the source of legitimacy for all other laws. It also can be seen as a system of governance, a statement of the rules by which a country is to operate. It is the charter that founds and authorizes the various governmental institutions. It is a declaration of the rights—or in the case of an authoritarian constitution, the absence of rights—of the people. More broadly, if it is a constitution democratically established, it may become an expression of the legal and political spirit of a nation. Or even if it is not democratically established, it may become such an expression over time.

But in the context of the history of a country, a new constitution can be seen also as a political act, a seizure of power. Or rather, it may be an attempt to institutionalize a seizure of power. This has been true ever since King John of England "with trembling hand" signed the Magna Carta in 1215.

When we evaluate a constitution, we ask many sorts of questions. Are its rules just? Does it provide for the public welfare? Is it workable? Does it accurately reflect the thinking of the nation? But viewing it as a political act allows us to ask a different sort of question: In this constitution, just *who* is wresting *what* power from *whom*? Read in this way, a constitution will be seen to have a momentum, a pull, a tension built into its structure.

This can be illustrated by contrasting the Constitution of Japan with that of the United States. What the latter institutionalized, it should be remembered, was not the American Revolution but the (relatively mild, but real) counter-revolution that followed it. The revolution was institutionalized in the Articles of Confederation, which established the sovereign independence of the thirteen colonies as states, and joined them in a league whose power resembled that of today's United Nations. It was this system, not British colonial rule, that the Constitution of 1789 replaced. The Articles of Confederation institutionalized the seizure of sovereign power from the British king and placed it with the states; the Constitution took away some of that power from the states and relocated it with the federal government. This is made clear in James Madison's *Notes of Debates in the Federal Convention of 1787*, in which it is reported that the first days of these debates were devoted to the delegates' confirming among themselves that this was what they wanted to do. Elbridge Gerry put it succinctly: "The evils we experience flow from the excess of democracy," to which the solution, according to Edmund Randolph, would be to establish "a *national* Government . . . consisting of a supreme Legislature, Executive, and Judiciary." When delegates asked that this be clarified, Gouverneur Morris "explained the distinction between a *federal* and *national, supreme*, Govt; the former being a mere compact resting on the good faith of the parties; the latter having a compleat and *compulsive* operation."[3] (Italics in original)

And indeed, that is what the delegates wrote: a constitution whose principal theme is power, detailing which branch of government is empowered to do what. Article I section 8 lists the eighteen powers of Congress, followed by section 9, which lists nine things Congress may not do. Article II grants executive power to the president; Article III grants judicial power to the courts. No powers are granted to the states; on the contrary, article I section 10 lists the powers of which they are to be deprived.

Thus the US Constitution contains a centripetal dynamic, which was the main reason the anti-federalists opposed ratification, some saying that the president as described in it looked to them like an elected king. (For example, Patrick Henry said, "There is to be a great and mighty President, with very extensive powers: the powers of a King: he is to be supported in extravagant magnificence.")[4]

In contrast to this, the Japanese Constitution amounts to a seizure of power from the central government, and in particular from the emperor. The momentum of this is striking: The first forty articles, with only three exceptions (article 27 [the right and obligation to work], article 24 [marriage by mutual consent], and article 30 [obligation to pay taxes]), are devoted to wresting power from the center. Power is taken from the emperor and handed to the elected government; power is taken from the cabinet and given to the diet; power is taken from the government itself and given to the people. The articles from 10 to 40 (again with the abovementioned exceptions) are a detailed list of basic human rights that, seen in the context of a document allotting powers, amount to a list of things the government may *not* do. No, you may not arrest people for things they have said or written, or for gathering to talk about public issues (article 21). No, you may not establish a system of slavery (article 18). No, you may not punish people except through due process of law (article 31). And so on.

Of course, some Japanese criticize the Constitution for the one great compromise on which it is based: its failure to abolish the emperor system entirely. This is a serious charge, and it may turn out that leaving that system partly intact admitted the virus that has been eating away at Japan's democracy ever since. But still, the change in the emperor's status stipulated in this Constitution was not trivial.

Concerning the emperor, the Constitution of the Empire of Japan (Meiji Constitution, 1889) contains the following provisions, among others:

Article I: The Empire of Japan shall be ruled over by Emperors of the dynasty, which has reigned in an unbroken line of descent for ages past.

Article III: The person of the Emperor is sacred and inviolable.

Article IV: The Emperor being the Head of the Empire the rights of sovereignty are invested in him, and he exercises them in accordance with the provisions of the present Constitution.

Article V: The Emperor exercises the legislative power with the consent of the Imperial Diet.

Article VI: The Emperor gives sanction to laws, and orders them to be promulgated and put into force.

Article VII: In case of urgent necessity, when the Imperial Diet is not sitting, the Emperor, in order to maintain the public safety or to avert a public danger, has the power to issue Imperial Ordinances, which will take the place of laws [which the Diet may declare invalid in its next session].

Article X: The Emperor determines the organization of the different branches of the Administration; he fixes the salaries of all civil and military officers, and appoints and dismisses the same.

Article XI: The Emperor has the supreme command of the army and navy.

Article XIII: The Emperor declares war, makes peace, and concludes treaties.

Article XIV: The Emperor proclaims the law of siege. The conditions and operation of the law of siege shall be determined by law.

Perhaps more important than these specific articles is the fact that the preamble to the Constitution is written as the emperor's command (in the jargon of linguistics, a performative utterance), which identifies him as lawgiver and therefore prior to the law. I shall return to this point.

The new Constitution places the emperor inside the framework of the law:

Article 1: The Emperor shall be the symbol of the state and of the unity of the people, deriving his position from the will of the people with whom resides sovereignty.

Article 3: The advice and approval of the Cabinet shall be required for all acts of the Emperor in matters of state, and the Cabinet shall be responsible therefor.

Article 4: The Emperor shall perform only such acts in matters of state as are provided in this Constitution and he shall not have powers related to government.

Article 7: [Lists ten actions, mainly ceremonial, that the emperor may take "with the advice and approval of the Cabinet."]

Article 99: [Includes the emperor among the public officials who "have the obligation to respect and uphold this Constitution."]

The Meiji Constitution nowhere states that the emperor has the obligation to obey the Constitution, which, after all, is formally written as the emperor's command; nor, for that matter, is he anywhere described as a "public official."

Of course, in granting, in the Meiji Constitution, all those powers plus the semi-theocratic qualities of sacredness and inviolability to this man called emperor, its authors were actually infusing the Japanese state with these qualities—which in practice became their own powers they could use to extract obedience from the people. And while it is certainly true that the postwar Constitution reduces and limits the emperor's powers as a matter of law, whether the Constitution limits them "enough" is a question on which opinions differ in Japan.

The Constitution does not, for example, abolish the office of emperor and then reestablish it under a different name or on a different legal basis. It preserves the office of emperor, and changes the rules that surround it. But it's the same office and, as it happened, it was the same person. That office, and even its name (in Japanese, *Tenno*), carry a heavy baggage into the postwar Japanese state. This mysterious aura famously activates Japan's ultra-rightists but also adds to the difficulty ordinary people have in standing up to their government.

With this in mind, it is still true that on the whole, the Constitution, with its shift to the principle of popular sovereignty, its long list of guaranteed human rights, and its renunciation of war, amounted to a major seizure of power from the Japanese government and the institutionalization of that seizure. Article 9 should be seen in that context.

This seizure was first carried out by the Allied military forces. In this sense, the whole operation can be seen as an extension of the Allied war effort: The Allies fought the Pacific war to reduce the power of the Japanese imperial government, and after their victory institutionalized that reduction in the form of the Constitution. This is the view of Japan's conservatives and is a big part of what they don't like about the Constitution. Their "forced Constitution" doctrine is not so much a theory as an expression of what the government bureaucrats experienced at the time and have been experiencing ever since. For their part, they acted and are continuing to act just as Rousseau predicted government ministers would if confronted by a proposal for perpetual peace: trying to prevent it with all the means at their disposal. Unquestionably, the Occupation used force, but what force? The force that proved decisive was the force of Japanese public opinion, and after the US changed its mind and began lobbying the Japanese government to forget Article 9 and build a proper military, Japanese public opinion was the only force left to prevent that from happening. I have no knowledge of whether MacArthur or any of the staff members he appointed to the constitutional drafting committee had ever read Kant on perpetual peace, but their practice followed his idea: To establish peace, you must transfer the power to make war from the government leaders to the people. The Constitution has built into it a two-pronged strategy: Article 9, rejecting the right of belligerency, and the many human-rights clauses, giving the citizens the tools they would need to defend Article 9 after the Occupation departed.

The process by which the Supreme Commander for Allied Powers (SCAP), MacArthur, carried this out was no model of democratic procedure. He did not call for a national referendum or a constitutional convention. He did not try hard to "reach out" to the general public, though he did read translations from, and plant articles in, the daily papers. But when a delegation from the Far Eastern Commission (FEC) came to Japan to urge the SCAP to push through strict reforms including a revised Constitution, MacArthur responded that as to the latter he had issued no orders, only "suggestions." "He stated that it was his belief, that it was his conviction, that a constitution, no matter how good, no matter how well written, forced upon the Japanese by bayonet would last just as long as bayonets were present."[5] This statement by

MacArthur was, as we shall see, not entirely honest. He and other members of the Government Section were quite willing to use force against the government when needed. At the same time, the fear that reforms enacted by force alone would be swept away the moment that force was removed was well grounded. The problem was how to get the Constitution approved without triggering that reaction.

The Basic Initial Post-Surrender Directive, Washington's mandate to SCAP, contained a hint as to how this might be accomplished. The directive contains these sentences:

> Changes in the form of government initiated by the Japanese people or government in the direction of modifying its feudal and authoritarian tendencies are to be permitted and favored. In the event that the effectuation of such changes involves the *use of force* by the Japanese people or government against persons opposed thereto, the Supreme Commander should intervene only where necessary to ensure the security of his forces and the attainment of all other objectives of the occupation[6] (italics added).

The Japanese people could be seen as, and used as, part of the "force." A movement by the Japanese people to overthrow their wartime regime by force was conceivable to the US authorities and—at least in this original policy directive—something with which SCAP was not to interfere. This could be seen as growing out of the US democratic ideology and the revolutionary experience behind it, or it could be seen as a realpolitik use of any means available to weaken the enemy state—a sort of nonviolent fifth-column action. But from the standpoint of evaluating the result, America's motivations are not the issue. What matters is what was done.

On February 1, 1946, the same day the FEC delegation departed from Yokohama, the *Mainichi Shimbun* published a scoop: the text of the constitutional draft that Government Minister Matsumoto Joji had been preparing. The Matsumoto Draft was the Meiji Constitution all over again, with just a few revisions. This triggered a storm of criticism, in newspaper editorials and from the general public.[7] As a result, the Occupation was saved from being placed in the position of rejecting the first government draft all alone: The public outcry gave it great support. This was so convenient for SCAP that scholars debate whether the scoop was simple serendipity or whether it was arranged. Whichever it was, it provided the occasion for the Occupation's Government Section to reconstitute itself as drafting committee.

BASKING IN THE ATOMIC SUNSHINE

After twelve days of labor, General Courtney Whitney and two others of the Government Section drafting committee had a meeting with Foreign Minister (later Prime Minister) Yoshida Shigeru, State Minister Matsumoto Joji, who had been working on revising his unpopular draft, and two other government officials. In his *Japan Diary*, Mark Gayn, an American newsman who was in Japan covering the Occupation at that time, describes what he heard about that meeting. Whitney was carrying the constitutional draft that the Government Section had secretly written. The Japanese officials assumed the meeting was to discuss the Matsumoto proposal and had the Constitutional draft open on the table as the American officers entered. Gayn quotes Whitney as saying, "Gentlemen, the Supreme Commander has studied the draft prepared by you. He finds it totally unacceptable. I've brought with me a document which has the approval of the Supreme Commander. I'll leave it with you for fifteen minutes, so that you can read it before we discuss it." The Americans then stepped out to the porch. While they were there, a US bomber buzzed the house. When the time was up, they went back inside, and Whitney said, "We've just been basking in the warmth of the atomic sunshine."[8]

GOOD COP, BAD COP

The same meeting is described in Koseki Shoichi's definitive *The Birth of Japan's Postwar Constitution*. The account is about the same. Koseki, looking at documents that Gayn didn't have, quotes Whitney explaining that this constitutional proposal is MacArthur's strategy, and indeed the only strategy, to rescue the emperor from being tried as a war criminal. And from this Koseki argues, "There is no evidence to conclude that SCAP 'forced' the American draft on the Japanese."[9] He's right in the sense that the Americans didn't enter the room accompanied by military police carrying rifles with fixed bayonets. The "force" was carried out at a different level. Whitney's statement that this constitutional proposal is intended to protect the emperor from being charged as a war criminal is simultaneously MacArthur's threat to have the emperor so indicted if it is not accepted. The unspoken message is that MacArthur has the power to have these ministers handed over to the Tokyo War Crimes Tribunal as well. Whitney and MacArthur were playing the good cop, bad cop game, the method regularly used by American police to persuade criminals to turn state's evidence: "cooperate with me and I can keep you out of jail"—which in this case included the real possibility of the gallows.

But MacArthur knew that openly threatening violence to get the constitution accepted would be bad political theater, and would probably backfire. He needed to persuade the Japanese officials at least to put on a public show of agreeing to the American proposal. So, while the threat of arrest was always in the background, the *open* threat that he had Whitney make was that if the Japanese government would not make the American proposal public, MacArthur would. But why was this an effective threat? The answer is that MacArthur and his advisors believed, and the government ministers feared, that the American proposal would be so popular with the general public that once it was made known to the public, there could be no turning back: The slightly revised Meiji Constitution, which the government officials were hoping for, would be impossible, and the officials who were promoting that option would be discredited. This was a gamble, GHQ's ace in the hole.

What grounds did the Occupation authorities have for this optimistic belief? First of all, there was the mood of the times. Koseki writes, "The people, liberated from war and oppressive government, were delighted when the constitution took effect. They sang and danced; young people in remote mountain villages organized groups to study the Constitution. The sight of them entering essay-writing contests about the constitution had never before, or since, been seen in modern Japanese history."[10] This admittedly is a description of the mood after the Constitution was enacted, but also before that, while discussions were going on between the Occupation and the Japanese government, there was much discussion in the newspapers. A number of organizations and ad hoc groups, some conservative but also including the Socialist Party, the Communist Party, and an anarchist group, began drafting their own constitutional proposals, citing the Weimar Constitution, the Webbs' *A Constitution for the Socialist Commonwealth of Great Britain*, and the People's Rights Movements of the Meiji era. Some of these proposals were read and appreciated by the Occupation drafting committee.

As for attitudes toward the emperor, on February 4, 1946, *Mainichi Shimbun* published the results of a public-opinion poll in which 16 percent supported the emperor system unchanged, 28 percent favored sharing political power between the emperor and the diet, and 45 percent "wanted the emperor to be outside the realm of politics and to be a patriarch and moral center for the Japanese."[11] The people were not demanding that the office be abolished, but the great majority favored a reduction of its powers.

On the whole, GHQ's gamble paid off. In the experience of the Japanese government officials, it was indeed a "forced constitution," but to the public it was not—or if it was, they were part of the force. It was upon receiving MacArthur's threat to go directly to the public that the Japanese government discarded the Matsumoto proposal and turned its attention to trying to make changes in the GHQ proposal.

Thus the Constitution, in addition to being a set of legal principles, was a transfer of real political power, in two senses. One, in the text of the Constitution, real limits are placed on what the government is allowed to do, which amount to real powers placed in the hands of the people, the legal structure that makes it possible to develop an active civil society. Two, the civil society that formed itself with the help of that legal structure, which has been the principal "force" preventing the government from amending the Constitution from that day to this. I'll discuss some of the characteristics and (sometimes-quite-bizarre) effects of this long struggle in the following chapter.

NOTES

1. *Nihonkoku Kenpo* [The constitution of Japan] (Tokyo: Shogakkan: Sharaku Books, 1982).

2. Douglas Lummis, "Japan's Radical Constitution," trans. Kaji Etsuko, *Science of Thought* (January 1983). Published in English in *Reading the Constitution of Japan* (Tokyo: Kashiwa Shobo, 1993).

3. James Madison, *Notes of Debates in the Federal Convention of 1787* (Norton: Ohio University, 1966), 39, 34, 35.

4. "Speeches of Patrick Henry in the Virginia State Legislature," in *The Anti-Federalist: Writings by the Opponents of the Constitution*, ed. Herbert J. Storing (Chicago: The University of Chicago Press, 1985), 308.

5. Koseki Shoichi, *The Birth of Japan's Postwar Constitution*, ed. and trans. Ray A. Moore (Boulder, CO: Westview Press, 1997), 75–6, n. 23.

6. "Basic Initial Post-Surrender Directive," in *The Japan Reader 2: Postwar Japan, 1945 to the Present*, eds. Jon Livingston, Joe Moore, and Felicia Oldfather (New York: Pantheon Books, 1973), 9.

7. Koseki, *Japan's Postwar Constitution*, 76 ff.

8. Mark Gayn, *Japan Diary* (Rutland: Charles E. Tuttle, 1981), 128–9.

9. Koseki, *Japan's Postwar Constitution*, 101.

10. Koseki, *Japan's Postwar Constitution*, 5.

11. Koseki, *Japan's Postwar Constitution*, 138, n. 37.

Chapter 11

Article 9 Meets Humpty Dumpty

> When I use a word . . . it means just what I choose it to mean—neither more nor less.
>
> —Humpty Dumpty, according to Lewis Carroll

THE REVERSE COURSE

By 1947, GHQ had fundamentally changed its policy. In the US's view, Japan was reconceived from an enemy whose government was to be weakened to a Cold War ally whose government and economy were to be strengthened. The breaking up of the zaibatsu monopolies was abandoned. GHQ began depurging war criminals and purging communists. In 1950, GHQ had the Japanese government establish the paramilitary National Police Reserve, whose job was to ensure domestic security while the US military was busy in Korea. This organization soon metamorphosed into the Self-Defense Forces (SDF) under the widely accepted reasoning that if you rename military action as self-defense, it might not have any need for the right of belligerency. This collection of policies, which, taken together, came to be called the Reverse Course, not only increased the coercive power of the government but also created the political and economic conditions under which Japan's old ruling class, now firmly allied with the US through the ruling Liberal Democratic Party (LDP) and the resurgent zaibatsu, could remain in power. And to institutionalize this alliance, the two governments established the Japan-US Security Treaty (AMPO), which gives the US permission to keep military bases and station US forces in Japan, signed along with the 1952 Peace Treaty as a condition for returning sovereignty to Japan. The Security Treaty is, in effect, a major amendment to the Constitution, as it hands over to Washington the power to determine a big part of Japan's foreign policy. So long as US military bases are in Japan, whoever the US decides are enemies to America automatically become Japan's enemies as well, which is about as fundamental a foreign-policy decision as there is. So, while the Constitution does not hand over any part of Japanese state sovereignty to the US, the AMPO treaty does.

LEGITIMATION THROUGH STRUGGLE

The Constitution was formally adopted in 1946 according to the provisions for amendment set down in the Meiji Constitution, which means that it was approved by the diet, and there was no popular referendum. There were public demonstrations in favor of it, the mass media largely supported it, and the diet approved it, after some debate, by a big majority, but as all this was under the domination of the Occupation forces, if you focus only on 1946 the conservative argument that the Constitution was never freely and spontaneously adopted looks strong. But if you look at the history of the country since then, the picture changes. Under the new Constitution, Japan developed a politically active civil society, and this civil society for decades has made protection—for some, full implementation—of the Constitution its main piece of business. The country's ruling elites made the amendment of Article 9 and the full remilitarization of the country its first goal as far back as the 1950s; civil society has so far prevented this project from being carried entirely to completion.

If the Constitution was not legitimized by the diet vote in 1947, it surely was legitimized in the decades of struggle by civil society to preserve it. When Shinzo Abe resigned as prime minister in 2020, he said he regretted having been unable to fulfill his dream of amending the Constitution, and gave public opposition as the main reason. So, the "forcing" of the "forced Constitution" continues to this day. This was made easier by the fact that the Constitution is designed to protect this kind of "forcing." And the key to that was the redefining of the Constitution itself as the speech act of a sovereign people.

THE CONSTITUTION AND ITS SPEAKER

To say that the creation of a constitution is a political act is different from saying that it is established as the result of political action (which is obvious). A constitution is itself a political act. Enacting a constitution is first of all an act of language—a speech act—and, if properly written, the constitution will have written into it a speaker, one whose declaration establishes it as a "constitution." This speaker is not necessarily the author of the constitution, nor is it required that the speaker do a public reading of the whole thing. The speaker, in the protocol of lawgiving, is the one whose speech act, especially the reading of the preamble, transforms the constitutional proposal into a constitution.

In the case of the Constitution of the Empire of Japan, the speaker was Emperor Meiji. The first word in that Constitution is *chin*, a peculiar word in the Japanese language that means "I," but only if spoken by the emperor. Thus all that follows is spoken (not actually, but formally) in the emperor's voice; its provisions are, taken together, declared by him to be "the Constitution." This mode of speech was called by language philosopher John Austin "performative utterance."[1] A performative utterance is not an observation. It does not state a fact; it creates one. Examples are "I now pronounce you man and wife," which words (if spoken by a person with the authority to speak them) change the legal status of the two people referred to, as well as of any children they may parent; or the words "You are under arrest," which (again, if spoken by a person with the authority) also change the legal status of the person addressed. In the case of a constitution, the difference can be clarified by comparing the words "This is the Japanese Constitution" as spoken in a preamble by a person or persons believed to have sovereign authority and as spoken later by, say, a schoolteacher teaching constitutional law.

The Imperial Constitution was a command of the emperor. For this to be possible, the emperor had to be understood as prior to the law, which is one of the ways sovereignty is defined. Meiji-era legal scholars argued that the emperor could not be held accountable to the law, as it is nonsense to say that a commander is obligated to obey his own commands. After all, the commander, who has the power to alter or rescind his commands, cannot also be bound by them. It all makes perfect sense.

Hermann Roesler, the Prussian legal scholar who served as advisor to Itō Hirobumi and the other authors of the Meiji Constitution, wrote of the emperor, "Being the fountain of all jurisdiction, criminal and civil, there can be no human judge over Himself, excepting on His own allowance."[2]

In the English version of the preamble to the present Japanese Constitution, *chin* is replaced by "We, the Japanese people." In the Japanese version, syntax requires that the "we" be postponed a bit, so the first words are, "The Japanese people." But it is clear that this Constitution begins with a 180-degree change from the Constitution it replaces: its speaker, and therefore the sovereign, is "we, the Japanese people."

Thus, in this Constitution, as in that of the US and in many other constitutions, popular sovereignty is not merely a stated principle or an aspiration; it is structurally built into the law itself as that which is prior to the law—that which makes the law law. The people are the sovereign and the Constitution is the vehicle of their command. Their status as prior to the law is preserved in the fact that it is only with their consent that the Constitution can be amended. Amending a constitution is a (legal) form of disobeying it, an act that can be taken only by the sovereign.[3] And it is only by understanding the clarity with which this Constitution establishes the sovereignty of the people that one can understand the clarity with which it abrogates the right of belligerency.

AMENDMENT BY INTERPRETATION

Article 9: "Aspiring sincerely to an international peace based on justice and order, the Japanese people forever renounce war as a sovereign right of the nation and the threat or use of force as a means of settling international disputes.

"In order to accomplish the aim of the preceding paragraph, land, sea, and air forces, as well as other war potential, will never be maintained. The right of belligerency of the state will not be recognized."

Article 9 of the Japanese Constitution constitutes a kind of test of the ability to read. On the one hand, it is written with admirable simplicity and directness. I believe that any sixth-grader of average ability, reading it in English or Japanese, could understand its meaning without difficulty. On the other hand, it seems that many people who have graduated from law school, and in particular those who have found employment in Japan's defense or foreign ministries, have lost this ability. They read it, as it were, deductively. Judging from what they have learned about law and politics, Article 9 could not possibly say what it says; therefore, they conclude, it does not. For example, in the Defense Ministry's white paper for 2022, we read, "Under the Constitution, Japan is permitted to possess the required minimum self-defense capability. The specific limit is subject to change according to the prevailing international situation, the level of military technologies, and various other factors."

On what basis could the authors come by such an interpretation? The word "permitted" appears nowhere in Article 9, nor is there any mention of "minimum self-defense capability" or of "limiting" that capability to some "level." That is, there is no discussion of degree. The operative expressions in Article 9 are "forever renounce," "never be maintained," and "not be recognized."

This qualifies as an example of what has been called by linguists the Humpty Dumpty Theory of Language, after Lewis Carroll's account of the exchange that personage had with Alice during her journey through Wonderland:

> "When *I* use a word," Humpty Dumpty said in a rather scornful tone, "it means just what I choose it to mean—neither more nor less."

"The question is," said Alice, "whether you *can* make words mean so many different things."

"The question is," said Humpty Dumpty, "which is to be master—that's all."

Except there's a difference: The words of Article 9 are not words uttered by Humpty Dumpty; they are words written by someone else. The Defense Ministry officials look at the words and say what they wish were written there, or what they would have written there had they been the authors. In a way, this is understandable, as the words of Article 9 violate the "common sense" of contemporary political science and international law. They violate the very definition of the state as given us by Max Weber: the social organization that "successfully claims" a monopoly of legitimate violence. To people educated in the context of a legal and political paradigm in which Weber's definition is treated as an axiom, what Article 9 says makes no sense—from which they deduce that it ought not to, and therefore does not, say what it says.

What about the argument that the right of people to defend themselves is inalienable—so fundamental that it cannot be renounced no matter what the Constitution says? I think it's undeniable that the right to defend our lives is built into our nature as sentient beings. It is another way of saying that we have the right to go on living. But this is a right that the state, being an artifice and not a living being, does not inherently have. Article 9 says nothing about taking away the *people's* right to self-defense. To say that the Constitution takes away the people's right of self-defense would be to say that the Constitution is a higher power than the people, which it cannot be. The Constitution, to repeat, is a list of powers that the people do and do not grant to the state, and the Constitution makes clear that the right to make war is not among those that it does grant. The key sentence is "The Japanese people forever renounce war as a sovereign right of the *nation*" (italics added). The English word "nation" is ambiguous, as it can mean a people, a country, or a state. The Japanese text is written more clearly, substituting for "right of the nation" the term *kokken*, which means "the right of the state," as opposed to *minken*, "the right of the people." The right of self-defense as *minken* (which in extreme cases can mean the people's right of self-defense *against* the government) is not abrogated; rather, it is simply not delegated to the government. It is held in abeyance and (despite the futile term "forever") could again be granted to the government should the people choose to amend the Constitution. At least that's what the words mean, if you read them with the straightforward honesty of Alice.

If there is any part of Article 9 that the abovementioned sixth-grader might have trouble understanding, it would be the final sentence: "The right of belligerency of the state will not be recognized." "Belligerency" is not a word we use often in daily life, and many people, not only children, don't quite understand it. Let's begin by looking at the definition given it in the 2022 white paper.

> Article 9, Paragraph 2 of the Constitution prescribes that "the right of belligerency of the state will not be recognized." However, the "right of belligerency" does not mean the right to engage in battle; rather, it is a general term for various rights that a belligerent nation has under international law, including the authority to inflict casualties and damage upon the enemy's military force and to occupy enemy territory.[4]

One would expect officials of the Defense Ministry to be people who have thought carefully and deeply about military defense. Here they wish to make a distinction between "the right to engage in battle" and "the authority to inflict casualties and damage upon the enemy's military force." But they give us no hint as to what that difference might be, nor could they, because engaging in battle and inflicting casualties and damage upon the enemy's military force are the same thing. As I wrote in chapter 2 and elsewhere, the right of belligerency is, essentially, the right of soldiers to kill enemy soldiers and civilians without being guilty of murder. It is distinct from the right of individuals to defend themselves from direct attack, or of police to use violence to prevent crimes. It includes the right to shoot enemy soldiers who are not threatening you in any way, as when they are running away, watching a ball game on TV, or sleeping. Without that right, you cannot "engage in battle"; without that right, soldiers ordered to do the things required to engage in battle would surely refuse. The white paper continues:

> On the other hand, Japan may of course use the minimum level of force necessary to defend itself. For example, if Japan inflicts casualties and damage upon the enemy's military force in exercising its right of self-defense, this is conceptually distinguished from the exercise of the right of belligerency, even though those actions do not appear to be different. Occupation of enemy territory, however, would exceed the minimum necessary level of self-defense and is not permissible.[5]

Indeed, "those actions do not appear to be different," because they are not. As for the right "to occupy enemy territory," if the Self-Defense Forces are to be put into action only if Japan is invaded, "enemy territory" would not be an issue; if the Forces mean to follow the US military on its various overseas adventures, it's a right they would certainly need. As for "the minimum necessary level" of force, this is, as Clausewitz argued, one of the most deceptive terms in military discourse. "Minimum" sounds small, but in war, the minimum necessary goal is to prevail over the enemy; anything short of that is to lose. Against a powerful enemy, the "minimum necessary" can be huge.

BELLIGERENCY AND SELF-DEFENSE

Interestingly, while Japan's conservative legislators and bureaucrats have willfully refused to admit that Article 9 presents any major obstacle to their building up the SDF into one of the world's major military organizations, there was a time when they seemed to have accepted that the SDF did not, at least when sent abroad, have the full right of belligerency. Beginning with the International Peace Cooperation Law (aka the Peacekeeping Law) passed by the diet on the occasion of the dispatch of SDF units for duty as peacekeepers in Cambodia in 1992, a series of laws passed by the diet allowing the SDF to operate abroad each included a clause titled "Use of Weapons." And this clause invariably contained the provision that weapons may not be used to harm anyone except in situations in which article 36 or 37 of the Criminal Code (dating from 1907) would apply. Article 36 stipulates the right of individual self-defense, article 37 the right to defend another person under attack. These are rights that every person in Japan (and in most other countries) has, and they are very different from the right of belligerency. For example, in Japan, if it is possible to protect your safety by moving away from an attacker, but you choose instead to stand and fight, your right of self-defense will probably not be recognized by a court of law. Certainly it will not be recognized if you shoot a likely attacker with a sniper rifle from the safety of a bunker, or with a howitzer from a thousand yards or from an airplane. Even less will it be recognized if you shoot people who happen to be standing near your likely attacker. But these are things that are allowed under the right of belligerency.

I had occasion, after the UN Cambodia peacekeeping operation was over, to talk to the Australian general who had been in command of the military units there. He told me that a major part of their job was to protect polling places against attack, but he could not assign SDF troops to this duty because if an attack did come, those troops would be legally required to withdraw, whereas the job of the PKO (Peacekeeping Operation) troops would be to hold the line and repel the attack with gunfire. In a lowered voice, he said to me, "I had to wrap them in *cotton wool*." He told me that he solved the problem by assigning the Japanese Self-Defense Force troops to road construction. As I discussed in chapter 9, the United Nations does not have the right of belligerency, and UN peacekeeping (or sometimes, as in the Korean War, war-making) troops act under the right of belligerency of the states of which they are citizens. Peacekeepers from Japan, at least up to that time, had no such right.

JAPANESE PARTICIPANTS IN THE KOREAN WAR

Some have argued that the secret use by the US military of Japanese citizens in the Korean War delivered the death blow to Article 9. In her study of that incident, Tessa Morris-Suzuki wrote, "The Korean war is the only war from 1945 to the present day [meaning 2018] in which Japanese sent overseas in combat and combat support roles with the knowledge of their government, have been killed or injured."[6] She estimates that some eight thousand Japanese were recruited for this work, some working on minesweepers or even on landing craft during the Inchon landing, others actually entering Korean territory.[7] The number killed, she estimates, was "in the dozens."[8] However, you don't need the right of belligerency to be killed in a war zone; the right of belligerency is not the right to die but the right to kill. Morris-Suzuki cites the cases of several Japanese citizens, one who was hired as an interpreter, and several children who were working as houseboys, who said they had been issued guns, and used them. Quite probably there were more.[9] But this doesn't amount to a revival of the Japanese state's right of belligerency. These Japanese citizens were working, formally or informally, for the US military, not for the Japanese government. Moreover, they and others who were returned to Japan by the US military were "firmly instructed" to keep the whole thing secret.[10] This means that the US military command understood that these citizens' presence in Korean war zones was illegal, which in turn means that they understood Article 9 to be in effect.

SHINZO ABE'S FINAL INTERPRETATION?

But things have changed. In 2015, the Shinzo Abe administration, frustrated in its efforts to pass an amendment to the Constitution that would change the SDF into a military organization, resorted again to its "amendment by interpretation" strategy. This took the form of the omnibus, variously titled, "Law for Peace and Independence of Japan and Maintenance of the Nation and People's Security in Armed Attack Situations," aka "Peace and Security Legislation Development Act." This amends, and bundles together, ten already existing laws. In it, the reference to articles 36 and 37, on the right of individual self-defense, has disappeared. Weapons can be used not only to save your own life or that of someone nearby but also to help a close ally (mainly meaning the US) who is being attacked. The US military newspaper *Stars and Stripes*, in its edition published just after the bill was passed, wrote that this meant an SDF ship "could fire on an enemy attacking a US vessel."[11] The "Armed Attack Situations" referred to in the title include "imminent" or "expected" situations.[12] The right to use weapons is expanded to include the "right to use weapons for the purpose of execution of missions," including "to repel obstructions of the performance of the duties of SDF members."[13] The bill also contains a number of detailed and complex expansions of the SDF's Rules of Engagement. We can see in these developments the working out of Clausewitz's laws of war: Once you admit the principle of war, there is an inevitable escalation in the direction of the extreme case. The Rules of Engagement of the SDF are slightly stricter than those of other countries, which is a (slightly) good thing. When the SDF follows the US into its next military adventure, we may see those rules blown away altogether.

ARTICLE 9 AS US GRAND STRATEGY

I can imagine more than one of his colleagues in the US Army officer class confronting General MacArthur with the question "What in hell were you thinking?" It's no use to speculate about what may have been going on in his head when he proposed and approved the inclusion of Article 9 in the Japanese Constitution. As Supreme Commander for Allied Powers, he was in no position to be truthful about such matters in his public statements. To get his work done, he had chosen the method of "bad cop, good cop," which is a performance; there's no reason to suppose there was anything real behind the "good cop" side of that performance.

Of his views in 1948, however, we have documentary evidence. In March 1948, the U.S. Department of State sent a delegation to Tokyo to persuade MacArthur to scrap Article 9 and establish "a small defensive force for Japan." The delegation consisted of Brigadier General C. V. R. Schuyler, Under Secretary of the Army William H. Draper, and the State Department's top diplomat at the time, the author of America's Cold War containment strategy, George Kennan. The fact that their mission was to persuade rather than to command is testimony to the immense power then wielded by the Supreme Commander.

MacArthur refused, and helpfully numbered his reasons for doing so: (1) To do so would be to violate America's international commitments and alienate Japan's neighbors, "all of whom are still mortally fearful of a remilitarized Japan"; (2) To do so would be to violate SCAP's basic principles "and would place us in a ridiculous light before the Japanese people"; (3) In any case, impoverished Japan would not be able to muster enough military power to be of any use; (4) To attempt to do so now would bankrupt the Japanese government; and (5) The Japanese have adopted the principle of Article 9 as their own and would not support rebuilding their military unless America forced them to, which America should not do. This last makes it seem as though

MacArthur was supporting the Japanese people's postwar pacifism, but it wasn't so simple. He gave one more reason for not scrapping Article 9, to which he did not give a number: There's no need to scrap it, he says, because we've got Okinawa.

In other words, MacArthur's paternalistic stance of sympathy toward the Japanese people didn't go so far as to respect their opinions. He asserted (in complete contradiction to the spirit of the Japanese Constitution) that of course Japan needs to be defended by military power, but don't worry, this can be done from Okinawa. In this age of air power, US air bases in Okinawa "could assure the destruction of enemy forces or harbor facilities along the Asiatic coast from Vladivostock to Singapore." America's "outer line of defense" had moved west from California and Hawaii and now passed through Japan and Okinawa, and to the south through the Philippines and beyond. Put differently, Japan and Okinawa (and the Philippines, etc.) were transformed into America's outermost defense line; that their residents were also to be "defended" (if indeed they were) was a side effect. MacArthur ended by urging the US government to "reach a decision now" (underlining in original) to transform Okinawa into a "permanent garrison." The government followed that advice, and the garrison remains in Okinawa to this day.[14]

A PERSON ABLE TO RETURN THE GAZE OF THE STATE: THE CITIZEN

I began the previous chapter by describing how in 1961 students of what later came to be called the "1960 AMPO Generation" explained Article 9 as meaning, first of all, "I will not go to war." They saw Article 9 not as a constitutional provision that laid upon them the duty to refuse military service, but rather as an expression of their prior resolution to do so. Historians will object that this is not what the record shows: The Constitution was drafted not by a nongovernmental citizens group (although other drafts were submitted by such groups) but by MacArthur's staff, with a few alterations proposed by and negotiated with the national diet.[15] But it was welcomed by the general public. To borrow John Dower's felicitous expression, the people "embraced" it. And this leads us to another effect this Constitution has had in addition to, while not fully prohibiting, at least placing some limits on, Japanese military activity. For in "embracing"—and fighting to preserve—this Constitution, the people changed themselves as political persons and formed (for a while, anyway) a politically active civil society. To understand this, it's useful to understand another difference between the Meiji Constitution and the present one.

The Meiji Constitution not only reconstructed the government but also redefined the people. During the Edo period (1603–1868), the people were divided into four classes, each with its own rights and privileges: samurai, farmers, craftspeople, and merchants—plus, at the very bottom, outcastes, with virtually no rights at all. The right of legitimate violence (including the right to own a sword), and the complex system of loyalties and obligations that went with that—so called *Bushido*—applied to the samurai class. To build Japan into a capitalist, industrial, militarily powerful state, the Meiji elites needed—or believed they needed—the full loyalty of everyone. They began by abolishing the four classes and merging the people into a single entity, to which they gave a new name, *"shinmin,"* which translates into English as "subject" but carries an even heavier burden of duties than does the English word. The first character, *"shin,"* means "retainer" and thus brings with it the whole *Bushido* ethic of duties and self-sacrifice; the second character, *"min,"* is the word for "ordinary people." Combining the two as a single word expressed the desire of the Meiji elites to mobilize the entire population as loyal subjects of the emperor—and therefore as obedient servants of the state. We encounter the word as early as 1871, in the Family Register Law, which abolished the four classes, as the name of the collectivity into which the four classes were to be dissolved. In the Meiji Constitution of 1889, the people are officially defined as *"shinmin"* in chapter II, article 18.

The word had a short life in Japanese history. The authoritative Japanese dictionary *Kojien* defines it as "Under the Meiji Constitution, the Japanese people. People other than the Emperor and the Imperial Family." With the disappearance of the Meiji Constitution, the word no longer has a referent. The present Constitution does not use the term; the Japanese people are called by the (relatively) neutral name *"kokumin,"* literally "the country's people." Though *"kokumin"* does imply that the people take on their identity by virtue of their membership in the country, it doesn't have servility built into it. But still, *"kokumin"* is a rather legalistic term; for the people who saw the rights guaranteed in the Constitution as an opportunity for personal liberation, a new term was needed. The term chosen in Japan was *"shimin,"* which, like its English equivalent, "citizen," literally means "city-person" but also implies people aware of their rights and who have an active public persona, the people who together make up "civil society." Before the 1960 AMPO uprising, the protest movements tended to use the terminology provided by the Japan Communist Party (JCP): The protesters were "workers," "farmers," or "students"; taken together, they were "the masses." It was from around 1960 that the term "citizens' movement" came into common use.

The context for this was the 1960 anti-AMPO struggle. The Japan-US Security Treaty—AMPO, which was signed a few hours after the signing of the San Francisco Peace Treaty and which permitted US military bases to remain in Japan—was set to expire in 1960 and to be replaced by a revised version. This was wildly unpopular and triggered a protest movement unprecedented in Japan's history. As the diet debated the issue, hundreds of thousands gathered outside, joined marches and rallies, and engaged in shoving matches with the police. People who couldn't come to Tokyo joined protests where they lived; ten million signed petitions. Inside the diet, the government decided to ram the AMPO bill through anyway while opposition diet members tried to prevent the vote with a sit-in. The government had those members carried out by the police and passed the bill in their absence. Prime Minister Kishi Nobusuke—an accused but pardoned war criminal—had to resign his office and US president Dwight Eisenhower had to cancel his planned visit (he went to Okinawa instead), but the AMPO treaty was renewed and remains in force to this day.

Unsurprisingly, many of the people who participated in these protests found their lives changed by the experience. Writing just a few days after the AMPO bill was passed, philosopher and gadfly Tsurumi Shunsuke chronicled the mood of that summer. In an essay titled *"Nemoto kara no Minshushugi"* ("Radical Democracy"), Tsurumi argued that the defeat in the Fifteen Years War (the name he gave it so as to include the long war with China prior to Pearl Harbor) had put Japan in the position in which a revolution in the tradition of the English Revolution ought to have been possible.[16] To bring that about, the first issue should have been to make clear who had been responsible for that war. However, as the public discourse was at that time dominated by the JCP and other Marxist intellectuals, the "enemy" came to be defined as those who would not support the JCP. Then there was the fact that the Constitution, while with its human rights and its peace clause was welcome, had not been directly enacted by the people. These two factors put the people in the position of (Tsurumi's metaphor) "having to build our building on unstable ground." But now, he wrote, the opportunity to carry out this revolution had arrived. To Tsurumi, "revolution" meant full realization of the Constitution.

> Demanding the full realization of the Constitution that we already have is the master principle by which the present government can be uprooted and fundamentally changed. It contains the promise of Japan's reincarnation as a country of culture and peace, whose citizens can enjoy human rights and have private lives, and also—in a world where militarism and nationalism seem inevitable—it violates this common sense by outlawing armaments.[17]

But "we cannot protect the Constitution by the method of 'protecting the Constitution.' We need to act in the spirit of people establishing a Constitution." For as we didn't establish it on our own, "that means we have to establish it now. If our present movement has a revolutionary content, that is because it is a movement to establish this Constitution."[18]

This formulation fits well with the way the students I met in Osaka the year after Tsurumi wrote described their relationship with the Constitution: The Constitution does not exist as something to be obeyed but is something that exists as a result of their collective conviction. But Tsurumi also was aware that the absence of a regime change in 1945 was a big part of the problem.

> The present movement can be seen as a battle between the Japanese state that existed before the defeat and the one that exists after. The spirit of this movement is not one of enjoying private life protected by the state, but of becoming a person able to return the gaze of the state.[19]

Perhaps a better translation would be "able to stare down the state." Tsurumi saw the fight to put into actual practice the principles set down in the Constitution as a fight in the process of which the fighters were evolving into a kind of citizen rarely seen in earlier Japanese history.

> What we must do is rebuild our public policy on the foundation of our convictions. If we call this democracy from the roots—"radical democracy"—then we must take this form that the mass movement has become, now, on June 19, 1960, and spread it out to become, as is, the form of all Japan. That is our goal today. . . . That is how we can isolate as the enemy the bureaucratism that has been dominating Japan up to now, and defeat it.[20]

Interestingly, there was a kind of evolution that took place within the 1960 movement itself. While, as the ten million petition signatures shows, opposition to extending the Security Treaty was widespread, the actual demonstrations and marches were, in a way, "bureaucratized." Workers marched under the flags of their various unions, students under the flags of their various student organizations, Marxists under the flags of their various parties and sects. And also, as there was a lot of pushing and shoving, one needed to be in pretty good physical shape. As the story-become-legend goes, a small group of people from the journal *Shiso no Kagaku (Science of Thought)* were on a commuter train together and talking about the demonstration they were heading for when an elderly lady sitting nearby said, "Do your best!" They answered, "Thank you. And how about you?" The lady said, "Oh, I'm too old." From this, they had an insight: As the demonstrations were organized, there was no space for older people, unaffiliated people, or parents with children to participate. For the next march, they prepared a banner with the words "Anyone Can Join—Voiceless Voices Society." But because of a miscommunication, when the person with the banner arrived at the meeting place, there was only one other person. The two of them bravely raised the banner and began walking at the very tail end of the procession, with five or six people they didn't know walking behind them. By the time they passed the national diet building, there were thirty, and soon they were a long procession. Among them were high school students, office workers in business suits and uniforms, and mothers with children. Some of them assumed leadership positions, talking into a microphone for the first time in their lives. When they arrived at the march's destination, they were three hundred strong.

This was the birth of a new kind of movement, a mode of acting together without having to submit to ideological discipline and which people would be free to join or leave. The many movements that appeared in the 1960s and 1970s—the anti-Vietnam War movement, the environmental movement, the women's liberation movement, the various antidiscrimination movements—mostly took this form. Even today, though people's movements in Japan have nowhere near the power they had in those years, when people do gather to protest, this is generally the form the gatherings take—people not acting as instructed but acting on their convictions.[21]

ARTICLE 9 AS DECADENCE

With just a bit of simplification, one could say that after World War II, Japan underwent constitutional change without regime change. Former prime minister Shinzo Abe's grandfather, Kishi Nobusuke, was never tried for his war crimes and served as prime minister during the 1960 anti-AMPO uprising (and in fact was brought down by that uprising). Many other members of today's ruling elite have ancestors who participated in the wartime government and some even in the Meiji Restoration. Many of them are unhappy with the Constitution and for decades have been announcing periodically that they are "about to" change it. It's not just that they find it out of the question for a state to abrogate the right to make war. Nor are they (with a few exceptions) all that eager to get Japan involved in another war. Rather, their focus is, I believe, not so much international as domestic. As the popular expression has it, they want to make Japan back into "a country that can make war." This means, to them, a country where the people are organized along military lines, from top to bottom, and do what they are told. As Rousseau understood, the threat of war, real or imagined, is one of the classic ways to persuade people to accept this degree of organization. During Japan's militaristic period, just about every social organization—economic, religious, artistic, educational, athletic, and even the family—was made over so as to serve the state, with the result that civil society properly so called no longer existed; the state penetrated everything. With this as its model, Japan's ruling elites see the country's vigorous postwar civil society not as a gathering of citizens but as decadence itself, and the Constitution, with its assertion that the people's rights are universal, as the root cause of this decadence. Their analysis that it is the combination of Article 9, the human-rights clauses, and the active civil society fighting to preserve them that are the cause of their troubles is accurate; their only error is to consider this decadence.

And the cure for this decadence begins with the revision of Article 9 so as to make war again a genuine possibility, which (they hope) will, as before, place the military at the center of society as the model of proper social organization. (This is made clear in the Liberal Democratic Party's 2012 highly detailed proposal for a revised Constitution, which reads like a model for dystopia. To my knowledge, this has never been formally placed before the diet.)[22]

A CONSCIENTIOUS OBJECTOR COUNTRY?

Among the many defenders of Japan's Article 9, one of the most eloquent and interesting is the essayist and activist Oda Makoto. Oda (along with Tsurumi Shunsuke) was one of the founders, in 1965, of the Peace in Vietnam! Citizen's League, known in Japanese by the acronym Beheiren, of which he was for many years the almost-charismatic leader. It is significant that the word "citizen" is in the title of the organization as the members' self-image. Beheiren proudly considered itself as an outgrowth of the Voiceless Voices Society. All one needed to be a member was to be opposed to the Vietnam War and to the US bases in Japan. Oda insisted that the true peacemakers are not the power brokers who move armies, launch bombs, and negotiate treaties but the ordinary people, the "little people." He had an old and bedraggled copy of a *New York Times* front page that had a photograph of the last bombing of Osaka in August 1945. At the beginning of his talks, he would hold it up to the audience (though from a distance you couldn't really see what it was), point his finger at the murky center of it, and say, "This is Osaka burning. You can see the smoke rising up. I'll show you where I was. I was down there. You see? Down there. When I talk about war, when I look at war, that's where I'm standing. Down there."

When you tell stories like this, you usually end up feeling you haven't got your point across. Probably for that reason, Oda told this story many times. In a newspaper article he published late in his life, he told it again:

> At the end of the war the US carried out seven huge bombing raids on Osaka that burned down the city—one-sided massacre and destruction. I was there for three of them, but I lived. The last bombing was carried out twenty hours before the war officially ended, on the afternoon of 14 August. The Americans dropped one-ton bombs and leaflets announcing, "The war is over." I picked some up.

I survived this bombing that took place after the war was over; many others of "the little people" were killed. I was thirteen then, a junior high school student.[23]

Most war stories, including most anti-war stories, are told by ex-soldiers, but the overwhelming majority of the people who have lived through war are noncombatants. Airmen who have served on bombing runs may develop a sincere hatred of war, but their experience is different from that of the people in the burning city. Undergoing a bomb attack, hovering in bomb shelters if they are lucky, they are experiencing powerlessness in its extreme form. But as Václav Havel understood (at least during his period as an antiestablishment activist), the "powerless" people also possess a potential power that in some situations can be decisive. This is the power, when called upon to be a cog in the power machine, to say no. Ironically, it is only the powerless who have this power: The powerless are the essential building material out of which power machines are constructed; it is their powerlessness that holds it all together. And it is the powerless who have the numbers, such that if enough of them say no, in certain circumstances, their powerlessness becomes their power.

In the case of the war machine, this is the power of conscientious objection: In the 1960 anti-war uprising in Japan, "We will not again go to war" was the starting point. But at that time (and still today), Japan had no draft that one could refuse with a clear no. The first time Japan's postwar peace movement had a direct encounter with conscientious objection was in 1967 when four US sailors opposed to the Vietnam War deserted from the carrier *Intrepid*, wandered into Tokyo, asked for help, and were taken to Beheiren. Oda and the others in the Beheiren leadership jumped at this opportunity to participate in anti-war direct action and managed to get the four smuggled across the Eurasian continent to Sweden, where they were given amnesty. From that beginning, Beheiren for a while ran an underground railroad that succeeded in getting eighteen US deserters to Sweden; when that became impossible, they hid people in their homes.

After the Vietnam War ended, there were no more US deserters, and anti-war people in Japan continued with the tasks of opposing AMPO and protecting Article 9 against amendment; saying no was changed from a decisive action (noncooperation) to an expression of opinion. Perhaps it was to revive "saying no" as an action that Oda began promoting the idea of Japan with its Peace Constitution as a "conscientious objector nation." In a newspaper article he published in 2000 (one of many), he begins by discussing the conscientious objector situation in Germany. Germany's post–World War II constitution provides for military conscription but also has a clause guaranteeing the right of conscientious objection. At the time he wrote, Germany was experiencing a conscientious-objector boom. "In 1999 the number of young people who had chosen refusal increased by more than 7000 over the year before and exceeded 174,000."[24] He points out that the people who refuse military service don't get a free pass. "Refusal" doesn't just mean not taking up a gun.

> In place of their military service they are obligated to carry out civilian service. For a longer period than they would have served in the military, they take care of handicapped people, do rescue service, peace education and other things that contribute to society. Draft refusers make up a significant percentage of Germany's old people's caregivers. . . . This is not passive behavior. One refuser said to me, "If we do military service, the world doesn't change. When we do civilian service based on peace, society gets better, and the world changes."[25]

Oda then proposes this as a model.

> I believe that Japan should take its situation as an extension of the reasoning behind conscientious objection, and should actualize its pacifism by becoming an objector country. Japan has its Peace Constitution and the pacifism that is based on it, and we refuse military service, but the country on the whole does not follow a policy of peace.[26]

On the contrary, the country follows the warlike policies of the US. Pacifism, he argues, is not just the passive behavior of not taking up arms; it must include the second part: civilian service, which in the case of a country would mean making peace action the basis of the country's foreign policy. A noble vision, held still today by a small number of Japanese peace activists, mostly stubborn, gray-haired veterans of the anti-war struggles of the 1960s and 1970s.

A PERFECT MUDDLE

Surely Japan today has one of the oddest defense policies in the world. On the one hand, there is the SDF: They dress like military, are organized and disciplined like military, train like military, wear military insignia, and (unlike the Boy Scouts or the Salvation Army) are armed with real projectiles and explosives, with the firearms, rockets, and aircraft to deliver them, but it's not clear whether they have the full right of belligerency; as far as we know, they have no experience of full participation in military action. And while the Constitution prohibits a defense policy based on war and threat of war, the country hosts dozens of US military bases occupied by military forces treaty-bound to defend Japan against attack, and which keep the country under the US "nuclear umbrella." Nobody planned it this way; rather than a contradiction, it is better described as a stalemate among people with conflicting ideas of what the country should be. If the Japanese government elites' plans had gone as expected, the Constitution would have been amended by now, and the SDF would be legal and blooded. If the country's anti-war civil society's movement had succeeded, the SDF would either not exist at all or else would have been reorganized as an international fire-and-rescue squad, flying to people's aid wherever there is an earthquake, tsunami, or forest fire.

As it is, while the SDF is not a rescue squad, it does do rescue work, which is said to be the only useful thing it ever does. And while the Japanese government supports just about every military adventure the US undertakes (excepting those in the Americas), which from an ethical standpoint makes Japan complicit in these wars, from a military standpoint the SDF has not proved itself to be effective in actual combat on the ground. This "failure" allows the US to extort fabulous sums of money from Japan to pay for its bases in the country and its various adventures abroad.

And as a bizarre side effect, Japan's government conservatives and ultra-rightists, who as rightists ought to be devoted nationalists, find themselves in the awkward position of flying the stars and stripes—the flag of a foreign military with bases in their country—from their sound trucks.

The Japanese anti-war civil society, for its part, has failed to prevent the establishment and growth of the SDF, but has succeeded at least in delaying the granting to it of the full right of belligerency, though the SDF continues inching toward that unhappy goal. The anti-war movement has so far held what amounts to their last line of defense: In all the years since World War II, (again, so far as we know) no human being has been killed under the authority of the right of belligerency of the Japanese state. That is an achievement no one could have predicted in, say, 1939. On the other hand, the SDF, following the US military here and there around the world, has been complicit in many deaths.

To its believers, Article 9 is straightforward, innocence itself. To government officials who yearn to be at the head of a real war machine, it is so wildly absurd that they can scarcely form its various aspects into coherent words and sentences. To MacArthur, Article 9 and the US bases in Okinawa were two aspects of the same policy. To many Japanese, US military bases are okay so long as they are kept mostly in Okinawa. Yet to the Japanese Self-Defense Forces, it still stands between them and full participation in real war. (Some SDF troops, we hear, are grateful for this, some not.)

The LDP government continues to announce that it means to begin the constitutional amendment process soon—as it has been announcing for decades. Quite possibly someday it will. If so, the result will be a historical showdown between the government and its supporters, and the anti-war civil society. During such a struggle, it is possible that some of the political entanglements described above will begin to come untangled, and the people's various political positions will become clearer. But until that happens, any attempt at a definitive conclusion to this chapter would be premature. At present, it's a perfect muddle.

NOTES

1. J. L. Austin, *How To Do Things with Words*, eds. J. O. Urmson and Marina Sbisa (Cambridge: Harvard University, 1962), passim.

2. Johannes Siemes, *Hermann Roesler and the Making of the Meiji State* (Tokyo: Sophia University in cooperation with Charles E. Tuttle Co., 1968), 62.

3. In the Magna Carta (1215), the first word, and (grammatically) the speaker, is "John." Some other examples:

English Bill of Rights (1689): "Representatives of all estates of the people."

Virginia Declaration of Rights (1776): "Representatives of the people of Virginia."

US Declaration of Independence (1776): "Representatives of the thirteen states."

US Constitution (1789): "We the People of the United States."

UN Charter (1945): "We the Peoples of the United Nations."

Republic of Korea (1948): "We, the People of Korea."

Iraq (2005): "We the People."

Cuba (1976/2002): "We, Cuban Citizens."

Vietnam (1986): "We, the Vietnamese People."

Republic of South Africa (1996): "We, the people of South Africa."

Then there are some exceptions.

In the constitutions of China (1982), the Democratic People's Republic of Korea (1948), and Iran (1979), there is no speaker. In the case of the first two, perhaps historical materialism persuaded them that history is the speaker.

In the constitution of Thailand (2007), the speaker is the king, though he declares that the people are sovereign. Saudi Arabia has no constitution; at the command of the king, it is governed by the basic law found in the Koran.

4. Japan Ministry of Defense White Paper, *Defense of Japan* (2022 digest), 192.
5. Japan Ministry of Defense White Paper, 193.
6. Tessa Morris-Suzuki, *The Korean War in Asia* (Lanham, Maryland: Rowman & Littlefield, 2018).
7. Morris-Suzuki, *The Korean War*, 8.
8. Morris-Suzuki, *The Korean War*, 12.
9. Morris-Suzuki, *The Korean War*, 25.

10. Morris-Suzuki, *The Korean War*, 21–2.

11. Eric Slavin, "What Japanese defense forces can do under new legislation," *The Stars and Stripes*, September 19, 2015.

12. Japan Ministry of Defense White Paper (2020), 231.

13. Japan Ministry of Defense White Paper (2020), 214, n. 1.

14. Annex B, "Views of General of the Army Douglas MacArthur on Rearmament of Japan," in JCS 1380/48, "Note by the Secretaries to the Joint Chiefs of Staff on Limited Military Armament for Japan," 398–9 (October 25, 1948). Few if any people in Japan knew of this meeting until Koseki Shoichi discovered this document and made it public.

15. Koseki, *Japan's Postwar Constitution*, chapter 6 ff.

16. Tsurumi Shunsuke, "Radical Democracy," in *Anti-war Thought and Action*, ed. Yoshikawa Yuichi (Tokyo: Shakai Hyoronsha Publishers, 1995), 131–2.

17. Tsurumi, "Radical Democracy," 132.

18. Tsurumi, "Radical Democracy," 132.

19. Tsurumi, "Radical Democracy," 132.

20. Tsurumi, "Radical Democracy," 134.

21. Kobayashi Tomi, "The Action of the Voiceless Voices," in Yoshikawa, *Anti-war Thought*, 135.

22. Liberal Democratic Party, Constitutional Revision Drafting Committee, *Comparison Chart for Draft Revision of Constitution of Japan* (2012). For an analysis of this draft, see C. Douglas Lummis, *A Constitution is a Command to the Government: Expanded Version* (Tokyo: Heibonsha Library, 2013).

23. Oda Makoto, "Where my 'Anti-War' Began," *Nine-One-One and Article 9* (Tokyo: Otsuki Publishing, 2006), 397–9.

24. Oda Makoto, "Toward a Conscientious Objector Country," *Nine-One-One and Article 9* (Tokyo: Otsuki Publishing, 2006), 372.

25. Oda, "Toward," 373.

26. Oda, "Toward," 373.

Chapter 12

Commonsense Peace

What if they gave a war and nobody came?

—Traditional

War is hell. But unlike Holy Hell, it's not a place where people get what they deserve. The people sent to war don't deserve that, and the people who never went to war but are surrounded by it deserve it even less.

War is a hell where those sent to it are both tortured as if by demons and required to do the work of demons. Unlike the Holy Hell we imagine, the hell of war neither is ordained by a sacred force nor does it serve a sacred purpose. It is a hell entirely fashioned and carried out by human beings.

Those who think up the reasons for war, those who make the plans for war, and those who carry out war are all people like us. So, why don't we quit? Most people—at least most people with a grain of common sense—think we should. And we have been trying to, from long ago.

WHY ISN'T IT WORKING?

There are many reasons. One, there is the contradiction in our main method for keeping the peace. When people threaten war, we preserve the peace by threatening war on them; when people wage war, we restore the peace by waging war on them. When people launch hell on earth, we respond by raining hell on them. The problem is not hard to see.

But another reason is our belief that the peace achieved by war is sometimes worth having. Peace established by war is not always desolation; or rather, the war situation itself is sometimes so desolate that "not so hurtful as the want of it" can seem an attractive option. It brings us our best days, generally remembered by later generations as "the good old days before the war." But it doesn't last: However sincerely the robber band may labor to establish lasting peace, the best it can do is establish "a time between wars." Peace-established-by-war has the next war built into it: the military organizations, the weapons, the nationalism, the state itself whose identity requires an enemy, the state whose nature cannot be explained without using the word "war." Still, the times between wars are the best, and it is right to make good use of them and to try to make them last.

Another reason for war's persistence is that in addition to the reestablishment of peace, there are other things worth having that it sometimes seems we can't have without fighting for them. Freedom, equality, justice, ending discrimination, ending exploitation—the list is long. Many people believe the only effective way to fight for these is through violent action. If, in the end, war is the only thing that works, then giving up war would mean giving up the good fight—giving the robber band a free hand. But this is the fatal mistake. As a means of getting these things, war, far from being the only thing that works, works badly, if at all. The point is not that we should stop fighting for a better world but that the nonviolent methods are the most effective ways to do that.

VIOLENCE AND POWER

In her essay "On Violence," Hannah Arendt writes, "The chief reason warfare is still with us is neither a secret death wish of the human species, nor an irrepressible instinct of aggression, nor finally and more plausibly, the serious social and economic dangers inherent in disarmament, but the simple fact that no substitute for this final arbiter in international affairs has yet appeared on the political scene."[1]

Presumably by "substitute" Arendt is not referring to William James's search for an activity that can match war's (alleged) grandeur and romance. Rather she is making the remarkable claim—especially remarkable in the context of the essay in which it appears—that as an "arbiter in international affairs," war works. Yet she devotes much of this 1971 essay to arguing that modern war has lost its effectiveness. This is not only because to launch a nuclear war is an act that could be carried out only by a mad person (which is not, despite what many think, a guarantee that it will not happen). It is also because we have entered an age of guerilla warfare, resulting in "a complete reversal in the relationship between power and violence, foreshadowing another reversal in the relationship between small and great powers."[2] Arendt wrote this before the US was driven out of Vietnam, when that result was predicted by few other than the Vietnamese. And even after Vietnam's victory, the belief in the effectiveness of modernized military power remains strong enough to prevent us from noticing that the greatest military power in the history of the human race has not gained a clear victory in any of its major wars since 1945. The Korean War ended in a draw. The Vietnam War was for the US a humiliating defeat. In the first Gulf War, the US did succeed in driving the Iraqi military out of Kuwait, but this led directly to the Iraqi War, in which, measured against their various war aims, all sides were defeated, the country was destroyed as a country, and as I write the fighting continues. Similarly in the Afghan War, all sides were defeated, the country was destroyed, and the war goes on. As for the "War on Terror," this is a war designed never to end—the weapons industry's dream.

In addition to arguing that the destructiveness of nuclear weapons plus the refusal of guerilla fighters to follow the rules of the war game have made it impossible for the big powers to achieve their aims by warfare, Arendt makes a more radical claim. This is that what in her special vocabulary she calls "power" is something that *in principle* violence cannot bring about.

Nonviolent methods suffer under a reputation of weakness. The "strong" are those who lobby for, and go to, war. Gandhi, who, judging from his writings, was not so free of irritation as his saintly reputation would suggest, was especially irritated when the method of nonviolent resistance he advocated was described as the method of the weak. Repeatedly, he argued not only that it requires great personal strength to carry out but also that it generates real power.

Is there a relationship between Gandhi's notion of nonviolent action and Arendt's notion of power? Arendt, like most Western political writers, did her best to keep Gandhi at a distance. Even in her essay "Civil Disobedience," Gandhi is never quoted, and his name is mentioned only twice. In the essay "On Violence," she manages to suggest a strong connection between her thought and that of Gandhi, and then immediately to dismiss him from consideration, all in a single sentence: "If Gandhi's enormously powerful and successful strategy of non-violent resistance had met with a different enemy—Stalin's Russia, Hitler's Germany, even prewar Japan, instead of England—the outcome would not have been decolonization, but massacre and submission."[3] "Enormously powerful"—these words planted smack in the middle of her discussion of what "power" means when the word is properly used. One might expect this to be followed by some elaboration at least, but instead she cuts off discussion with something one rarely finds in Arendt's writing, a platitude—the standard platitude used to keep Gandhi out of the conversation. But is it true? Gandhi's followers did suffer massacres, yet the movement was not broken by them. And submission was their starting point, the condition that the Indian National Congress had to overcome to begin their resistance and had to struggle against to the end. It is bizarre to attribute the Indian people's victory in this agonizing struggle, in which thousands were beaten, jailed, broken, and killed, to the kindliness of the British. Gene Sharp wrote that in putting down the Indian nonviolent movement, the British

> were by no means as brutal as they *could* have been, and as they in fact *were* in putting down the 1857 uprising in India and the Mau Mau movement in Kenya, or in the bombing of German cities in World War II. At least a major part of the reason for the comparative British restraint . . . was that the Indians' continuing nonviolence limited the British in the means of repression which were effectively open to them.[4]

Would a Gandhian resistance have been defeated in Stalinist Russia, Nazi Germany, or militarist Japan? As with most counterfactual speculations, the answer is, Maybe. The image we have of these regimes is, naturally enough, as they in fact were: unified, with no large nonviolent resistance movement within them. Arendt's (not my) counterfactual speculation asks, What if there had been such a movement? How large should we suppose this counterfactual movement to be? If it is one hundred or one thousand people, most likely it would have been crushed, as the platitude has it. If it is one or two million people, and the soldiers and police are beginning to find its arguments persuasive—who knows?

Stranger still, this is the same Arendt who in her *Eichmann in Jerusalem* devoted a good part of a chapter to detailing cases in which nonviolent resistance to Nazism did have real success—by people under Nazi occupation, and also by people in Italy, resisting Nazi orders to round up their countries' Jews and send them to Germany. In most countries, she wrote, this was not done by open resistance but by deception, foot dragging, intentional inefficiency. "Italy and Bulgaria sabotaged German orders and indulged in a complicated game of double-dealing and double-crossing, saving their Jews by a tour de force of sheer ingenuity" while pretending to support the policy.[5] On the other hand, Denmark, which was in the German sphere of influence but had an independent government, resisted openly. On this, Arendt wrote:

> The story of the Danish Jews is sui generis, and the behavior of the Danish people and their government was unique among all the countries of Europe—whether occupied, or a partner of the Axis, or neutral and truly independent. One is tempted to recommend the story as required reading in political science for all students who wish to learn something about the enormous power potential inherent in non-violent action and in resistance to an opponent possessing vastly superior means of violence.[6]

The Danish government refused to require Jews to wear yellow badges, refused to enforce a distinction between Danish Jews and Jewish refugees, and when German police arrived from Germany to round up the Jews (because the Danish police could not be trusted to do so), the Danish government revealed the plan to the Jewish leaders, who passed the information on to the community so that almost all were able to hide out in Danish people's homes. Some stayed in hiding until the end of the war; others were taken to neutral Sweden in fishing boats. In the end, only a few hundred were shipped to Germany. Arendt continues:

> It is the only case we know of in which the Nazis met with open resistance, and the result seems to have been that those exposed to it changed their minds. . . . They had met resistance based on principle, their "toughness" had melted like butter in the sun, they had even been able to show a few timid beginnings of genuine courage.[7]

YOU CAN'T GET THERE FROM HERE

Arendt's main theoretical task in the essay "On Violence" is to clarify the differences between power, strength, force, authority, and violence. The essay can be read as a summary and extension of the analysis of power she made in *The Human Condition*. Her purpose in taking up the issue again in 1971 was to counter what she saw as the glorification of violence in Frantz Fanon's *The Wretched of the Earth* and in Jean-Paul Sartre's preface to it, and, more troublingly, by many new-left readers of those works, expressed in the often-repeated slogan of Mao Tse Tung, "Political power grows out of the barrel of a gun." Far from being so intimately connected, she argues, "power and violence are opposites; where the one rules absolutely, the other is absent."[8] Power is generated when people act together. "When we say of somebody that he is 'in power' we actually refer to his being empowered by a certain number of people to act in their name."[9] And if those people withdraw that support and walk away, the leader's power melts "like butter in the sun." These observations are not exactly Arendt's discovery, though she found wonderful ways of expressing them. Politicians have always known consciously or instinctively that their power is in their support. Weber's trinity—traditional, charismatic, and legal authority—are three methods for gaining and maintaining that support. A dictator can use violence and threat of violence to obtain obedience, but "everything depends on the power behind the violence." You can send the infantry to crush the people storming the Bastille, but if the soldiers join the stormers (as happened July 14, 1789), you will regret having done so.

As the Bastille example shows, in the real world, as opposed to the world of ideal types, power and violence usually come mixed together. Military commanders have always known that effectiveness depends on something called morale, and that if your organization holds together and causes the other side to become a scattered crowd of fleeing individuals, you will have won the day.

This crucial fact, that power is not a characteristic of the ruler but is given—whether willingly, reluctantly, mistakenly, or unconsciously—to the ruler by the ruled, is something both well known and easily forgotten. Dictators need to persuade their subjects that they are powerless, and to persuade their police and military that their power flows into them from the dictator rather than the reverse. For leaders of democratization or anti-colonial movements, persuading the people that people's power is real is the central task of political education, so-called conscientization. But what concerned Arendt, and motivated her to write this essay, was the fact that many such activists were (and still are) convinced that the only way to empower the powerless is to persuade them to take up arms.

Violence can do what violence can do. If a person is acting against your interest, you can solve that problem by killing that person (assuming you get away with it). If there is a government official who is especially odious, assassination will rid the world of him or her (but will not prevent the appointment of a still more odious replacement). If there is a mass demonstration that threatens to overthrow your government, machine-gun fire can disperse that demonstration (assuming the machine gunners don't go over to the other side).

In short, "violence can destroy power: it is utterly incapable of creating it."[10] It is not in the nature of violence to do so. So there is what can be called the "You Can't Get There from Here" problem. The robber band can create a situation in which order is enforced by the robber band; Leviathan can establish Leviathan. If a measure of peace grows up within a polity so established, it was grown by the people in spite of, or in resistance to, the violent state.

GANDHI AND THE VIOLENT STATE

I understand that for me to write about Gandhi is foolhardy. Millions of words have been written about this man, most by people who know him better than I do. As a means of mitigating this foolhardiness, what I propose to do is not so much to offer an analysis as to tell a story. Analysis is a zero-sum game: To prove one's thesis is correct, you must show that the other theses are wrong. Stories, however, admit of different tellings, each reflecting the perspective of the storyteller. My perspective is that of one who spent many years teaching Western political theory in a country whose constitution denies one of Western political theory's founding principles: that a state without the right of belligerency is no state at all. From this contradictory and therefore awkward standpoint, perhaps I may be able to tell this story in a manner somewhat different from the way it has been told by others, without denying the truth-value of those other renderings. I will title this story:

GANDHI AND THE FOUNDING OF THE VIOLENT STATE

To set the tone, I take as my texts Machiavelli's *The Prince* and his "Discourses on Livy." This may seem a strange choice, until one remembers that Machiavelli is the premier theorist on the subject of founding. This is often obscured by his reputation as the theorist of "the end justifies the means." I take it that the main message of his work is that the founding of a new state or the restoration of an old one is almost impossible except under the leadership of one man (I use the gender advisedly), whom he called the prince and modern political scientists call the charismatic leader. Looking from this perspective, one could see the twentieth century as Machiavelli's century, for never have so many new states been founded in so short a time, and one would be hard pressed to think of one of those new states that does not have the name of such a leader attached to its founding. Think Ataturk, Lenin, Nasser, Sukarno, Kenyatta, Senghor, Nkrumah, Mao, U Nu, Ho Chi Minh, Tito, Kim Il-Sung, and Castro, to mention only some of the more prominent figures. In the case of India, the name of course is Gandhi.

With the exception of Gandhi, all these figures match well with Machiavelli's model, as set out in *The Prince*, of political brilliance and political ruthlessness. Gandhi alone seems out of place. The difference can be brought into focus by recalling Machiavelli's words on the dilemma posed by the radical restoration of a state, which also can be taken as the dilemma of founding.

"And as the reformation of the political condition of a state presupposes a good man, whilst the making of himself prince of a republic by violence naturally presupposes a bad one, it will consequently be exceedingly rare that a good man should be found willing to employ wicked means to become prince, even though his final object be good; or that a bad man, after having become prince, should be willing to labor for good ends, and that it should enter his mind to use for good purposes the authority which he has acquired by evil means."[11]

Much has been written about the varying degrees of success or lack thereof with which the abovementioned founders were able to overcome the dilemma between what they (believed they) had to do to make themselves "princes" of their new/revolutionary states, and what kind of government was needed after the convulsion of founding/revolution was over. For Gandhi, the dilemma was reversed. That is, while his denial of Machiavelli was complete, it was so complete that it came back to haunt him standing, as it were, on its head. For Gandhi discovered that it was possible—or rather, he *made* it possible—to lead India from colonial subjection to independence without committing the crimes of violence that Machiavelli believed were indispensable. But the founding of independent India eventually led, with its success, to the founding of yet another violent state. Gandhi is seen as the father of his country, or of his nation, but it was entirely against his nature to become the father of the state. Alone among the great founders of the twentieth century, as the moment of the transfer of power approached, Gandhi backed off, not only not becoming head of state but taking no post at all either in the new government or in the Constituent Assembly. He didn't attend the independence ceremony of August 15, 1947.[12] And he even made an alternative constitutional proposal (of which more is below) but he was realistic enough to know it was not going to be adopted. Thus for him, the Machiavellian dilemma must be stated the other way around: How is it possible for a person who has led a nation to independence using nonviolent means to adopt, after independence is achieved, the wicked means of the violent state? Gandhi was incapable of making that transformation, and while he remained the adviser and father figure for many of the government leaders, the state itself had no place for him.

GANDHI AND POWER

Mohandas Gandhi became the effective leader of the Indian National Congress at the time when Lenin was consolidating his position as leader of the Russian Revolution, Mao Tse Tung was emerging as a revolutionary leader in China, and Michael Collins was leading Ireland's war for independence. At that time, India could be described as a vast collection of villages dominated by what amounted to a robber band. That is, this was a rare moment in history when the transformation described in Original Position 2 (see chapter 1) would, with a few adjustments, have fit India's situation fairly closely. One of the adjustments would be that, as Gandhi was fond of saying, since India had some seven hundred thousand villages, it was not within the power of the British robber band to manage each in detail. Even under the Raj, the villages maintained much of their traditional economic, cultural, and political autonomy. Gandhi's political philosophy, in addition to its being a contribution to political philosophy generally, also was a strategy for action in that particular situation.

In the dialogue between the Editor and the Reader depicted in Gandhi's *Hind Swaraj*, both agree that the robber band must be driven out; the question is how to do it. The Reader argues that India must study what gives the Raj its overwhelming economic, political, and, above all, military power, and use this knowledge to transform itself into a force powerful enough to drive the British out.

> READER: We may get [self-government] when we have arms and ammunition even as they have. . . . As is Japan, so must India be. We must own our navy, our army, and we must have our own splendour, and then will India's voice ring through the world.
>
> EDITOR: You have well drawn the picture. In effect it means this: that we want English rule without the Englishman. You want the tiger's nature, but not the tiger, that is to say, you would make India English, and when it becomes English, it will be called not Hindustan but Englistan.[13]

The Reader's solution, replacing the British robber band with an Indian robber band, is seen by the Editor as a catastrophe. This difference with the Reader is not just an ethical one; it is also a disagreement as to the facts, for the Editor has a different way of defining the situation. He agrees with the Reader that it is necessary to analyze the source of British power, but the conclusion he draws from that is based on an understanding of power much closer to the one later propagated by Arendt.

The Reader asks how it could have been possible for England to have taken India.

> EDITOR: The English have not taken India; we have given it to them. They are not in India because of their strength, but because we keep them. . . . Who assisted the Company's officers? Who was tempted at the sight of their silver? Who bought their goods? History testifies that we did all this.[14]

The Reader then asks how they are able to retain India.

> EDITOR: The causes that gave them India enable them to retain it. Some Englishmen state that they took, and they hold, India by the sword. Both these statements are wrong. The sword is entirely useless for holding India. We alone keep them.[15]

This answer may sound dangerously close to blaming the victim, and perhaps to some extent it is that. But more importantly, it is a theory of where the robber band's power comes from that yields a different strategy for driving the robber band out. If cooperation is the source of their power, noncooperation should leave them powerless. And noncooperation, it should be noted, is not nonviolent by ethical command; refusing to cooperate is simply not an action that entails violence.

This argument has obvious resemblance to Marx's analysis of the dialectic of alienated labor. According to Marx, factory workers may be persuaded to believe that the power of capitalists somehow grows out of their nature as capitalists, but actually capitalists' power is their wealth, and their wealth is produced by the work the workers do, extracted in the form of surplus value. So the harder the workers work, the more power they give to the system that is forcing them to work so hard. And Marx's solution, like Gandhi's, is noncooperation. Marx was not ethically committed to nonviolence, and strikes—especially general strikes—were often accompanied by violence, but the act of striking itself—refusing to work—is an act not of violence but of noncooperation. Marx's revolution was violent in that when policemen or soldiers or goons attacked, the strikers would fight back, whereas Gandhi's followers would (usually) not. But the power of the workers' movement grew not out of the street fights (which they usually lost) but out of their noncooperation: the strike itself, which shut off the capitalists' power at the source.

As I wrote in chapter 2, Gandhi's contemporary, Max Weber, argued that any person who imagines that it is possible to take effective political action while refusing to use the "satanic powers" that lurk behind political power—specifically, refusing to use violence—has failed to understand the first thing about politics and is a political "infant." Mature political actors will be concerned with the consequences of their actions and will do what it takes to achieve the consequences they aim for. One of the ways later political scientists have justified ignoring Gandhi has been to think of him as a mainly religious leader who chose the ethic of the saint, and therefore stands outside the sphere of realistic political action. But as can be seen in the *Hind Swaraj* dialogue (not to mention Gandhi's entire political history), this is not the case. His lifetime search was for a way to escape the dilemma. He was clearly committed to consequences: He passionately wanted India to drive out its oppressor, and at the same time to avoid India's becoming an imitation of its oppressor—as he put it pithily, Englistan. Violence might yield the former result, but not the latter. Violence was to be avoided *because of the consequences* that invariably come with it.

NONVIOLENCE FOR THE ORDINARY PEOPLE

The claim that Gandhi was, or aspired to be, a saint, made by both his supporters and his detractors, serves as a basis for excluding his thought from the main body of political theory. Yet he himself denied the label: "I am not a visionary. I claim to be a practical idealist. The religion of non-violence is not meant to be merely for the rishis and the saints. It is meant for the common people as well."[16]

As the present work aims to be of some use to people who don't aspire to saintliness, it is the latter of these uses that concerns us here. And when ordinary, non-saintly people (quite naturally) aspire for peace, they are talking not about a condition of their souls but about an actually existing social and political condition. As "Mahatma," Gandhi distanced himself from many commonsense social norms and practices. But as activist he threw himself into the society of his time. From this position, paradoxically, he had a clearer, more realistic grasp of the political situation than many self-proclaimed "realists."

For example, there is his description of the state: "The State represents violence in a concentrated and organized form. The individual has a soul, but the state is a soulless machine; it can never be weaned from violence to which it owes its very existence."[17]

In his assertion that the state and violence are inextricably bound together, Gandhi is in agreement with Max Weber's definition, the main difference being that Gandhi does not use the value term "legitimate." Of course, Weber did not use that term as a value judgment. He wrote that the state "(successfully) claims" (the parentheses are Weber's) the right of legitimate violence, which is an assertion of fact: The claim has been successful. But in addition to its alleged facticity, the term hints at a value judgment: State violence *can* be legitimate, adding an element of state-romantic hope, compared to which Gandhi's statement is the more courageously realistic. (On this, Arendt was unconditional: "Violence can be justifiable, but it never will be legitimate.")[18]

Hobbes, also, would find little with which to disagree in Gandhi's statement, except he would want to add that life under the state is "less hurtful" than life without it. And here is where Gandhi parts company with Hobbes and with mainstream (Western) political philosophy. Rather than seeking ways to make the state a little less hurtful, he proposed doing without it. But coming to this conclusion took time.

GANDHI AND CONSTITUTIONS

Before Gandhi became India's political and spiritual leader or was called Mahatma, he was a British-trained lawyer. When he was in South Africa, the appeals he made to the British government were written in lawyer-like language and showed great respect for the British Constitution. Consider:

> The cherished maxim of the British Constitution, namely, that every man is to be presumed innocent until he is proven guilty, and that, rather than an innocent man should suffer, guilty ones should go unpunished.[19]

The British Constitution teaches us, it taught me while yet a child, that British subject was to be treated on a footing of equality in the eye of the law, and I do demand equality in the eye of the law in the Transvaal also.[20]

If the orders of the Revenue Department or any other Government orders are not revised despite petitions, it is not the spirit of the British Constitution that they must be obeyed meekly. There is no such political doctrine. It is the birth-right and the duty of the people to disobey orders which, on mature consideration, they regard as unjust or oppressive.[21]

The last quotation is especially striking. Gandhi is widely believed to have gotten his ideas of civil disobedience from Tolstoy, Thoreau, and/or the Hindu religion, but here he seems to be saying that it came from his British legal training. Of course, these statements are in the context of appeals to the British authorities, so holding them to their own principles is a smart tactic. But Gandhi was neither cynical about British legal principles nor naïve about the Empire's actual practices: "We fought to keep the theory of the British Constitution intact so that practice may someday approach the theory as near as possible."[22]

In *Hind Swaraj*, Gandhi was no longer talking about the British Constitution Solution. Rather, making India over in the image of Great Britain now appeared to him as the Englistan Solution (i.e., the worst version of the robber band solution: the Village re-forming *itself* into a robber band), against which he laid down in simple terms the theoretical groundwork for the Village Solution. Later, when he became a leader in the Indian National Congress, this picture of India's situation became the basis for a simple strategy for achieving self-governance.

In 1919, Gandhi and many other Indians believed that their support of Great Britain in World War I would be rewarded by better—possibly even equal—treatment within the Empire. In the event, things got worse. In March, the Rowlatt Act was passed, effectively placing the country under martial law. The Congress responded by calling a *hartal*, a national day of prayer, which would also serve as a one-day national general strike. This took place on April 6. It was a gigantic event, largely but not entirely nonviolent: There also were riots and deaths. Gandhi called it off, labeling it a "Himalayan blunder." But immediately following this, on April 10, came the Amritsar Massacre. A military unit of Gurkha and Balochi troops, commanded by Brigadier General Reginald Dyer, fired into a crowd of civilians gathered to celebrate a Sikh festival in Amritsar, killing 379 of them. And a few days later, Dyer, apparently feeling that his point had not been made, issued the Crawling Order, commanding all Indians passing down a certain street where an English woman had been assaulted to crawl on their hands and knees. Indians were enraged, and many resorted to violence. For the next year, Gandhi and the Congress sought a way to channel their pain and humiliation in a nonviolent way. Satyagraha campaigns were announced, and canceled when violence broke out. A one-man Satyagraha campaign was tried—Gandhi's first political fast. This was the period when the khadi movement began—the spinning wheel as a symbol of self-sufficiency and dignity and as a device for calming a troubled mind.

In 1920, Gandhi began promoting a slightly different version of Satyagraha, based on the theory of power he had set out in *Hind Swaraj*: pure noncooperation. Satyagraha as positive interference in the operations of the Empire required people to gather in public places, and invited retaliation, which can lead to riots. Noncooperation, being not a "doing" but a "not-doing," should be easier to carry out nonviolently. Or so it was hoped.

This strategy fit with Gandhi's belief that political action must seek two consequences: ending the oppression by the colonizers and establishing or maintaining the colonized as a peaceful, self-sufficient community. Gandhi believed, and for a time was successful in persuading the Congress leadership to believe, that it was still possible to rescue India's identity as a vast collection of villages, not with a massive uprising but by reasserting their character as self-sufficient villages, and withdrawing their cooperation from the robber band. His insistence on nonviolence was not a position of "may the consequences be damned." On the contrary, given the consequences he was aiming for, he believed that a national noncooperation movement was the best method by which those consequences could be attained.

By the end of 1920, noncooperation had evolved from theory to strategy to Indian National Congress policy to active campaign. In September, it was adopted as policy at a special meeting of the Congress. In December, it was adopted at the annual national meeting. It was inserted as a clause in their new Constitution making a pledge of noncooperation a condition of membership. The astoundingly optimistic goal of this movement was, as Gandhi repeatedly wrote, to achieve *swaraj* (self-sufficiency) in one year. To capture the remarkable character of this revolutionary effort, I quote some of Gandhi's writings from that time.

> The days of merely passing resolutions during the Christmas week and sleeping over till the next Christmas are gone. . . . Everyone is called upon to withdraw their children from Government-managed or controlled schools. Everyone is called upon to use as few foreign articles as possible and to use only hand-woven cloth made from hand-spun yarn. Everyone is called upon to subscribe to the Tilak Memorial Swaraj Fund. . . . The new constitution enables workers to organize the nation within one year for carrying out the program in detail and if the vast body of the people make a conscious effort, nothing can thwart its

> legitimate wish for self-determination. If we nationalize schools, boycott law courts, and manufacture all the cloth we need, we will have created our right to govern ourselves and no army in the world can possibly defeat our purpose.[23]
>
> It is necessary for us to understand the meaning of the Congress constitution. This constitution has been so drawn up that we may be able to win *swaraj* at an early date. If, in accordance with that constitution, we can form a Congress Committee in every town, and succeed in having the name of every man and woman of twenty-one years [and over], it will mean Congress' authority respected in everything simultaneously with the Government's. The latter is aintained by force. When, in one and the same place, another authority comes to be, the authority of the Government, if it is not accepted by the people, will not last even a moment. This is to say, if we see the Congress constitution functioning on a country-wide scale, we may take it that swaraj will have been established that very day.[24]
>
> If [the constitution] is honestly worked and commands confidence and respect, it can oust the present Government without the slightest difficulty. For, the latter has no power except through the cooperation, willing or forced, of the people. The force it exercises is almost [entirely] through our own people. One lakh [100,000] of Europeans, without our help, can only hold one-seventh of our villages each, and it would be difficult, for one man, even when physically present, to impose his will on, say, four hundred men and women—the average population of an Indian village.[25]

Of course, the key word, repeated in each of these statements, is "if." And the actions that followed this word did not happen on the scale that Gandhi and the Congress hoped for. Not all the children were taken out of the British-run schools, not all the lawyers and politicians quit their jobs, not all the people wore homespun, and, most importantly, there were outbreaks of violence, capped by the massacre of some police officers who had fired into a crowd in the town of Chauri Chaura, which caused Gandhi (over the objections of many of the Congress leaders) to call off the campaign. This in turn emboldened the government to sentence him to six years in prison.

But the fact that the campaign failed to achieve "*swaraj* in one year" does not disprove Gandhi's theory of power, nor does it prove that a campaign based on that theory can never succeed. Every political theory that has an action element is based on an if-then, from "if philosophers become kings," through "if xx type of social contract is agreed to," through "if the workers in the most developed countries do xx," through "if people behave in accordance with xx model of rationality"—and so on. What the 1920 campaign showed was that an effective noncooperation campaign is difficult, not that it is impossible.

With this campaign, Gandhi invented the "self-limiting revolution" more than half a century before the term was coined in Poland. The differences between the situations in India and Poland are huge, but also there are important similarities. In both cases, the countries were dominated by foreign powers whose domination was carried out by cooperating nationals, some of who believed in the superiority of the foreign power, others who were opportunists. In both cases, there was no realistic possibility of ejecting the invader militarily. In both cases, the principal method of combating the government was noncooperation (in India, as described above; in Poland, the strike). In both cases, the nonviolence was justified by some as practical, by others as ethical, probably by most as both (the ethical aspect supported in India by Hinduism and Islam; in Poland by the Catholic church). In both cases, opposition was organized both in the form of large units (the Congress, Solidarity) and small, face-to-face ones (in India, villages; in Poland, "civil society" organizations [Jacek Kuron: "Set up your own committees instead of burning down party committees!"[26]]); in both, a campaign of consciousness raising (in India, the campaign against the colonized consciousness; in Poland, refusing to live inside the "Big Lie"). Most importantly, both aimed not to overthrow the government but to delegitimize it, to render it powerless by *empowering the society* over which it had been ruling. And in both cases, the heroic phase of this effort was brief. Both were smashed in classic martial-law fashion, their leaders thrown in prison, the effort declared a failure. But in both cases, some years later, the dominating foreign power gave up and withdrew. In both cases, the process leading up to this result was complex, and this is not the place to attempt to recount it in detail, but it seems that in the background is the fact that neither government was able to recover from the delegitimizing campaign; both realized that, realistically, they had no choice but to withdraw. Not the cleanest, most dramatic, or most complete form of victory, but victory nonetheless.

This strategy also can be compared with that used by the Democratic Republic of Vietnam (DRVN) in their war to drive the French out of Vietnam, called by the French *hierarchies paralleles*. According to Bernard Fall, far more important than the establishment of an on-paper revolutionary government in the south was "the establishment of small but efficient administrative units that duplicated the existing Franco-Vietnamese administration. . . . These, rather than the existence of guerilla battalions, were the source of France's defeat."[27]

The DRVN was by no means nonviolent and had as its chief war aim the seizure of the state. But the case supports Arendt's assertion that it is collective action rather than violence that generates real power and decides revolutions.

A NOTE ON SATYAGRAHA AND THE RIGHT OF BELLIGERENCY

I wrote above that when Weber asserts that the state "successfully" claims a monopoly of legitimate violence, he is not making a value statement but asserting a fact. But like most political facts, this one is only partly factual. In some states, the claim is largely successful, in others less so. In so-called "failed states," achieving this monopoly is precisely what they have failed at. Within these states, members of national liberation, separatist, and revolutionary movements also sometimes claim that right. In a sense, this is simply an extension of the logic of the right of belligerency of the state: Because these movements aim to become the state where there is none or seize it where it exists, and are typically infused with the faith that they will surely succeed, from that assumed legitimacy they simply apply the state's right of belligerency to themselves in advance.

This right is to some extent recognized in international law. The 1948 Geneva Convention on the treatment of prisoners of war stipulates that members of "organized resistance movements" must, when captured, be given prisoner-of-war status if they meet certain conditions. Being granted prisoner-of-war status means that the killing they have been engaging in is not murder but war, justified by the right of belligerency.

Satyagraha refuses to claim this right. The effect of this on the soldiers of the other side is usually described in ethical or religious terms, but it also can be described in terms of just war theory. As I wrote in the chapter on just war, one of the ways to explain why just war can be considered just and accepted as legal is that it follows the logic of the duel. Both sides know what kind of game this is, and both sides have accepted the rules. The rules are cruel, painful, life threatening, but fair: The people you are trying to kill are also trying to kill you. This scenario (which, as we have seen, does not always describe what actually happens on the ground) is at the heart of just war theory, both in its international-law form and in the form it takes in the consciences of individual soldiers.

Satyagraha spoils this game. By renouncing the right to attempt to kill the enemy, Satyagraha denies the other side its primal justification to use violence. By the very rules of war, what the soldiers are doing ceases to be war and begins to look like murder: the killing of noncombatants. This puts pressure both on individual soldiers and on their commanders. One imagines them longing for just one act of violence from the Satyagrahis so the situation can be fitted back into their notion of how war is carried out. This may help to explain Gandhi's controversial decision to call off the noncooperation campaign when violence broke out on the anti-government side. Just one act of violence and the game is restored: "Murder" again becomes "war."

GANDHIAN CONSTITUTION FOR A FREE INDIA

As World War II came to an end, it became clear that Gandhi's dream of driving England out of India was going to succeed, but his dream of avoiding the founding of Englistan was not. Thus while the Constituent Assembly was sanctifying Gandhi as the father of the nation and writing a constitution for India as an ordinary violent state, Gandhi had a different constitutional proposal, from which the Constituent Assembly averted its eyes. The most systematic statement of this proposal was that compiled by Shriman Narayan Agarwal, from various public statements Gandhi had made, into the book *Gandhian Constitution for Free India*.[28]

It is remarkable that this book, which should stand alongside the works of More, Morris, Owen, Fourier, and Kropotkin as a major proposal for an ideal polity, is virtually unknown, difficult to find, and generally brushed aside in works on Gandhi. Perhaps this is because it is so radical that it is unthinkable, which means that people will generally do their best not to think it.

The essence of the proposal is contained in the following simple statement, written in 1947, just before independence: "Independence must begin at the bottom. Thus every village will be a republic or panchayat with full powers."[29]

Admirers of Gandhi who find it difficult or inconvenient to believe he ever said such a thing sometimes avoid the problem by having him say something else. In his *Gandhi's Political Philosophy*, Bikhu Parekh has Gandhi proposing a polity made up of "self-determining communities."[30] Yet Gandhi said "republics." Surely he chose this word carefully, in full awareness of what it implies. A republic is not a "community" or an "administrative unit"; it is a sovereign entity.

Now, Gandhi was fond of saying that India had seven hundred thousand villages. Taken literally, he was proposing that the number of sovereign states in the world would be increased from the something around seventy-six that it was in 1947 to 700,076. If each sent an ambassador to the United Nations, not only would there be no hall or even stadium to hold them, but also the population of New York City would have been increased by almost 10 percent.

But Gandhi's proposal was not a scheme to pack the United Nations. The seven hundred thousand village republics were to be joined in a federation. Village Panchayat presidents would join to form a Taluka Panchayat (about twenty villages), the presidents of these would form a District Panchayat, and on through Provincial and finally to the All-India Panchayat. Presumably it would be the All-India Panchayat that would send an ambassador to the United Nations.

This does not mean that Gandhi accepted the state after all. As he and Agarwal describe it, the organization above the Village Panchayat is analogous to the United Nations—an international body with considerable authority but without sovereignty, and without the right to infringe on the sovereignty of its member states. Agarwal does not use the word "sovereignty," and what he writes on this point is sometimes ambiguous, but in the following passage he makes the point clear enough: "The functions of these higher bodies shall be advisory and not mandatory; they shall guide, advise and supervise, not command the lower Panchayat."[31]

In the dominant Western theory of the state, sovereignty rests with the people, but in practice this is realized mainly as the right to participate in elections. The Gandhian constitution gives popular sovereignty a different structure by placing it not with that vague entity "the people" but rather within a multiplicity of actually existing organizations, the villages. Here popular sovereignty is not the myth by which the state is legitimized but is built into the structure of political society. It is not something that slips out of the people's hands and reappears, monstrously larger, in the capital city; it is there where the people live, where they can hold on to it.

Coming from Gandhi, the idea may seem easily dismissed, but it's worth noting that it is structurally similar to what Hannah Arendt called "the lost treasure of the revolutionary tradition," the small, face-to-face "publics" that (she said) inevitably crop up in revolutionary periods (and did during the American, French, and Russian) and which she called the council system. The only writer she was able to identify who took these councils seriously as a desirable basis for a polity was Thomas Jefferson, who called them, among other things, "elementary republics."[32] According to historian Gordon Wood, after the Jefferson-authored Declaration of Independence became official, social-contract-believing New Hampshire citizens argued that the Declaration had transformed their towns into little sovereign states. While the contract binding them to England had been dissolved, the social contracts binding townspeople to one another were still in force.[33] Perhaps this memory gave Jefferson the image of the sovereign town. It was later in his life that he argued that these "elementary republics" would give each citizen an opportunity to participate in the debates on public matters not just on election day but as part of daily life, giving them a share in—in Arendt's terminology—public freedom and public happiness. Like Gandhi, Jefferson envisioned a polity organized as a "gradation of authorities," with the "little republics" at the bottom, above that the ward, then the county, then the state, and finally the union.[34] Jefferson saw this system as "peaceable," "a nonviolent alternative to his earlier notions about the desirability of recurring revolutions."

Both Jefferson's proposals and the actual appearance of such councils in the revolutionary process (one could add many other examples occurring since Arendt wrote) have been "utterly neglected by statesmen, historians, political theorists and, most importantly, the revolutionary tradition itself."[35] Arendt concluded, "The spectacular success of the party system and the no less spectacular failure of the council system, were both due to the rise of the nation-state, which elevated the one and crushed the other."[36] This generalization fits India's case nicely.

A somewhat different idea to compare with that of Gandhi comes from what Teodor Shanin called the Late Marx. Basing his case mainly on the research of the Japanese historian Wada Haruki, Shanin argued that in his last years, Marx was persuaded by the Narodnik position that it could be possible to build their new society in Russia on the basis of the "primitive communism" that still existed in the village communities there, and thus avoid going through the horrors of industrialization under the violent state.[37] It is surely one of the great ironies of history that Lenin and his fellow Bolsheviks never learned that their master had come to this view—or if any did, they learned it too late. (The letters in which Marx expressed these views came to light only in 1924—but this is not the place, nor am I the person, to pursue this question further.) What matters here is this question: Would the All-India Panchayat have an army?

In his book on the Gandhian constitution, in the section "National Defense," Agarwal writes, "He would like Free India not to maintain any armed defense against foreign aggression. Gandhiji wants India to develop disciplined non-violent power to face invasions bravely and successfully."[38] But then he goes on to quote Gandhi's words from 1920: "Alas! In my *Swaraj* of today there is a room for soldiers. . . . Under *Swaraj*, you and I shall have a disciplined, intelligent, educated police force that would keep order within and fight raiders from without, if by that time I or someone else does not show a better way of dealing with either."[39]

So, which is it? The nonviolent case is helped some by the fact that the "soldiers" are quickly transformed into "police," limited by a series of modifiers ("disciplined, intelligent, educated"), and as we learn later "believers in non-violence." It's true that over the course of his long life, Gandhi wavered on the question of a military. He admired the bravery and discipline of soldiers, and while in South Africa participated in the Zulu war as part of an ambulance corps. It is significant that Agarwal had to dig back to 1920 to find this quotation allowing a much-modified military force. But the question cannot be resolved by searching through Gandhi's one-hundred-volume *Complete Works* for all the times he said there would be soldiers and lining them up against all the times he said there would not. What matters is that a collectivity of sovereign villages organized in the manner described by

Gandhi and Agarwal would be structurally incapable of raising or commanding a national army. To do this, the All-India Panchayat would need the state's right of belligerency. A body with only advisory powers standing over a collectivity of village republics would not have the authority to recruit an army, to command it, or to delegate to it the right to kill people and destroy property. There can be no military without the power to command. Command, and the power to punish disobedience to command, are the essence of military organization, and obtaining the power to command the enemy on pain of death is the object of military action. Moreover, if the All-India Panchayat does not have the power of command, then the people, unlike the people of most countries, will not have been trained in obedience to central command. This would put any invader at great disadvantage. In most wars, if the central command is captured, the war is won. But how would it be possible to conquer seven hundred thousand republics? Where, for example, would one find enough paper on which to write seven hundred thousand surrender instruments? And if we suppose, as Gandhi surely did, that the citizens of each of these republics are trained in Satyagraha, what invader would be so foolish as to catch hold of this porcupine?

GANDHI AND THE ART OF THE POSSIBLE

The works of Thomas More and other authors of plans for ideal polities are read for their theoretical interest; few people see them as proposals worth considering. Gandhi, however, believed that his federation of Panchayat republics was a real possibility for the subcontinent if the leaders of the Congress could only gather the political will to make it so, and was deeply disappointed when they did not. It was his intention not to write a utopian proposal "of theoretical interest" but to propose a working constitution for India. This plan did not presuppose some radical transformation of human nature or giant leap in consciousness to a level heretofore unknown in history. It was rooted in the reality of the Indian village. Here Gandhi was influenced by Henry Sumner Maine's *Village-communities in the East and West*, which described the remarkable degree of self-sufficiency of the traditional village, which in turn was informed by Maine's years living in India.[40]

It probably would have entailed less violent a change in consciousness and custom than what did happen: the founding of the Indian state, and the introduction of the European industrial revolution into India. And probably it also would have avoided the horror of the partition.

Moreover, the puzzle plaguing all utopian proposals—by what agency of change could such a thing ever be brought about?—had a plausible solution. The agency would be Gandhi, or, more accurately, the Gandhi phenomenon:

Gandhi and his supporters in the Congress and in the public. For it had already been proven to the world that, for reasons no one has ever been able fully to explain, this combination of the Congress with Gandhi at its head had the power to transform impossibilities into possibilities and then into accomplished facts. For Gandhi, politics as the art of the possible took on a different meaning. Under his leadership, things hitherto dismissed as impossible in the real world of politics were brought into being. Again and again, people who mocked his "unrealism" were forced to eat crow. Surely this is part of the reason his constitutional proposal inspires a feeling of unease that other utopian proposals do not. For while it is difficult to imagine his constitution being realized in the India of today (except in scattered ashrams), it was imaginable then, or would have been had the leaders of the Congress not deserted Gandhi and opted for an ordinary (violent) state.

Yet if the founding of the Gandhian constitution is hardly imaginable now, shouldn't that transform it into a mere curiosity, without the power to make us feel uneasy? But the very fact that it was a possibility in the recent past upsets an axiom of our political belief: that the (violent) nation-state is inevitable and necessary; that it is not to be doubted; that it has no alternative; that the establishment of the state, including the Indian state, was not a human choice but a destiny (as in Nehru's "tryst with . . . "). The Gandhian constitution forces us to realize that, at that time, it was a choice. It is poignant to think that this shabby, little-known, and lesser-read book on my desk outlines India's road not taken.

HOBBESIAN WAR, RADICAL PEACE

But enough of speculating about what might have happened; it is time to return our attention to what did happen. And what did happen was that the leadership in both the Congress and the Muslim League opted for the modern state structure, resulting directly, as happens so often when the modern state is imposed on a region artificially unified by colonial power, in a demand for partition and horrific communal bloodshed. Gandhi was heartbroken. When the Congress accepted partition, he began speaking obsessively about his death. "What sin," he asked Sardar Patel, "must I have committed that He should have kept me alive to witness these horrors?"[41]

Gandhi had more than one reason to be horrified. For aside from the awfulness of the communal violence itself, it also threatened to bring his political dreams to a catastrophic end. Communal violence was rapidly reducing Indian society to something close to a Hobbesian state of nature, a condition for which, Hobbes had so persuasively argued, state domination is the appropriate solution. Communal violence is not, strictly speaking, a war of each against all, but it is close enough to make the organized and "legitimate" violence of police and armies look like peace by comparison. And that is how the state did react, sending police and the army out to stop the violence with greater violence. Nehru even threatened to bomb Bihar.[42] Faced with the stark fact of communal violence, Gandhi's talk of a nonviolent state began to seem like utter fluff.

Seen in this context, what Gandhi did next was one of the most extraordinary political actions ever undertaken. If the fact of communal violence provided overwhelming justification for the violent state, Gandhi began a one-man campaign to change that fact. Walking from village to village in Noakhali, setting up household with a Muslim comrade in the most riot-torn area of Calcutta, walking again from district to district in rioting Delhi, heedless to the danger to his life, he poured all the powers of his being into persuading people to stop the killing. He met with bitter setbacks and stunning successes. Viceroy Mountbatten, in his note congratulating Gandhi's "miraculous" success in bringing peace to Calcutta, showed that he partly understood what was at stake, but muddled it: "In the Punjab we have 55 thousand soldiers and large-scale rioting on our hands. In Bengal our forces consist of one man, and there is no rioting. As a serving officer, as well as an administrator, may I be allowed to pay my tribute to the one-man boundary force!"[43] But Gandhi was no "boundary force," nor was he seeking only to stop the fighting where the soldiers had failed to do so: He was working to establish a kind of peace that soldiers can never achieve, however successful they may be in stopping overt rioting. In the written pledge that ended his last fast in Delhi, he even insisted that the difference be included as a clause: "We give assurance that all these things will be done by our personal efforts and not with the help of the police or the military."[44] Thus, when he walked from village to village, from district to district, he was struggling to refute the Hobbesian worldview not by making arguments against it but by creating facts that contradict it, creating, that is, a peace that did not depend upon the violent state for its enforcement. Of course, such action is subversive, for actually to create such a peace would be to eliminate the need for the violent state. And that was how Gandhi understood it: His attack on the rioting was also aimed at undermining the "necessity" for state military dominance that the rioting seemed to produce. As he put it in Calcutta, "How nice it looks when soldiers march in step! I am opposed to military power, for it results in killing human beings. There is only one way to vanquish military power, and it is this."[45]

And while he was not able to bring this peace to all of India—without the support of his party, how could he?—his local, partial successes showed that in principle it could be done. Once again, he was transforming impossibilities into possibilities, in this case demonstrating the possibility, even in the most bitterly violent of situations, of establishing a non-Hobbesian peace, peace from the bottom up, what could be called radical peace. At the same time, he was founding, village by village, the essence of his Panchayat Raj Constitution. It was while he was in the midst of this activity that he was assassinated.

THE LAST CONSTITUTION

On the morning of January 30, 1948, Acharya Jugal Kishore, then general secretary of the AICC (All-India Congress Committee), received from Gandhi a proposal for a new constitution for the Congress, which Gandhi had just completed. According to his secretary Pyarelal, Gandhi, though exhausted, had stayed up late the night before to get it done. Gandhi was behaving as though he knew what was coming. That morning he had stopped his helper Manuben from preparing medicine for the evening, saying, "Who knows, what is going to happen before nightfall, or even whether I shall be alive? If at night I am still alive you can easily prepare some then."[46]

The document was a bombshell, or would have been had Nathuram Godse not defused it. Despairing at the sight of what attachment to the state was doing to his beloved Congress, and despairing of the state's capacity to reform, Gandhi proposed that the Congress withdraw from the state altogether and return to the villages.

> Though split into two, India having attained political independence through means devised by the Indian National Congress, the Congress in its present shape and form, i.e., as a propaganda vehicle and parliamentary machine, has outlived its use. India has still to attain social, moral and economic independence in terms of its seven hundred thousand villages, as distinguished from its cities and towns. The struggle for the ascendancy of civil over military power is bound to take place in India's progress towards its democratic goal. It [the Congress] must be kept out of unhealthy competition with political parties and communal bodies. For these and other reasons, the A.I.C.C. resolves to disband the existing Congress organization and flower into a Lok Sevak Sangh [people's service organization] under the following rules. . . . [47]

What follows is a restatement of his long-cherished constitutional model, a tiered system with five-person Panchayats at the base, elected second-level leaders over them, and so on, expanded until it covers all of India. Gandhi's idea seems to have been that if Panchayat Raj could not be established in place of the state, then the situation would move back to what it had been in 1920, when there was nothing for it but to establish Panchayat Raj *within* the state, as a separate authority. From that position, it could devote itself to "constructive work"—build the concrete economic and social base for autonomy in the villages—and at the same time "struggle for the ascendancy of civil over [state] military power."

The idea is stunning. Imagine what would have happened if it had been carried out as Gandhi conceived it. If the Congress, which at that time was almost synonymous with India's political class, had vacated the government and returned to the villages, what a massive shift in power, not lateral but from top to bottom, that would have been. It would have brought about a revolution of a sort never before seen—not the people at the bottom rising up and seizing the state, but the people who have just seized the state walking away from it and joining the people at the bottom. Such a move would not, of course, be without its dangers—the danger, for example, that the offices vacated by Congress members might be quickly occupied by generals and colonels (Gandhi's proposal doesn't say what should be done with the military, except that it should be struggled against). But as a revolutionary model, it is essentially the same as that by which Gandhi hoped to take down the British Raj in 1920. Only this time, its target was the government of independent India, which he and the Congress had just succeeded in establishing—and which to Gandhi looked like Englistan.

It is not likely that many members of the Congress would have found the proposal attractive. But the question was soon moot. Within hours of the moment the proposal was handed to the AICC chairman, its author was dead.

FOUNDING AND SACRIFICE

Sacrifice: The slaughter of an animal or a person (often including the subsequent consumption of it by fire) as an offering to a God or a deity.

On the morning of the penultimate day of his life, Gandhi was visited by Indira Gandhi and her son Rajiv. It was a remarkable last meeting of India's three great modern assassinees. Rajiv, then four, began wrapping flowers around Gandhi's bare ankles and feet, but the old man scolded him and pulled his ear, saying, "You must not do that. One only puts flowers round dead people's feet."[48]

By all accounts, there was something strange about Gandhi's assassination. There is the fact that even though, a full ten days earlier, the police had arrested one of the conspirators when he exploded a bomb at Gandhi's prayer meeting, and the man had talked, they proceeded with remarkable lethargy, and they were somehow unable to track down the others or to prevent the arrested man's fellow assassin from entering the Birla House garden carrying a pistol on January 30. In his biography of Gandhi, Robert Payne, after detailing the inertia of the police, concluded, "There were people in high places who acted as though they had no business interfering with a conspiracy which must be permitted to take its course" and to describe the phenomenon coined "permissive assassination."[49] The person heading the government department most responsible for Gandhi's safety was Home Minister Sardar Patel, who had been one of Gandhi's most devoted disciples and who as the "Iron Man" of the new government most sharply disagreed with him. After the assassination, Patel was accused of "inefficiency," and his colleague Maulana Azad believed that it was this accusation that caused Patel's heart attack two months later, which eventually led to his death.[50] It is not my purpose here to go through the evidence attesting to the strangeness of the assassination; that has been done elsewhere. Ashis Nandy, in his elegant essay on the subject, argued that it was Gandhi's challenge to the deep structure of mainstream Hinduism that made him intolerable to a large part of that community, even including those who, with political correctness, continued to hail him as Mahatma and father of the nation. The assassin Nathuram Godse, Nandy said, far from being a marginal outsider, "was a representative of the centre of the society that Gandhi was trying to turn into the periphery."[51] I have no quarrel with this thesis but only wish to point out that it does not fully account for the timing of the assassination, namely, the moment at which the state was being newly founded, and while the Constitution was still being debated. If there was, as Nandy argued, a conflict between Gandhi and middle-class Hinduism on the issue of that class's domination of society and on the role and meaning of womanhood, that must have been an ongoing, if hidden, conflict going back to the 1920s or before. But if there was a conflict between the father of the nation and the emerging state, wouldn't that have been a national crisis that, even if largely unconscious, demanded an immediate solution?

The subject of Gandhi's death had become a public topic long before the assassination. People were shouting "Death to Gandhi!" or, when he went on his fasts to death, "Let Gandhi die!" Bricks and stones were thrown at him, and some came close. But perhaps the person most obsessed with the subject of Gandhi's death was Gandhi. He continuously talked about it, sometimes in a mood of depression ("What sin must I have committed that He should have kept me alive to witness these horrors?"), sometimes enigmatically ("It might be that it would be more valuable to humanity for me to die"), sometimes as the apotheosis of his life ("If someone shot at me and I received his bullet in my bare chest without a sigh and with Rama's name on my lips, only then should you say that I was a true Mahatma").[52]

But not only that; it was Gandhi who forced his death on the attention of the nation by making it a public issue. When he went on one of his "fasts to death," the last one of which he said was "directed against everybody," no one doubted his readiness to die if his conditions were not met.[53] In a remarkable passage, Rajni Kothari wrote that at the end of Gandhi's life, Gandhi carried out three "heroic acts": his pilgrimage through Noakhali, his "fast to death" against the government in Delhi, "and finally being shot to death by a fanatic Hindu."[54] Gandhi's assassination is characterized as one of his "acts"; it is as if he had flung himself at the bullets, rather than the bullets coming to him.

Consider the situation of those who were directly engaged in the building of the new Indian state. The chief leaders among them were some of Gandhi's closest associates and disciples. By all indications, they genuinely loved him. Though he had no official position in the government, they consulted with him at every opportunity and even had what amounted to cabinet meetings in his presence. At the same time, he was the most maddening obstacle to their project. Again and again, he made proposals and even demands that flew in the face of state-power logic: Give the whole government to the Muslim League; remove the police and army from rioting areas; give Pakistan its share of the national treasury, despite the war (this demand enforced by the abovementioned last "fast to death"); on and on. Even if they never allowed the word "death" to escape their lips, surely they must have often found themselves wishing he would just . . . go away.

Of the Hindu middle class, Nandy wrote, "If not their conscious minds, their primitive selves were demanding his blood."[55] As the sharpest of political observers have noted, from ancient times it has not been unusual for political foundings to be accompanied by blood sacrifice. For Freud, founding takes place through patricide (the sons murder the father-king), for Augustine and Arendt it is fratricide (Cain killed Abel, Romulus killed Remus), for Machiavelli—but let us look at Machiavelli a bit closer. How would Machiavelli have read this story?

One can find a clue in the tale told by Livy of how, after Brutus drove out the Tarquin monarchy, Brutus's sons participated in a conspiracy to bring it back. Brutus had them condemned to death, and stood witness to their execution, his face, Livy tells us, showing both his agony as a father and his grim determination as head of state. In his "Discourses on Livy," Machiavelli mentions this story and judges Brutus's action as "not only useful, but necessary."[56]

He explains, "Every student of ancient history well knows that any change of government, be it from a republic to a tyranny, or from a tyranny to a republic, must necessarily be followed by some terrible punishment of the enemies of the existing state of things. And whoever makes himself tyrant of a state and does not kill Brutus, or whoever restores liberty to a state and does not immolate his sons, will not maintain himself in his position long."[57]

This is the primal political sacrifice, which Machiavelli took to be essential to the task of foundation. It is not simply a matter of purging the state of its present and potential enemies, though that is part of it. At a deeper level, it is also a means of driving into the consciousness of the people *what the state is*: not only a violent institution that will not hesitate to use violence to establish itself and to protect itself, but also one whose violence is enshrouded in the mystical cloak of sovereignty, which places the state outside the realm of human judgment and gives its agents the authority to carry out acts that would not be permitted to ordinary human beings. Thus it will not allow itself to be interfered with by ties of friendship, love, or blood: When you act in the name of the state, you must be ready to destroy your friend, your father, your sister, or your son.[58]

For Machiavelli, it is not enough simply to explain this in words. It must be acted out in bloody ritual sacrifice. And for the purposes of the sacrifice, the more intimate the victim, the better.

It will be objected that Nathuram Godse was no agent of the state but an assassin acting outside the law, who was tried and executed by the state for his crime. This is true, so for the above thesis to apply to his act, it would be necessary to show at least (1) that Godse saw himself as acting in the name of the state, and (2) that there were those among the agents of the state who, if not positively demanding Gandhi's blood, were troubled enough by his existence that they could not bring themselves to take strong measures against the one who was coming to shed it. As for the first, Godse's words were clear, and even eloquent. Godse, like most assassins, was depicted by many as a demented fanatic, but if you read his own account of his action and his reasons for it, he appears as intelligent, articulate, clear headed, patriotic, and courageous. (According to all accounts, before shooting the father of the nation, he put his hands together in respectful greeting; according to his own account, after the shooting, he raised his hand with the pistol into the air and shouted, "Police!") Nandy insists that Godse "more than any other person" knew what he was doing.[59] Surely, then, we ought to take Godse's words seriously. In his statement in English to the court, Godse said the following:

> Briefly speaking, I thought to myself and foresaw that I shall be totally ruined and the only thing that I could expect from the people would be nothing but hatred and that I shall have lost all my honour even more valuable than my life, if I were for [*sic*] kill Gandhiji. But at the same time I felt that the Indian politics in the absence of Gandhiji would surely be practical, able to retaliate, and would be powerful with armed forces. No doubt my own future would be ruined but the nation would be saved.[60]

He wrote that it gave him "complete satisfaction" that everything had turned out just as he had expected. For example:

> The problem of the State of Hyderabad which had been unnecessarily delayed and postponed has been rightly solved by our Government by the use of armed force after the demise of Gandhiji. The present Government of the remaining India is seen taking the course of practical politics. The Home Member [Home Minister Patel?] is said to have expressed the view that the nation must be possessed of armies fully equipped with modern arms and fighting machinery. While giving out such expressions he does say that such a step would be in keeping with the ideals of Gandhiji. He may say so for his satisfaction.[61]

With Gandhi gone, the government was now able to arm itself without reserve, and to use its military in a "practical," that is, realpolitik, manner. Godse was not surprised that government spokesmen now claimed that such actions were "in keeping with the ideals of Gandhiji"; he knew that had Gandhi been still alive, they would not have been able to say such a thing. Must we not admit that, from Godse's point of view, the assassination was a crashing success?

As for the second point, while there is no decisive evidence (only Godse held a smoking gun), there is plenty of circumstantial evidence, much of which has already been mentioned. Given the terrible double bind they had been in, the impossible contradiction between the demands of raison d'état and the demands of their beloved leader, who can doubt that, entwined within the turmoil of mixed emotions they must have felt after the murder was done, there was also an overwhelming feeling of release? Now they could get on with the business they had set themselves, build a powerfully armed state, send the troops out against enemies domestic and foreign, transform Panchayat Raj into "local administration," tell the people that Gandhi would have approved of it all, and build monuments to him, without the old crank interfering at every step. Surely from their standpoint, his assassin was a well-named Godse(nd).

Machiavelli drew from the story of Brutus what he believed to be a general law of politics: If you wish to found a tyranny, you must kill Brutus; if you wish to found a republic, you must kill his sons. Had Machiavelli been alive to witness the events in India at the middle of the twentieth century, would he not have formulated another, more fundamental, general law? That is, if you wish to found a violent state, you must kill Gandhi. By "violent state," I do not mean here a tyranny, or a militaristic state, or a warmongering state. I mean a perfectly ordinary state, one that fits Max Weber's definition as an organization claiming a monopoly of legitimate violence. Godse was not trying to found some kind of extremist or fundamentalist state; he claimed to be quite satisfied with the Indian state as it evolved under Nehru and Patel after Gandhi's death, and believed that it was his action that had made it possible. So he for one agreed with the above general law, and acted according to it.

Arguably, Gandhi also would have understood this general law. Certainly as it became increasingly clear what kind of state independent India was going to become, he spoke constantly of his waning influence, describing himself as a "back number" and (in a remarkable choice of words) a "spent bullet," and, as mentioned above, in a variety of ways expressed a wish to die, and even a wish to be killed. He genuinely loved as his own sons the men who were building the new state; he said again and again that he didn't want to interfere with their work, but being who he was, he could not stop himself. Thus, his "fast to death" to force the government to honor its obligation to hand over to Pakistan its share of the national treasury—from the standpoint of state reasoning, absurd behavior in time of war—can be seen as a pure manifestation of the above general law: "You wish to engage in that kind of realpolitik? Over my dead body!" In any event, the government backed down and paid the money. It is said that this was the incident that persuaded Nathuram Godse to carry out the assassination.

In what Robert Payne described as an "irony" of history, Gandhi's funeral was arranged by the Indian military.[62] In his chapter titled "The Burning," Payne described the arrangements. The body was to be placed on top of a huge weapons carrier and pulled by two hundred soldiers, sailors, and airmen. "Four thousand soldiers, a thousand airmen, a thousand policemen, and a hundred sailors would march in front of or behind the weapons carrier, and in addition there would be a cavalry escort from the bodyguards of the Governor General." Air force planes were sent to fly over and drop roses.[63] Payne wrote, "There were many who wondered whether the government had acted wisely in ordering the Defense Ministry to take command of the funeral."[64] But to Nathuram Godse, the arrangements must have seemed perfect beyond his wildest dreams. While a million people watched, the military carried Mahatma Gandhi off to be burned. Payne said the procession resembled a "triumph." Indeed.

It is said that after the cremation there was "a dramatic cessation of communal riots throughout the country."[65] One wonders, were the rioting elements shamed, or sated?

NOTES

1. Hannah Arendt, "On Violence," in *Crisis of the Republic* (San Diego, New York, London: Harvest HBJ [Orig. New York Review of Books, 1971]), 107.
2. Arendt, "On Violence," 107.
3. Arendt, "On Violence," 112.

4. Gene Sharp, *The Politics of Nonviolent Action* (Boston: Porter Sargent, 1973), 584.

5. Hannah Arendt, *Eichmann in Jerusalem: A Report on the Banality of Evil* (New York: Viking, 1963), 171.

6. Arendt, *Eichmann*, 171.

7. Arendt, *Eichmann*, 175.

8. Arendt, "On Violence," 155.

9. Arendt, "On Violence," 143.

10. Arendt, "On Violence," 143.

11. Niccolo Machiavelli, "The Discourses on Livy," in *The Prince and the Discourses*, trans. Luigi Ricci (New York: The Modern Library, 1950), 171.

12. Louis Fischer, *The Life of Mahatma Gandhi* (New York: Harper and Row, 1950), 473; Manubehn Gandhi, *Last Glimpses of Bapu* (Delhi: Agarwala, 1962), 297–8.

13. Gandhi, *Hind Swaraj*, 24.

14. Gandhi, *Hind Swaraj*, 34.

15. Gandhi, *Hind Swaraj*, 35.

16. M. K. Gandhi, "The Doctrine of the Sword" (*Young India*, August 11, 1920), in *Collected Works of Mahatma Gandhi*, vol. 21, electronic book version (New Delhi, Publications Division), 134. For a critique of what I call the "common-sense position," see Joan V. Bondurant, *Conquest of Violence: The Gandhian Philosophy of Conflict* (Berkeley: UC Press, 1971). Bondurant sees *satyagraha* not only as a tactic but also as a practice of self-realization. She writes that while there is no need for everyone to try to adopt all of Gandhi's ascetic practices, it is important to understand the difference between *satyagraha* and *duragraha*, the latter defined as "symbolic violence" (Bondurant, *Conquest*, ix). She examines five of the well-known movements of Gandhi's time to identify those that "do not measure up in essentials to the genuine Gandhian technique" (Bondurant, *Conquest*, 42). The conditions she sets down for qualifying as "genuine" are pretty severe.

17. M. K. Gandhi, "Interview to Nirmal Kumar Bose" (*The Hindustani Times*, October 17, 1935), in *Collected Works of Mahatma Gandhi*, vol. 65, 318.

18. Arendt, "On Violence."

19. M. K. Gandhi, "Lord Amphill" (*Indian Opinion*, June 29, 1907), in *Collected Works of Mahatma Gandhi*, vol. 7.

20. M. K. Gandhi, "Speech at a Mass Meeting" (*Indian Opinion*, August 23, 1908), in *Collected Works of Mahatma Gandhi*, vol. 9, 88.

21. M. K. Gandhi, "Message to Satyagraha Agriculturalists" (Gujarati, Mahadevbhaini Diary, vol. IV, April 17, 1918), in *Collected Works of Mahatma Gandhi*, vol. 26, 433.

22. M. K. Gandhi, "Letter to J.B. Petit, June 16, 1951," in *Collected Works of Mahatma Gandhi*, vol. 15, 17.

23. M. K. Gandhi, "How to Finance the Movement" (*Young India*, January 12, 1921), in *Collected Works of Mahatma Gandhi*, vol. 22, 204.

24. M. K. Gandhi, "Congress Constitution" (Gujarati, Narajiran, March 20, 1921), in *Collected Works of Mahatma Gandhi*, vol. 22, 447.

25. Gandhi, "Congress Constitution," 475.

26. Aleksander Smolar, "Towards 'Self-limiting Revolution': Poland, 1970–89," in *Civil Resistance and Power Politics*, eds. Adam Roberts and Timothy Garton Ash (Oxford: Oxford University Press, 2009), 132–3.

27. Bernard Fall, *The Two Viet-nams: A Political and Military Analysis*, revised edition (New York: Praeger, 1965).

28. Shriman Narayan Agarwal, *Gandhian Constitution for Free India* (Allahabad: Kitabistan, 1946). Reprinted by Atlantic Books in 1998, and under the title *The Gandhian Plan* by Forgotten Books in 2012. All three seem to be out of print.

29. M. K. Gandhi, "Independence" (*Panchgani*, July 21, 1946; *Harijan*, July 28, 1946), in *Collected Works of Mahatma Gandhi*, vol. 91, 325.

30. Bikhu Parekh, *Gandhi's Political Philosophy* (Notre Dame: University of Notre Dame Press, 1989), 114.

31. Agarwal, *Gandhian Constitution*, 85.

32. Hannah Arendt, *On Revolution* (New York: Viking Press, 1963), 252, 254.

33. Gordon S. Wood, *The Creation of the American Republic* (Chapel Hill: University of North Carolina Press, 1969), 288.

34. Arendt, *On Revolution*, 258.

35. Arendt, *On Revolution*, 252.

36. Arendt, *On Revolution*, 251.

37. Teodor Shanin, *Late Marx and the Russian Road* (New York: Monthly Review Press, 1983).

38. Agarwal, *Gandhian Constitution*, 109.

39. Agarwal, *Gandhian Constitution*, 111.

40. Henry Sumner Maine, *Village-communities in the East and West: Six Lectures Delivered at Oxford to Which Are Added Other Lectures, Addresses and Essays by Sir Henry Sumner Maine* (New York: Henry Holt, 1889). Gandhi acknowledged his debt to Maine: "Maine has said that India was a congeries of village republics. The towns were then subservient to the village. They were the emporia for the surplus village products and beautiful manufactures. This is the skeleton of my picture to serve as a pattern for Independent India" ("Speech at Meeting of Deccan Princes" [*The Hindu*, August 1, 1946], in *Collected Works of Mahatma Gandhi*, vol. 85).

41. Pyarelal, *Mahatma Gandhi, vol. 10, The Last Phase*, Part II (Ahmedabad: Navajivan Publishing House, 1958), in *Collected Works of Mahatma Gandhi*, vol. 97, 382.

42. Fischer, *Life of Mahatma Gandhi*, 447.

43. Robert Payne, *The Life and Death of Mahatma Gandhi* (New York: Dutton, 1969), 565.

44. Manubehn Gandhi, *The Miracle of Calcutta* (Ahmedabad: Navajivan Publishing House, 1951), 50.

45. Manubehn Gandhi, *Miracle*, 50.

46. Pyarelal, *The Last Phase*, 767.

47. M. K. Gandhi, "Draft Constitution of Congress" (*Harijan*, February 5, 1948), in *Collected Works of Mahatma Gandhi*, vol. 98, 333.

48. Krishna Nehru Huthseeing, *We Nehrus* (New York: Holt, Rinehart & Winston, 1967), 222, quoted in Payne, *Life and Death*, 577.

49. Payne, *Life and Death*, 630.

50. Maulana Abul Kalam Azad, *India Wins Freedom: An Autobiographical Narrative* (Bombay: Orient Longmans, 1959), 225.

51. Ashis Nandy, "Final Encounter: The Politics of the Assassination of Gandhi," in *Exiled at Home* (Delhi: Oxford University Press, 1988), 76.

52. Vincent Sheehan, *Lead, Kindly Light* (New York: Random House, 1949), 183, quoted in Payne, *Life and Death*, 576.

53. Manubehn Gandhi, *Last Glimpses*, 297–8.

54. Rajni Kothari, *Politics in India* (New Delhi: Orient Longmans, 1970), 75.

55. Nandy, "Final Encounter," 91, n. 35.

56. Machiavelli, *Discourses*, 405.

57. Machiavelli, *Discourses*, 405.

58. Here I stick with the male gender intentionally. For whatever reason, it does seem that the sacrificial victim needs to be male. Joan of Arc may be the one great exception.

59. Nandy, "Final Encounter," 87.

60. Nathuram Godse, *May it Please Your Honor* (Delhi: Surya Bharti Prakashan, 1987), 154–5.

61. Godse, *May it Please*, 155–6.

62. Payne, *Life and Death*, 593.1.

63. Payne, *Life and Death*, 594.

64. Payne, *Life and Death*, 59.

65. Kothari, *Politics in India*, 75.

Chapter 13

Final Rumination

If the state is to survive, those who are ruled over must always acquiesce *in the authority that is claimed by the rulers of the day.*

—Max Weber

PEACE AS THE HUMAN THING

If war is hell, what is peace?

One answer, as we have seen, is that peace is when hell takes a holiday. A happy time indeed—but we know the demons will be back. If, as both Hobbes and Kant argued, war is the rule, then peace is the exception—a situation that must be artificially constructed and maintained. The artifice is fragile; a few missteps, and we fall back into our natural mode of living: war.

Must we replace hell with heaven then, and behave like saints? I know that for many people, religious faith is the key to peace. I respect that belief, when it is followed consistently. But as I have tried to remind readers in this book, religious faith is easily put to service as *jus ad bellum*. When religious faith is joined with "the right of legitimate violence," the result can be monstrous. The desire for peace is a secular desire, growing out of the human condition and grounded in secular common sense. It is not something we need to have explained to us by gods, nor is it something that the gods (as we variously imagine them) have been especially concerned about or diligent in explaining to us; peace is not included in the Ten Commandments. This is one way of reading the story told in the Old and New Testaments. In the Old Testament, while Yahweh was observing Earth from the safety of heaven, he was more a war god than a peacemaker, the very embodiment of legitimate violence. As the story goes, it was only after he decided, bravely, to take on human form, and to experience for himself things he could never experience as the *athanatos* God—most notably, fear of death—that he came to be called the Prince of Peace. This part of the story began in the Old Testament, not the New. It was Isaiah who, when he prophesied that "for unto us a child is born," gave that child the title Prince of Peace, apparently understanding that the experience of walking on the earth in a mortal body, and of being prepared for this by the mother who would raise him, would enable the Deity to appreciate the value that peace has for mortals (Isaiah 9:6).

To understand the value of peace, we need neither threats from hell nor instruction from heaven. Living as mortals on earth will do. The desire for peace is a human thing. Let's put it more strongly: It's *the* human thing.

Here I am returning to Gandhi's insight, mentioned in the introduction of this book. For Gandhi, that most people are nonviolent most of the time is proved by the fact that the human race is not extinct. And this survival is made possible by countless nonviolent acts. We don't think of them as "nonviolent" because they are not "negations of violence"; they are just the way things get done. Put differently, we don't think of them as nonviolence because they aren't a "not-doing" but rather a "doing": talking, listening, cooperating, bonding, teaching, apologizing, forgetting, ignoring, promising, thanking, forgiving, respecting, deferring, compromising, persuading, negotiating, trading (and perhaps also, less charmingly, deceiving, dissembling, evading, waffling, etc.)—the list (of which the above is only a small part) encompasses just about all the actions that human beings carry out that, taken together, we call "society." (Someone will ask, Shouldn't "loving" be included in this list? But the common characteristic of the items on this list is that they don't require love; they are actions that we can and do carry out even with people we don't particularly like. As for love, the list is a pretty good list of the actions lovers also need to continue to carry out if they want that love to last.)

Recognizing this is not enough to persuade us that violence is utterly against our nature, but it does remind us that however violently we may sometimes act, violence is an exception; for every violent act, there are, as it were, behind and beneath it countless not-violent behaviors that enable us to talk, think, learn, work, and relate to other human beings. Nonviolence is not something with which we are unfamiliar; it's what we mostly do. We are members of a peace-seeking, peace-dependent species.

This is the world picture brought into view by positing peace as the Original Position. We are reminded of the fact that, as every military drill instructor knows, even the most anger-driven recruit must be radically changed if he or she is to become an effective professional killer—and that many who have successfully completed this basic training and are sent into real combat spend the rest of their lives struggling with the resulting trauma.

But while violence may be the exception, there is still way too much of it, and Satyagraha is a method for consciously and deliberately dealing with that. Here Gandhi's distinction between Satyagraha for "saints and rishis" and that for ordinary people is useful. By taking the latter commonsense position, we can avoid being entrapped in

THE WHAT-IF GAME

There are people who, when encountering a person who for ethical reasons will not use violence under any circumstances, become stridently anxious to think up hypothetical situations—some wonderfully ingenious—designed to make the pacifist position look monstrous. The starting point is generally, "What if somebody is trying to rape your sister?" (to which the answer is, "I'd get in between"), but sometimes the situations get quite elaborate: "What if you see someone about to push a nuclear button that will destroy the world, and there is a high-powered rifle at your side; will you refuse to shoot?"—that kind of thing. Absolute pacifists may have trouble talking their way out of these dead-end situations, but a commonsense peace-lover should have no difficulty in picking up a board and knocking the rapist in the head or shooting the madman before he pushes the button. Or rather, "no difficulty" might be an exaggeration. A gentlehearted person may find it difficult to bash the rapist or even more to shoot the unsuspecting madman, and may have nightmares about it later, but will still accept that it was the best thing to do in that situation. The questioner wants to believe that once you have allowed violence in the most extreme case then the game is up, and you have admitted it for all the other cases. Whether that is true for the saints I will leave for the saints to worry about, but for the commonsense peace-lover, it is not a problem: For her or him, there is no need to see a contradiction between smacking the rapist with a heavy object and refusing to go to war.

NOTHING ALWAYS WORKS

But if the effectiveness of Gandhi's method of noncooperation can be explained by India's situation—the British Raj required India's cooperation—this raises the question of whether there are situations in which such methods would not be effective. Certainly if "cooperation" is understood in the broadest sense, it is hard to think of a situation of domination that does not depend at least in part on the cooperation of the dominated. It may be labor power, surplus value, military service, votes, taxes, obedience to oppressive laws, belief in religions or ideologies, the various obedient and servile behaviors that support people in dominating positions and persuade them that they really are "great," or failing that, at least generate the consent that persuades them that their power is legitimate. In these and similar cases, collectively refusing cooperation is depriving the dominator of real power.

This presupposes an established system of domination, but what about invasion? The answer implied in the Gandhian Constitution is that if a country is organized and trained in Satyagraha, nothing can be gained from invading it; rather, the invasion will turn out to be a great trouble, expense, and profitless burden, and an invader that realizes this in time will give up the idea, while one that doesn't will learn soon enough and withdraw quickly. Of course, this would require a high degree of national organization and training. But so does war.

But (another what-if) what about a situation in which the invader is not aiming to dominate and exploit the people, but rather either to steal their land and drive them off it, or worse, to eliminate them from the world for religious or racist reasons?

The example of Nazi-occupied Denmark given above was such a case. The Nazis were not mainly seeking the Jews' labor power. Although the Nazis were willing to use it, their main project was to rid the world of the Jews. But to achieve that in the real situation of Denmark, they required the cooperation of both the Danes and the Jews. They needed the Danes to turn over the Jews to them, and they needed the Jews to stay dutifully in their homes and await their incarceration. Neither cooperated, and as Arendt put it, when confronted by this kind of courage and principle, many of the Nazis saw their Nazi resolve melt "like butter in the sun." Even against Nazis, nonviolent resistance has been effective and can be again.

The response to this may be yes, sometimes, but sometimes not. To which all one can say is, "Of course." This is not the abstract world of ideal types but the real world of politics, where there is no such thing as a strategy that always works. Particularly notorious for its failure rate is warfare. In each war, where there is a winner there must also be a loser, which places the average odds of winning at fifty-fifty—not good at all. But worse yet, there are many wars—especially recently—in which there are no winners and no prospect of one emerging, if winning means achieving your war aims. So the fact that nonviolent action might not succeed does not distinguish it from war, threats of war, sanctions, diplomacy, or any other method used in international politics.

Still, it can't be denied that there might arise situations that will cause the most peacefully inclined people to take up arms. To repeat, this is the real world; who can say, who can guarantee, that such situations will never appear? As this book is not written from the standpoint of absolute pacifism, there is no call here to make an ethical critique in advance of all such decisions, especially as all possible situations cannot be known. What can be said, however, is that *the decision to take up arms will always come with a price*. First, there is the price of going to war that everyone knows about, or ought to: the suffering of battle, the wounds and deaths, the damage to the spirit that may follow veterans and civilian survivors to the grave, the often years of impoverishment after the war ends. These are risks that anyone going to war needs to be ready to take. But aside from these, there is the "you can't get there from here" problem. A genuinely peaceful society cannot be achieved by the method of war, even if you win, which you might not. War is the robber-band solution, and war re-empowers the robber band. The level of suspicion, rage, and hatred, and probably racism, in your country will rise, human rights will be curtailed, and the military, which carried out the war, will rise in prestige and, quietly or noisily, begin planning and training for the next war. The peace achieved by this method will be the one called "the time between wars," more bitterly "hell's week off."

But if war seems in some situations the only solution, it is usually war, or threat of war, that has created those situations. This bears repeating: War *creates* situations in which war becomes "unavoidable," or transforms situations that could be negotiated into war situations (e.g., the first world war spawned the second). "Escalation" is not just a matter of armaments and threats. It is a process that takes place in societies and in individual spirits. It transforms peaceable people into warmongers and soldiers, foreigners into enemies, dutiful soldiers into serial killers, and friends and relatives of the serially killed into righteous avengers. War creates itself out of thin air, pulls itself out of a hat, is a self-caused phenomenon. War is the original self-fulfilling prophecy: Shout "WAR!" and there will be war.

Nonviolent resistance has the power to break that cycle. It is not simply "a method that works in some situations"; it is a method for *creating situations in which it can work*. As I wrote earlier, Satyagrahis, by refusing to become combatants in a war, change the status of those attacking them from "soldiers" to "murderers." This doesn't guarantee that no one will be victimized, but in the long run, the use of intentional nonviolent resistance that is spreading around the world not only is effective in certain situations and locations but also is, slowly but surely, creating situations and locations where it is respected. In this sense, the intentionally nonviolent protest movements around the world, taken together, amount to a continuation of Gandhi's experiments with truth, and of his project of establishing peace not from the top by diplomats and politicians but on the ground.

TRAGEDY AND PROPHECY

In chapter 2, I touch on Max Weber's "Politics as a Vocation," originally a lecture to students. In it, he vividly describes "the tragedy in which all action is ensnared, political action above all."[1] By "tragedy" here he doesn't mean simply "likely to end unhappily" but rather that anyone who wishes both to live an ethical life and to bring some actual good into this world must confront the fact that "ethics" itself is divided into two "irreconcilably opposed" forms, between which one must make one's way. And each of these, carried out in real action, can turn into what, from the standpoint of the other, amounts to a horror. The end point of the ethic of the saint is expressed in the aphorism "*Fiat iustitia, et pereat mundus* (Let there be justice, though the world perish)." The ethic of the political actor leads to the notorious "the end justifies the means." Weber wants to disabuse the young students of any naive notion that in the political vocation, one can achieve ethical ends through the exclusive use of ethical means. The working out of cause and effect in society is blind to ethical considerations: Sometimes well-intentioned actions have horrendous results, while sometimes acts terrible in themselves bring about desirable results. The mature political actor, he argues, must have the grit to bear this contradiction, and the courage and honesty to take responsibility for the real effects of what he or she has done.

This is discussed in more detail in chapter 2 and needs no further elaboration here. But I do wish to suggest some qualifications. The first is a qualification made by Weber himself. While his essay seems to present this ethical dilemma as an unshakable aspect of the human condition, at the very beginning he says that while "politics" can refer to the "policies" of all sorts of social institutions and organizations, or even of individuals, "today we shall consider only the leadership, or the exercise of influence on the leadership, of a *political* organization, in other words a *state*"[2] (emphasis in original). This is followed by his celebrated definition of the state as the organization that (successfully) claims a monopoly of legitimate violence. Deliberately left out of this analysis is the vast body of human activities that, as Gandhi pointed out in *Hind Swaraj*, are nonviolent because they have nothing to do with violence, and yet can effectively generate real power.

And the main body of Weber's essay is devoted to demonstrating the historicity of the state, showing how it evolved from other political forms through a combination of intention and accident, which means that the state can (and surely someday will) evolve into something else. But he is not, in this essay, concerned with speculating about that "something else." He is seeking to make young people aware of the nature of the political careers that lie before them "today," which, of course, means political careers in the context of the state.

Not just "the state" but the German state, only months after Germany's defeat in the Great War. The country was in turmoil, violence was rampant, the government was shaky, the future was uncertain (inspiring Carl Schmitt to write essays about the state of exception). One can appreciate the intensity with which Weber sought to make his young listeners understand the severity of what they would be getting into should they decide on political careers in that country at that time. But in disabusing them of the idea that one can pursue a political career and still avoid all unethical behavior, he sometimes goes a little overboard. For example: "Anyone who wishes to act in accordance with ethic of the Gospel should abstain from going on strike—for strikes are a form of coercion. Instead he should join the company unions."[3]

This is not a slip. Throughout the essay, "violence," "power," and "coercion" are spoken of as though they are synonyms. Give up violence and you have given up all hope of acting powerfully in the world. This is Weber's fatal error, and it is an error of fact. It is simply not true that when you refuse to use violence, you render yourself powerless. The strike is one of the clearest examples of nonviolent power. It is one of the forms that the strategy of noncooperation can take, along with boycotts, civil disobedience, draft refusal, and resignation from not only company unions but all institutions designed to organize cooperation with the oppressor. These actions, as Gandhi showed, are not "the strategy of the weak" at all but rather generate power in its most elemental form by undermining, disassembling, and usurping the power of the dominator. Of course, Weber, one of the greatest analysts of political and social power, understood that power is created and sustained by consent and cooperation. As I mention in chapter 1, at the very beginning of "Politics as a Vocation," he states this clearly: "If the state is to survive, those who are ruled over must always *acquiesce* in the authority that is claimed by the rulers of the day"[4] (emphasis in original). This is the same insight as Gandhi's, but where Gandhi saw it as the latent power in the hands of "those who are ruled over" to refuse this "acquiescence" and force the state to change or even bring it down, Weber focuses on the means rulers use to prevent that from happening. From this comes one of Weber's central themes, his justly famous analysis of the three sorts of authority: traditional, charismatic, and legal. Looking at the same phenomenon—political authority—Gandhi studied and experimented with the ways it could be destroyed, while Weber studied the ways by which it is maintained. Despite his understanding that domination is built on acquiescence, Weber also writes that "in politics, the decisive means is the use of force."[5] Thus, people who have committed themselves to nonviolence have disempowered themselves altogether. He gives the example of the American Quakers, who "were unable to take up arms in defense of their ideals, even though it was those ideals that were being defended in that war [the war of independence]."[6] But it is simply not true that armed struggle is the only effective way that colonial domination can be resisted, as the Indian Congress demonstrated.

In "Politics as a Vocation," the word "tragedy" appears several times. Partly the essay describes a tragedy allegedly built into the human condition: There is no way a human being can satisfy both the ethic that requires us to avoid all sin and the ethic that requires us to seek to make the world a better place. This may be a fixed truth, but the essay also describes another tragedy, told in the form of a story: the story of the historical development of the state, and its gradual success in monopolizing legitimate ("believed to be legitimate," as Weber puts it) violence. The dominance of this organization may not be the cause of the dilemma Weber has described, but it has made it far more destructive than it need be. The notion that either we accept the notion of legitimate violence or we are powerless—either we fight using "satanic powers" or we don't fight at all—gave us the blood-spattered twentieth century and is now giving us the blood-spattered twenty-first.

A decade and a half before "Politics as a Vocation," in 1904–5, Weber published a different version of the same tragedy, the process of desacralization that gave us the capitalist industrial state. *The Protestant Ethic and the Spirit of Capitalism* is the story of how the ascetic spirit of early Protestantism evolved into the acquisitive work ethic that became the engine of capitalism. In perhaps his most famous passage, he wrote, "the care for external goods" should have been "like a light cloak, which can be thrown off at any moment. But fate decreed that the cloak should become an iron cage."[7] In his own time, Weber could imagine no escape from this cage, though in the future, he suggested, perhaps "new prophets will arise."[8]

The trouble with prophets, as Weber knew from his studies of ancient Judaism, is that they are usually ignored. Or even when they are celebrated as prophets, the hardest parts of their messages are evaded. Just a few years after Weber wrote these words, in 1909, Gandhi, native of a country then colonized and ruled by the inventor of "the spirit of capitalism," wrote in *Hind Swaraj* that he believed it was still possible for India to refuse to be dominated by that spirit and to avoid being transformed into "Englistan"—in short, to stay out of the cage. During the years that Weber was preparing his massive study of Indian religion and also developing his theory of the types of authority, Gandhi, with the help of Indian religion, was carrying out his experiments in noncooperation and civil disobedience, and effectively undermining the authority of what had been the most powerful empire in history.

Unbeknownst to Weber, the "new prophets" had already started to arise. If they were noticed at all, they were dismissed as caring only for their own souls and giving up the fight for a better world—a false charge, certainly.

Their message had nothing to do with giving up the fight but rather was based on the discovery that there is another, more effective way to fight, a way that has the potential to carry us to places violent struggle can never get us to.

In the context of today's world, radical peace is difficult to imagine either as a collection of peaceful villages founded at the bottom or as an international organization established by treaty at the top. Treaties are fine, preferable to wars, and worth working to achieve. What they give us is breathing space, precious indeed but which (so far, anyway) always comes to an end. Perhaps someday in the future a super treaty will be achieved and a different kind of peace will be inaugurated. But in the world as it is structured today, the most radical form of peace is neither a static model nor a deal struck among heads of state. Rather it is action, radical because it is action: not wishful thinking, but action that has real results: peacemaking. Peaceful resistance is not new in history, but the method of conscious, intentional, collective nonviolent resistance—noncooperation, civil disobedience, draft resistance, and so on—is something new. I repeat, these methods are not miraculous; they do not succeed in all situations: There is no such thing as a method that always works. But the particular character of these methods is that they have the power to change unpromising situations into situations in which these methods can be effective. In a large and increasing number of countries around the world, the method of nonviolent resistance is being adopted, and governments are finding it more difficult (though not impossible) to use violence to put these movements down. In this way, Gandhi's "experiments" are being continued, authority/legitimacy is slowly but steadily being transferred from the state to the grass roots, and territories of peace are being established. These territories are not all idyllic; some are scenes of bitter struggles. That's another thing we can learn from Gandhi's movement: "Peace" is not all gentle smiles and sweet words. It includes anger, tears, harsh language, disobedience, and sometimes physical pain and jail sentences. But let's give Weber the last word, only substituting for his word "politics" the word "peace."

> [Peace] means a slow, powerful drilling through hard boards.... It is absolutely true, and our entire historical experience confirms it, that what is possible could never have been achieved unless people had tried again and again to achieve the impossible in this world.[9]

THE END

NOTES

1. Weber, "Politics as a Vocation," 78.
2. Weber, "Politics as a Vocation," 77.
3. Weber, "Politics as a Vocation," 82.
4. Weber, "Politics as a Vocation," 34.
5. Weber, "Politics as a Vocation," 84. In the Gerth and Mills translation, *"Gewaltsamkeit"* is rendered "violence."
6. Weber, "Politics as a Vocation," 88.
7. Max Weber, *The Protestant Ethic and the Spirit of Capitalism*, trans. Talcott Parsons (New York: Scribner, 1958), 181.
8. Weber, *The Protestant Ethic*, 181.
9. Weber, "Politics as a Vocation," 93.

Appendix

The Phenomenon of Violence

Different languages emphasize different aspects of what we call in English "violence." Here I compare the definitions and examples of proper use of the word used to name the phenomenon in authoritative dictionaries in three languages. As a result, surprisingly different characteristics are revealed, but unsurprisingly, we also can discern a common core.

I will begin with the Japanese term, *boryoku*. In the *Kojien* [Japanese-Japanese] dictionary, the definition is simple and brief: "wild force; illegal force." The only two examples given are "violent revolution" and "violent gang." Both of these are illegal and anti-government. What, then, is "wild" *(ranbo)*? Again, the *Kojien* is brief: "rough behavior, illegal behavior." But it is more complex than that. This can be seen by using a Japanese-English dictionary, which, because the word has no exact equivalent in English, gives a larger number of possible translations and examples of usage than does the Japanese-Japanese. In the *Kenkyusha* Japanese-English dictionary, *ranbo* is defined as "wildness," "rampage," "riotous behavior," "disorderliness"; examples of usage include "Navvies have rude ways," "He gets violent when drunk," and "His grammar is shocking." The word implies a breakdown of order, a collapse of discipline, behavior that is chaotic and irrational.

The character for *bo*, which is shared by **boryoku** and **ranbo**, when used alone as a verb, is pronounced *abareru*, for which the Japanese-English dictionary offers the words "riot," "rage (about)," "rampage," "run amuck," and "be wild." Among the things mentioned that might behave in this way are typhoons, rivers, rogue horses, children, drunks, and students ("Some students went on a rampage and set fire to several buses").

We can see here a difficulty in using this word in Weber's definition, "legitimate violence." It does not describe the behavior expected of police, jailers, executioners, and military troops. Of course, sometimes these people do break discipline and run amuck. Police riot, jailers beat and torture prisoners, executioners use sadistic methods, soldiers rape and pillage. But these actions are not what these people are supposed to do; in fact, they are violations of the law. And the character *bo (abareru)* is applied to government only in the various words for "tyranny," that is, for a government that is *not* legitimate.

So, when "legitimate violence" *("legitimer physischer Gewaltsamkeit")* is translated into Japanese using the word *boryoku*, it becomes a contradiction; arguably some other word should be used. When Weber used the word *Gewalt*, he meant not wild behavior but the (usually) disciplined, orderly, and legal use of physical force by state employees. Nevertheless, *boryoku* is the standard translation and, as I shall argue below, at a fundamental level it does have something in common with what Weber meant.

A second aspect of *boryoku*, according to the *Kojien* dictionary, is that it is illegal (*muho*, literally "lawless"). In this word, *ho* is the term for law, and it has three forms. One is positive law, as established by the government. The second is Buddhist law. The third is *nori*, a different reading of the same character *ho*, defined as "form," "model" (to be followed), "example," or "standard."

Therefore, *muho* does not simply mean the violation of the criminal code. It means the violation of Buddhist ethics, and it also means the violation of something deeper still. The notion of *ho* as *nori* refers to a "law," an order, that is in the structure of the world itself, the integrity that is built into the nature of things. It suggests that there are forms that ought not to be violated, not only because to violate them is illegal or irreligious but also because they are what they are. Or to state the point more accurately, it is not that such things must under no circumstances be violated, but that to violate them is always a *violation*. I recognize that this is a tautology. Perhaps the following example will make it clear.

Suppose a bullet passes through a human body, breaks bones and tears organs apart, and then comes out the other side. This is a violation of the body: The bullet's chaotic action inside the body is *boryoku*; the bullet interferes with the laws (physiological laws) as to how the body must function to stay alive and healthy. Whether the gun was fired by a burglar, a policeman, a psychopathic killer, a jealous lover, or a president's bodyguard, the coroner will pronounce it a violent death.

Next, let's consider the English word, "violence." The *Oxford English Dictionary* (OED) defines it as follows:

> The exercise of physical force so as to inflict injury on, or cause damage to, persons or property; action or conduct characterized by this; treatment or usage tending to cause bodily injury or forcibly interfering with personal freedom.

This is strikingly different from the definition of *boryoku*. There is nothing here about disorder or chaos, nothing about wildness, irrationality, or loss of control. Moreover, there is no suggestion that violence by definition necessarily means disobedience to the laws of the state. In English, Weber's "legitimate violence," while shocking, is not—even if "legitimate" means "legal"—a logical contradiction. The OED definition describes accurately what police, jailers, executioners, and armies do. (It is interesting that the definition includes "forcibly interfering with personal freedom." Such behavior is not excluded from the Japanese term, but neither was it mentioned in any of the dictionaries I consulted.)

Another definition given by the OED is "improper treatment or use of a word." This is interesting to compare with the example given above, "His grammar is shocking" (a more literal translation of the Japanese would be "His grammar is wild"). Grammar (in Japanese, *bunpo*, literally "composition law") is "law" that is nowhere mentioned in any criminal code or religious or ethical set of rules; nevertheless, it is a law, and to violate it is both *ranbo* and violence.

Still another definition is given: "undue restraint applied to some natural process, habit, etc., so as to prevent its free development or exercise." Again, there is nothing here about either positive law or ethics. The key word is "natural." The idea is that there are processes in nature, that is, in reality itself, that ought not to be restrained "unduly." There are processes in nature that have their own integrity, that ought to be allowed to develop freely. It may be that when our own needs are great, and when they conflict with these natural processes, we will decide to put those processes under restraint. But even if that is "the best thing to do," the act itself, according to the OED definition, will still be violence.

It seems that *boryoku* describes the action of the assailant (is the action undisciplined, wild, irrational, uncontrolled; does it depart from the proper pattern of behavior; is it illegal; is it immoral?) whereas "violence" describes the effect on the victim (was there injury or damage; was personal freedom interfered with; was undue constraint applied?). *Boryoku* describes the character of the action; "violence" describes its consequences.

The difference becomes clearer when we examine the verb form of the word, "violate." The OED gives a number of definitions that are different yet connected. The first is "to break, infringe, or transgress unjustifiably." The image here is of using force to pass beyond a limit or a boundary that ought not to be crossed. If this sounds like rape, it's no coincidence: "To violate a woman" means just that.

The second is "to fail duly to keep or observe a) An oath or promise, one's faith, etc., b) A law, commandment, rule, etc., c) Abstract and moral qualities, etc." (examples given are "justice," "truth," and "chastity"). This somewhat resembles the notion of *muho*—lawlessness—described above.

The third is "to treat irreverently, to desecrate, dishonor, profane or defile." Other definitions are given, but these three catch the essence of the word.

What is important here is what these words presuppose about the world. For the verb "to violate," and hence for the noun "violence," to mean what they do mean, the world must be seen as a structure that contains boundaries. Some of these boundaries are artificially created (laws, rules, promises); some are natural (people's bodies, natural processes); as for the third type (abstract principles, such as truth, justice, moral principles), whether they are natural or artificial has been the subject of what may have been the longest debate in the history of philosophy. Here I will take no position on whether these boundaries have real, existential being. I only wish to point out that anyone who uses the words "violence" or "violate" is presupposing the existence of some such boundaries; otherwise, the words convey no meaning. I shall return to this point.

Next, let us look at *Gewalt*. Here the emphasis is not so much on disorder or lawlessness (as with *boryoku*) or on forcing through boundaries (as with "violence") but rather on domination. As with "violence," *Gewalt* can mean rape; as with both "violence" and *boryoku*, it can refer to forces of nature, such as storms; as with both, it can mean the use of physical force to harm another. But it does not always mean "to do harm"; it may also mean the use of physical force for the other's good. In the *Oxford-Harrap Standard German-English Dictionary*, the first example given is *göttliche Gewalt*, divine power. Other examples given include the domination of kings over subjects, feudal lords over tenants, conquering armies over the conquered, parents over children, and, most interestingly, the will over emotions (*"seine Gefühle in der Gewalt haben"*). For the English translation of this last, *Oxford-Harrap* gives "to have one's feelings under control." To attempt to express this notion using the word *boryoku* would produce an unintelligible sentence; to write it using the word "violence" would yield the opposite, "to do violence to one's feelings." Still, one can imagine a situation that could be described by either the German or the English expression, depending on the point of view of the speaker.

The theme shared by these examples is the use of physical force to have one's will against something that is resisting it (the exception is the storm, unless one takes an animistic view of nature). The big difference is that in some cases the use of force is seen not as disrupting order but rather as creating it. Another example is *"der Lehrer hatte die Gewalt über seine Hasse verloren"* ("The teacher had lost control over the class"). Here the idea is that if the pupils are allowed to have their way, the class will be disorderly, and to create order the teacher must use *Gewalt*. (I would not like to be a pupil in that class.)

Gewalt has legitimate and illegitimate forms. The illegitimate forms are clear: *"die Gewalt des Bösen"* ("the power of evil"), *"Gewaltherr"* ("tyrant"), *"Gewaltherrschaft"* ("despotism"). The legitimate forms are more complex. Presumably most people using the expression *göttliche Gewalt* consider this as something legitimate. But the question again is, What does this presuppose about the nature of the world? Why does God need *Gewalt* to rule his creatures? In the Christian view (and very strongly in the Protestant view), mankind is tainted with original sin, and left to themselves, human beings do not have the ability to establish orderly, just society. It is not enough for God simply to be persuasive; he must use power to overcome the stubborn, rebellious wills of sinful human beings. In this picture of the world, the same is true of governments, which can create order only by overpowering the stubborn wills of their subjects, and true of parents and teachers, who can establish discipline only by overpowering the wills of their children. I am not saying that this worldview is present in all uses of *Gewalt*, only that it is a theme that joins many of its "legitimate" forms. It is the presupposition to the reasoning that sees *Gewalt* as legitimate.

This picture reminds one of Hobbes: Without coercive power from the top, peace and order cannot be achieved. The big difference is that in the examples given under *Gewalt*, there is no indication that the coerced have given their consent; there is no social contract. And so the coercion is continuous.

And there is an important difference between *Gewalt* and both "violence" and *boryoku*. While the latter two tend to refer to actions—beating, shooting, restraining a person—the former often refers to a situation in which people are dominated by a force that has the means of physical coercion but is not necessarily using it. The difference is made clear in the following example given in *Oxford-Harrap*: *"nach langen Kämpfen Brachten, bekamen, sie das Land endlich unter ihre Gewalt"* ("After much fighting, they finally had the country under their power"). The word *Gewalt* here refers not to the fighting (which is *Kämpfen*) but rather to the situation after the fighting has ended. The conquering army is no longer shooting people or blowing off their arms and legs, but the fact that it had done this and could begin doing it again at any time are the sources of its *Gewalt*.

The differences between these three terms—"violence," *boryoku*, and *Gewalt*—are so great that one wonders why they are used as translations of each other. Rather than being different names for a single phenomenon, they seem to be distinct. Yet they share a common core. All refer to a use of physical force so as to damage, destroy, or suppress something of value. In the case of *boryoku*, the emphasis is on the character of the physical force itself, as something that is undisciplined and wild, which bursts into the orderly world from the chaotic outside. In the case of "violence," the emphasis is on the violation of a boundary, or on behavior that infringes on the integrity of things, in particular of human beings. *Gewalt* is used in these ways, but it is used also, as I have described, to mean a coercive domination of people "for their own good." And it is difficult to think of the overcoming of people's harmful impulses (the will to original sin, for example) as the destruction of "something of value." It is less difficult, however, if one remembers that coercion of people against their will is a violation of their freedom, no matter how mistaken or evil that will may be. These uses of *Gewalt* suggest a situation in which coercion is used because persuasion has failed (or has not been attempted); they come close to the last part of the OED definition of "violence": "forcibly interfering with personal freedom."

Another, simpler way to look at the matter is to shift attention away from the dictionary definitions of words and look at what people actually do in the name of the state, which is what Max Weber cared about. And it is clear that state-legitimized coercion has all the characteristics that these three words imply. Thus, at least in this case, these three words are the proper translations of one another.

Bibliography

Agamben, Giorgio. *The State of Exception*. Translated by Kevin Attell. Chicago: U. of Chicago, 2005.
Agarwal, Shriman Narayan. *Gandhian Constitution for Free India*. Allahabad: Kitabistan, 1946.
Aquinas, Thomas. *Summa Theologia*. Volume 1 of 5. Translated by Fathers of the English Dominican Province. New York: Christian Classics, 1948.
Arendt, Hannah. *Eichmann in Jerusalem: A Report on the Banality of Evil*. New York: Viking, 1965. Originally published in *The New Yorker*, 1964–5.
———. *The Human Condition*, 2nd edition (1998). Chicago: U. of Chicago, 1958.
———. *On Revolution*. New York: Viking Press, 1963.
———. "On Violence." In *Crises in the Republic*. San Diego: Harvest, 1972.
Arrowsmith, William. "Introduction to *Heracles*." In *The Complete Greek Tragedies*. Vol. 3, *Euripides*. Edited by David Grene and Richmond Lattimore. Chicago: U. of Chicago, 1992.
Augustine. *The City of God against the Pagans*. Edited and translated by R. W. Dyson. Cambridge: Cambridge University Press, 1998.
———. *Contra Faustum* XXII. In *The Political Writings of St. Augustine*. Edited by Henry Paolucci. Chicago: Henry Regnery, 1967.
Austin, J. L. *How To Do Things with Words*. Edited by J. O. Urmson and Marina Sbisa. Cambridge, MA: Harvard University, 1962.
Azad, Maulana Abul Kalam. *India Wins Freedom: An Autobiographical Narrative*. Bombay: Orient Longmans, 1959.
Barker, Pat. *Regeneration*. Plume/Penguin, 1993.
"Basic Initial Post-Surrender Directive." In *The Japan Reader 2: Postwar Japan, 1945 to the Present*, edited by Jon Livingston, Joe Moore, and Felicia Oldfather. New York: Pantheon Books, 1973.
Biddle, Tami Davis. "Air Power." In *The Laws of War: Constraints on Warfare in the Western World*, edited by Michael Howard, George J. Andreopoulos, and Mark R. Shulman. New Haven, CT: Yale University Press, 1994.
Biondi, Rick, and Alex Newman. *World Federalism 101*. Self-published, 2014.
Blake, William. *The Marriage of Heaven and Hell*. New York: Dover, 1994.

Bondurant, Joan V. *Conquest of Violence: The Gandhian Philosophy of Conflict.* Berkeley: UC Press, 1971.

Clark, Grenville, and Louis B. Sohn. *World Peace Through World Law.* Cambridge, MA: Harvard University Press, 1958.

Clausewitz, W. Carl von. *On War.* Edited by Anatol Rapoport. Translated by J. J. Graham. Penguin Books.

Derrida, Jacques. *The Death Penalty.* Translated by Peggy Kamuf. Chicago: U. of Chicago, 2013.

Duyvendak, J. J. L. *The Book of Lord Shang.* London: Probsthain, 1928.

Fall, Bernard. *The Two Viet-nams: A Political and Military Analysis, revised edition.* New York: Praeger, 1965.

Fischer, Louis. *The Life of Mahatma Gandhi.* New York: Harper and Row, 1950.

Galtung, Johan. *Peace by Peaceful Means.* London: Sage Publications, 1996.

Gandhi, M. K. "Congress Constitution." Gujarati, Narajiran, March 20, 1921. In *Collected Works of Mahatma Gandhi.* Vol. 22. New Delhi: Publications Division.

———. "The Congress Constitution." *Young India*, March 30, 1921. In *Collected Works of Mahatma Gandhi.* Vol. 22.

———. "The Doctrine of the Sword." *Young India*, August 11, 1920. In *Collected Works of Mahatma Gandhi.* Vol. 21. New Delhi: Publications Division.

———. "Draft Constitution of Congress." *Harijan*, February 5, 1948. In *Collected Works of Mahatma Gandhi.* Vol. 98.

———. *Hind Swaraj.* Edited by Suresh Sharma and Trid Suhrud. New Delhi: Orient Blackstone, 2010.

———. "How to Finance the Movement." *Young India*, January 12, 1921. In *Collected Works of Mahatma Gandhi.* Vol. 22.

———. "Independence." *Panchgani*, July 21, 1946; *Harijan*, July 28, 1946. In *Collected Works of Mahatma Gandhi.* Vol. 91.

———. "Interview to Nirmal Kumar Bose." *The Hindustani Times*, October 17, 1935. In *Collected Works of Mahatma Gandhi.* Vol. 65.

———. "Letter to J. B. Petit." June 16, 1915. In *Collected Works of Mahatma Gandhi.* Vol. 15.

———. "Lord Amphill." *Indian Opinion*, June 29, 1907. In *Collected Works of Mahatma Gandhi.* Vol. 7.

———. "Message to Satyagraha Agriculturalists." Gujarati, Mahadevbhaini Diary, vol. IV, April 17, 1918. In *Collected Works of Mahatma Gandhi.* Vol. 26.

———. "Speech at a Mass Meeting." *Indian Opinion*, August 23, 1908. In *Collected Works of Mahatma Gandhi.* Vol. 9.

Gandhi, Manubehn. *The Miracle of Calcutta.* Ahmedabad: Navajivan Publishing House, 1951.

———. *Last Glimpses of Bapu.* Delhi: Agarwala, 1962.

Gayn, Mark. *Japan Diary.* Rutland: Charles E. Tuttle, 1981.

Giedion, Sigfried. *Mechanization Takes Command: A Contribution to Anonymous History.* UK: Oxford Clarendon Press, 1970.

Godse, Nathuram. *May it Please Your Honor.* Delhi: Surya Bharti Prakashan, 1987.

Gray, J. Glen. *The Warriors: Reflections on Men in Battle*. Lincoln: U. of Nebraska, 1959.
Grossman, Dave. *On Killing*. Boston: Little, Brown, 1995.
Grotius. "Prolegomena, 28, The Rights of War and Peace." In *The Theory of International Relations*, edited by M. G. Forsyth, H. N. A. Keens-Soper, and P. Savigear. London: George Allen and Unwin, 1970.
Hedges, Chris. *War Is a Force That Gives Us Meaning*. New York: Random House, 2002.
———. *What Every Person Should Know about War*. New York: Free Press, 2003.
Hobbes, Thomas. *Leviathan: or The Matter, Forme and Power of a Commonwealth Ecclesiastical and Civil*. Edited by Michael Oakeshott. New York: Collier Books, 1962.
———. *Man and Citizen*. Edited by Sterling P. Lamprecht. Westport: Greenwood Press.
Homer. *The Iliad of Homer*. Translated by Richmond Lattimore. Chicago: U. Chicago Press, 1951.
Hulsey, Gary. Interview, CNN. www.youtube.com/watch?v=B1R-cEk5Fc.
Huthseeing, Krishna Nehru. *We Nehrus*. New York: Holt, Rinehart & Winston, 1967.
Huxley, Aldous. *Grey Eminence*. New York: Meridian Books, 1959. First published in Great Britain under the title *Grey Eminence: A Study in Religion and Politics* by Chatto and Windus.
Inoue, Kyoko. *MacArthur's Japanese Constitution: A Linguistic and Cultural Study of its Making*. Chicago: The University of Chicago Press.
James, William. "The Moral Equivalent of War." In *Pragmatism and other Essays*. New York: Washington Square Press, 1963 (originally published 1910).
Joas, Hans, and Wolsfanf Kuobl. *War in Social Thought*. Translated by Alex Skinner. Princeton, NJ: Princeton University Press, 2013.
Kant, Immanuel. "Idea for a Universal History from a Cosmo-political Point of View." In *The Theory of International Relations*, edited by M. G. Forsyth, H. N. A. Keens-Soper, and P. Savigear. London: George Allen and Unwin, 1970.
———. *Kant on History*. Edited by Lewis White Beck. Upper Saddle River: Prentice Hall, 2001.
———. "The Metaphysical Elements of Justice." In *The Theory of International Relations*, edited by M. G. Forsyth, H. N. A. Keens-Soper, and P. Savigear. London: George Allen and Unwin, 1970.
———. "On the Commonplace: That May Be Correct in Theory but Is Useless in Practice." In *The Theory of International Relations*, edited by M. G. Forsyth, H. N. A. Keens-Soper, and P. Savigear. London: George Allen and Unwin, 1970.
———. "Perpetual Peace: a Philosophical Essay." In *The Theory of International Relations*, edited by M. G. Forsyth, H. N. A. Keens-Soper, and P. Savigear. London: George Allen and Unwin, 1970.
Keegan, John. *The Face of Battle*. London: Penguin Books, 1978.
Kobayashi, Tomi. "The Action of the Voiceless Voices." In *Anti-war Thought and Action*. Edited by Yoshikawa Yuichi. Tokyo: Shakai Hyoronsha Publishers, 1995.

Koseki, Shoichi. *The Birth of Japan's Postwar Constitution*. Edited and translated by Ray A. Moore. Boulder, CO: Westview Press, 1997.

Kothari, Rajni. *Politics in India*. New Delhi: Orient Longmans, 1970.

Liberal Democratic Party, Constitutional Revision Drafting Committee. *Comparison Chart for Draft Revision of Constitution of Japan*. 2012.

Lindqvist, Sven. *A History of Bombing*. Translated by Linda Haverty Rugg. The New Press, 2003.

Lummis, Douglas. "The Empire's Clothes: Simple Disobedience Can Strip Government Institutions of Power." A review of Gene Sharp's *The Politics of Nonviolent Action* (1973). *Psychology Today* 7, no. 12 (May 1974): 18.

———. "Japan's Radical Constitution." Translated by Kaji Etsuko. *Science of Thought* (January 1983). Published in English in *Reading the Constitution of Japan* (Kashiwa Shobo, 1993).

———. *A Constitution is a Command to the Government: Expanded Version*. Tokyo: Heibonsha Library, 2013.

MacArthur, Douglas. "Views of General of the Army Douglas MacArthur on Rearmament of Japan." JCS 1380/48, "Note by the Secretaries to the Joint Chiefs of Staff on Limited Military Armament for Japan." Annex B. October 25, 1948.

Madison, James. *Notes of Debates in the Federal Convention of 1787*. Norton: Ohio University, 1966.

Maine, Henry Sumner. *Village-communities in the East and West: Six Lectures Delivered at Oxford to Which Are Added Other Lectures, Addresses and Essays by Sir Henry Sumner Maine*. New York: Henry Holt, 1889.

Marshall, S. L. A. *Men Against Fire: the problem of battle command*. Norman: U. of Oklahoma Press, 2000. Originally published in Washington, *Infantry Journal*. New York: William Morrow, c. 1947.

Mazower, Mark. *Governing the World: The History of an Idea, 1815 to the Present*. London: Allen Lane, 2012.

Meagher, Robert Emmet. *Herakles gone mad: rethinking heroism in an age of endless war*. Northampton, MA: Olive Branch Press, 2006.

Meron, Theodor. *Henry's Wars and Shakespeare's Laws: Perspectives on the Law of War in the Later Middle Ages*. Oxford: Oxford University Press, 1993.

Morris-Suzuki, Tessa. *The Korean War in Asia*. Lanham, MD: Rowman & Littlefield, 2018.

Morrison, Charles Clayton. *The Outlawry of War: A Constructive Policy for World Peace*. Willett, Clark and Colby, 1927.

Nandy, Ashis. "Final Encounter: The Politics of the Assassination of Gandhi." In *Exiled at Home*. Delhi: Oxford University Press, 1988.

Nelson, Allen. "You were never my enemy." Interview by Brian Covert. https://www.indybay.org/newsitems/2009/02/02/18567572.php.

Nietzsche, Friedrich. "The Geneology of Morals." In *The Birth of Tragedy and the Geneology of Morals*, translated by Francis Golffing. New York: Doubleday, 1956.

Nihonkoku Kenpo (The Constitution of Japan). Shogakkan: Sharaku Books, 1982.

Ninh, Bao. *The Sorrow of War*. Edited by Frank Palmos. Translated by Phan Than Hao. New York: Riverhead Books, 1996.

Oda, Makoto. *Nine-one-one and Article Nine*. Tokyo: Otsuki Publishing, 2006.
———. "Towards a Conscientious Objector Country." In *Nine-one-one and Article Nine*. Tokyo: Otsuki Publishing, 2006.
Paris, Roland. "The 'Responsibility to Protect' and the Structural Problems of Preventive Humanitarian Intervention." In *International Peacekeeping*. Vol. 21, 2014.
Plato. *The Republic of Plato*. Translated by Allan Bloom. New York: Basic Books, 1968.
Pyarelal. *Mahatma Gandhi, vol. 10, The Last Phase*. Part II. Ahmedabad: Navajivan Publishing House, 1958. In *Collected Works of Mahatma Gandhi*. Vol. 97.
Remarque, Erich Maria. *All Quiet on the Western Front*. Translated by A. W. Wheen. New York: Ballantine, 1982 (English original: Little, Brown, 1929).
Reves, Emery. *The Anatomy of Peace*. New York: The Viking Press, 1963 (originally printed by Harper and Row, 1945).
Rivers, W. H. R. "The Repression of War Experience." *The Lancet*, February 2, 1918.
Roberts, Adam. "Land Warfare." In *The Laws of War: Constraints on Warfare in the Western World*, edited by Michael Howard, George J. Andreopoulos, and Mark R. Shulman. New Haven, CT: Yale University Press, 1994.
Rogers, A. P. V. *Law on the Battlefield*. Manchester: Manchester U. Press, 1996.
Rousseau, Jean-Jacques. "Abstract of the Abbe de St Pierre's Project for Perpetual Peace." In *The Theory of International Relations*, edited by M. G. Forsyth, H. N. A. Keens-Soper, and P. Savigear. London: George Allen and Unwin, 1970.
———. "Judgment on Saint Pierre's Project for Perpetual Peace." In *The Theory of International Relations*, edited by M. G. Forsyth, H. N. A. Keens-Soper, and P. Savigear. London: George Allen and Unwin, 1970.
Rummel, R. J. *Death by Government: Genocide and Mass Murder since 1900*. Routledge, 1997.
Schmitt, Carl. *Political Theology: Four Chapters on the Concept of Sovereignty*. Translated by George Schwab. Chicago: U. of Chicago, 2006.
———. "The Turn to the Discriminating Concept of War." In *Writings on War*. Edited and translated by Timothy Nunan. Cambridge: Polity Press, 2011.
Shang Yang. *The Book of Lord Shang*. Translated by J. J. L. Duyvendak. Clark: The Lawbook Exchange Ltd, 2003 (originally published London: Probsthain, 1928).
Shanin, Teodor. *Late Marx and the Russian Road*. New York: Monthly Review Press, 1983.
Sharp, Gene. *Gandhi as Political Strategist*. Boston: Porter Sargent, 1979.
———. *The Politics of Nonviolent Action*. Boston: Porter Sargent, 1973.
Shay, Jonathan. *Achilles in Vietnam: Combat Trauma and the Undoing of Character*. New York: Atheneum, 1994.
Sherman, William T. *Memoirs of General W. T. Sherman*. New York: Renaissance Classics, 2012.
Siemes, Johannes. *Hermann Roesler and the Making of the Meiji State*. Tokyo: Sophia University in cooperation with Charles E. Tuttle Co., 1968.
Silko, Leslie Marmon. *Ceremony*. New York: Penguin, 1977.

Smolar, Aleksander. "Towards 'Self-limiting Revolution': Poland, 1970–89." In *Civil Resistance and Power Politics*, edited by Adam Roberts and Timothy Garton Ash. Oxford: Oxford University Press, 2009.

The Stars and Stripes. September 19, 2015.

Storing, Herbert J., ed. *The Anti-Federalist: Writings by the Opponents of the Constitution.* Chicago: The University of Chicago Press, 1985.

Streit, Clarence K. *Union Now: The Proposal for Inter-democracy Federal Union.* New York: Harper and Brothers, 1940.

Swank, Roy L., and Walter E. Marchand. "Combat Neuroses: Development of Combat Exhaustion." *Archives of Neurology and Psychology* 55 (March 1944).

Thucydides. *The Complete Writings of Thucydides: The Peloponnesian War*. Crowley translation. New York: Modern Library, 1954.

Tsurumi, Shunsuke. "Radical Democracy." In *Anti-war Thought and Action*. Edited by Yoshikawa Yuichi. Tokyo: Shakai Hyoronsha Publishers, 1995.

Walzer, Michael. *Just and Unjust Wars: A Moral Argument with Historical Illustrations*. New York: Basic Books, 1977.

Weber, Max. *Ancient Judaism*. Edited and translated by Hans H. Gerth and Don Martindale. New York: The Free Press.

———. "Politics as a Vocation." In *From Max Weber: Essays in Sociology*. Edited and translated by H. H. Gerth and C. Wright Mills. New York: Oxford, 1958.

———. "Politics as a Vocation." In *The Vocation Lectures*. Edited by David Owen and Tracy B. Strong. Translated by Rodney Livingstone. Hackett, 2004.

———. *The Protestant Ethic and the Spirit of Capitalism*. Translated by Talcott Parsons. New York: Scribner, 1958.

Weber, Thomas. "World Governance." In *The Oxford International Encyclopedia of Peace.* Vol. 4. Oxford: Oxford University Press, 2010.

Weiss, Thomas G., David P. Forsyth, Roger A. Coate, and Kelly-Kate Pease. *The United Nations and Changing World Politics*. Boulder, CO: Westview Press, 2014.

Wright, G. Ernest, and Reginald H. Fuller. *The Book of the Acts of God.* Garden City, NY: Doubleday, 1957.

Index

A
Abbé de Saint-Pierre;
    peace proposal, 104–105
    Rousseau's evaluation, 105–106
Achillius;
    "like a god", 31
Agamben, Giorgio;
    exception, state of, 96–97
    "law", force of, 96
Agarwal, Shriman Narayan. See
    Gandhian Constitution for Free India
Agincourt, battle of, 60–62
    duel writ large, 60
    laws of war broken, 61–62
    laws of war followed, 61
Air Warfare Rules, 1922;
    never ratified, 80
amendment by interpretation, 152
    Abe Shinzo's final attempt, 156–57
AMPO. *See* Japan-US Security Treaty
AMPO Generation, Japan;
    view of Constitution, 137–38, 158–62, 165
Annan, Kofi;
    Nobel Peace Prize awarded, 127
    Responsibility to Protect (R2P) program, 127–29
Aquinas, Saint Thomas;
    hell, moral dynamics of, 64–65
    plausible deniability, 64
Arendt, Hannah;
    Gandhi dismissed, 171
    Gandhi, theoretical agreement with, 173–76
    on Denmark's resistance to Nazism, 172–73
    power and violence, opposites, 173
Article 9. *See* Japanese Constitution
athanatos (immortality);
    disqualifies gods from "hero" status, 30–32
    sought after by warriors, 31
Augustine, Saint, 36–40
    just war theory, founder of, 39
    kill without sin, how to, 39–40
    kingdoms and robber bands, compared, 37
    the two cities, 37
Austin, John;
    on performative utterance, 151

B
balloon bombing
    moratorium, 1899, 78–79
Bao Dinh, Vietnam War veteran, North Vietnamese Army;

PTSD victim, 47–48
Barker, Pat, author of *Regeneration*,
  historical fiction on "shell-shock"
  treatment, World War I, 49
Basic Initial Post-Surrender
  Directive, 144
Beheiren (Peace in Vietnam! Citizens'
  League), 163
    See also Oda Makoto
belligerency, right of;
  defined and misdefined, 14–15,
    17–19, 153–55
  individual self-defense, how
    different, 155
  not recognized, Japanese
    Constitution, 152
bombing;
  before airplane invented, 77
  Jules Verne bombs Africa
    (1886), 77
  H. G. Wells bombs New York
    (1908), 77
bombing, where;
  European colonies
    (1912–35), 77–78
  German cities (1941), 81–83
bombing, who;
  enemy military only, 77
  the public (area bombing), 77
    See also Douhet, Brig.
      Gen. Giulio
bombing, why;
  close air support, 77
  infrastructure, 77
  terror, 77–78
    See also Trenchard, Maj. Gen.
      Hugh; Walzer, Michael
Bricker Amendment, 103

C
Caen, sacked by Henry V, 65
Cambodia;
  Japanese Self-Defense
    Forces in, 155
citizen;
  and "citizen's movement", 158–62
  and Japanese Constitution's
    human rights clauses, 146–49,
    151–52, 158–62
  targeted by LDP's amendment
    proposals, 162–63
    See also Japan, subject to citizen
Clark, Grenville and Henry Stimson,
  peace proposal, 116–18
  monopoly of legitimate
    violence, 117
  no POW rights, 118
  UN armed, 116
  war to disarm world (ten
    years), 117
Clausewitz, Carl von;
  just war impossible, 58
  law of war ineffective, 58
  logic of war leads to
    extreme, 58, 82–83
  Walzer critique, 58, 59
combat, sixty days continuous,
  effect of, 49
Commandments, Ten; "peace" not
  among them, 201
Concert of Europe;
  collapses with World War I, 110
Constitution of Japan;
  and civil society, 144, 146,
    150, 158–62
  legitimized by struggle, 150
  and MacArthur, 143, 145, 157–58
  and Okinawa, 157–58, 166
  as radical democracy, 160–62
Constitution of Japan, Article 9, as test
  of literacy, 152
Constitution of Japan as performative
  utterance, 150–52
    See also Austin, John
Constitution of Japan as power
  seizure, 139–44
  peace clause as seized power, 143
  rights clauses as seized
    power, 140–41

sovereignty transfer to people as
  seized power, 142, 150–52
war aims, allied, and
  Constitution, 143
Constitution of the United States as
  power seizure, 140
    powers transferred from states to
      center, 140
cooperation as generator of domination
  (Gandhi), 176–78
cooperation refusal as peaceful
  generator of people's power
  (Gandhi), 181–83
Corcyra, revolt of (Thucydides);
  model of "absolute war", 94
criminal code, Japan, articles 36
  and 37, 155

D

death, sheer, 33
democracy;
    Japanese Constitution as
      radical, 161
Denmark;
    nonviolent resistance to
      Nazism, 172–73
distance-collapse, examples;
    Bao Dinh, 47
    Herakles, 51–54
    Allen Nelson, 48
    Erich Maria Remarque, 46–47
    See also entries by name
distancing;
    defined, 43–44
    numbered by Lt. Col. Dave
      Grossman, 43
    taught by drill instructors
      (DIs), 45–46
Douhet, Brig. Gen. Giulio;
    "bomb everybody" theory, 77
    See also bombing, area
drill instructors (DIs), what they
  teach, 45–46
    See also distancing
dueling;

bound by rules, 59–60
just war, model for, 59
sports, contact, compared, 60
dumdum bullets;
    outlawed, 75
Dyer, Brig. Gen. Reginald E. H., 180
dystopia
    Japan Liberal Democratic Party's
      constitutional proposal as, 163

E

ecology of labor and robbery, 9
ecstasy of war. *See* war, alleged pleasure
Emperor of Japan, Meiji, 141–42
Emperor of Japan, Showa, 142–43
Englistan, Gandhi's dystopia, 177
    See also Hind Swaraj
Euripides. *See Herakles*
exception, state of, 94–97
    Agamben on, 96
    death penalty as (Derrida), 96
    Henry V speech at Harfleur
      (Shakespeare) as
      model for, 62–63
    Schmitt on, 94–95
    See also Thanatopia
executions as replacement for war
  (Schmitt), 119
Extraordinary Chambers in the Courts
  of Cambodia (ECCC), 125

F

Fanon, Frantz, 173
"fifteen democracies" rule, peace
  proposal by Clarence K.
  Streit, 112–13
    colonialism institutionalized, 113
    influence on Atlantic
      Alliance, 115–16
    world's wealth controlled, 113
Fluellen, character in Shakespeare's
  Henry V, on laws of war, 61
"force, minimum necessary," platitude
  unpacked, 154
founding, primal sacrifice, 192–95

G

Galtung, Johan, "institutional violence", 9
Gandhi, Mohandas, political theorist;
    Hannah Arendt, compared, 171–72
    Hind Swaraj theory of power, 176–78
    Marx, compared, 178
    "practical idealism", 178
    Self-Limiting Revolution, inventor, 183
    Poland case, compared, 183
    state, characterized, 179
    violence, ineffectiveness of, 176–78
Gandhi, Mohandas, twentieth-century nation builder, 175–76
    assassination as "final act", 194
    on British Constitution, 179–80
    and "ethic of consequences" (Weber), 198, 207
    head of state refused, 175–76
    noncooperation, 1920–1921; 181–83
    and "Prince's Dilemma" (Machiavelli), 175
    Self-Limiting Revolution, inventor of, 183
    violence, changing fact of, 189–91
Gandhian Constitution for Free India: sovereign village republics, 185–88
    Hannah Arendt "council system," compared, 186
    Thomas Jefferson "elementary republics," compared, 186
    Henry Sumner Maine, influence, 188
    "Late Marx" (Shanin/Wada), compared, 187
    Gordon Wood on 1777 New Hampshire, compared, 186
Gandhi's death wish, 193
Gandhi's funeral; called a "triumph", 197
Gandhi's last constitutional proposal; Congress of India to disband, return to villages, 191–92
Gandhi's "permissive" assassination, 193
    "his last act", 194
gaze of the state, returning, 158–61
Glenn, Russell W., on Lt. Gen. S. L. A. Marshall, 44–45
Godse, Nathuram, Gandhi's assassin;
    not a demented fanatic, 193–95
    enabler of India's armed forces, 195–96
    in his own words, 195–96
Goethe, soldier's ditty, 66
golden rule, reversed, 60
Grossman, Lt. Col. Dave. *See* distancing
Grotius;
    sought to limit, therefore allow, war, 71–72
Guantanamo Bay US Naval Base, why selected as prison, 133

H

Harfleur, Henry's speech at (Shakespeare), 62
    "military execution" accurately depicted, 63–64
    model of war at extreme limit, 63–64
    strictly speaking, not military action, 98
Henry V, king of England, depicted by Shakespeare;
    muddles rape of villages, women, 67
Henry V, king of England, invader of France;
    allowed looting, Harfleur, 62–63
    ordered "military execution," Caen, 65
    ordered prisoners killed at Agincourt, 62
Herakles (Euripides);

depicts PTSD-madness
  (Meagher), 51–54
hierarchies paralleles, Vietnam, 183
Hind Swaraj (Gandhi);
  nonviolence of daily life, 10–11
  on power, 176–78
  See also Gandhi, Mohandas,
    political theorist
Hobbes, Thomas;
  peace, defined, 1
  state of nature (war), 3
  presupposes prior state of
    peace, 2–8
  state power "not so hurtful as the
    want of it", 4
  two ways to found
    commonwealth, 123
Hook, Sidney, defines "violence", 14
Hulsey, Gary, PTSD victim, 50
Humpty Dumpty Theory of Language;
  used to interpret Japan's
    Article 9, 152–53

I

Iliad;
  a poem of killing, 30
India, independence, compared to
  Poland, 183
International Court of Justice
  (ICJ), 1946, 124–25
International Criminal Court
  (ICC), 2002, 125–26
    determines criminality, 125
    enforcement by member
      states, 126
International Criminal Tribunal for
  Yugoslavia (ICTY), 1993;
    determines criminality, 125–26
    enforcement by member
      states, 126

J

Japan;
  AMPO Generation, 137–38
  AMPO struggle, 1960–70, 158–62

Japan-US Security Treaty
  (AMPO), 1952, 149–50
"perfect muddle", 165–66
reverse course, 149–50
subject to citizen, 158–62
Japanese Constitution. *See*
  Constitution of Japan
Joe Gook, defined, 45–46
John, king of England;
  signed Magna Carta under
    duress, 139
Jones, James, author of *The
  Thin Red Line*;
    depicts war killing as
      "pleasure", 87–88
    See also war, alleged pleasure
jus ad bellum;
  differs in different ages, 72–73
  since 1945, only "defense"
    permitted, 73
jus in bello;
  disorderly jumble of rules, 74ff

K

Kant, Immanuel, peace proposal;
  "as though", 109, 110
  Hobbes's worldview,
    agrees with, 106
  intelligent devils, peace
    among, 107
  peace and progress
    theory, 109–110
  peaceful republics
    theory, 106–107
  right of violence not granted
    world government, 107
  who will watch the
    watchers?, 107–108
Katherine, French princess;
  King Henry's "spoils of war", 67
Keegan, John;
  battlefield as *dies* non, 62
Kellogg-Briand Pact, 112
killing, fear of. *See* Marshall, Brig. Gen.
  S. L. A., 44

Kishore, Acharya Jugal, 191
knowing as "not-knowing", 13–14
Koran, on heaven and hell, 43
Korean War, Japanese
    participation in, 156
Kuron, Jacek, 183

L

Law (xed out) in state of
    exception, 96–97
        See also Agamben, Giorgio
League of Nations;
    successes and failures, 110–11
legitimate violence, right of;
    "axiom" of political
        science, xiii–xiv
    birth of (model), 2–5
    enabler of war, xiii
    as hypothesis, 16–17
    as oxymoron, 14–15
    perception, effect on, 14–16
    three aspects, 14
    Weber's definition of state,
        key term, 13
Liberal Democratic Party (LDP, Japan)
    constitutional revision proposal as
        dystopia, 163
looting.
    See war, alleged pleasure

M

MacArthur, Gen. Douglas, and Japan
    Peace Constitution;
        bad cop, good cop, 145–46
        peace constitution and US
            war aims, 143
        threatens war crimes
            prosecution, 145–46
        uses people's power, 146–47
MacArthur, Gen. Douglas, on the
    Constitution and Okinawa, 157–58
Machiavelli, Niccolo;
    founding and sacrifice, 194–95
    prince's dilemma, 173
machine guns;
    industrialization of warfare, 76
    Maxim conveyer belt system, 76
Manuben, 191
Mao Tse Tung;
    political power, definition, 173
Marshall, Brig. Gen. S. L. A.;
    killing, fear of, 44–45
    training techniques, to cure
        killing fear, 44–46
Marx, Karl;
    general strike, Gandhi's
        "noncooperation,"
        compared, 178
Mazower, Mark, 110
Meagher, Robert Emmet, on Euripides's
    Herakles, 52
    See also *Herakles*
Meron, Theodor;
    Shakespeare's *Henry V* viewed
        through international law, 61
    See also entries for Henry V, king
        of England
Monopol legitimer Gewaltsamkeit
    (monopoly of legitimate violence);
    key words in Max Weber's
        definition of the state, 13
Morrison, Charles Clayton, peace
    proposal, 111–12
    force, "god of peace
        movement", 111
    Kellogg-Briand Pact,
        influence on, 113
    "national defense" OK, 112
Moses, rules for holy massacre, 34

N

Nandy, Ashis, on Nathuram Godse;
    not a "demented fanatic", 193–95
    See also Godse, Nathuram
National Police Reserve (Japan), 149
"natural man" (Hobbes);
    able to make promises, 5–6
    has wife and children, 5
Nelson, Allen, Vietnam
    veteran, USMC, 47–48

Nietzsche, Friedrich;
  right to make promises, 5
noncooperation;
  general strike as, 178, 207
  India, 1920-1921, 181-83
  power, source of, 176-78
  Self-Limiting Revolution as, 183
  See also cooperation refusal;
    Gandhi, Mohandas (both);
    Hind Swaraj
Nuremberg war-crimes trials, 124

O

Oda Makoto, Japan peace activist;
  Beheiren, founder, 163
  burning city, view from, 163
  conscientious objector country proposal, 165
  deserters, US Vietnam War, supported, 164
  See also Beheiren
Original Position: state of peace;
  implied in Hobbes's image, 3-5
  offers alternative world picture, 6-8
Original Position: state of war (Hobbes), 3-4;
  axiom of international political system, 4
  prior state of peace, necessary condition, 3-5
Osaka, bombing of, 138, 163-64
oxymoron, "legitimate violence" as.
  See also legitimate violence;
    Weber, Max

P

pacifism;
  not the stance of this book, xiii
  and "what-if game", 203
Paris, Roland, on R2P, 128-29
  See also Responsibility to Protect (R2P)
Payne, Robert;

Gandhi's funeral as "triumph", 197
"permissive assassination", 193
peace as "daily life";
  in *Hind Swaraj*, 10-11
peace, defined by Hobbes, 1-2
peace as "the human thing", 201-202
  "Prince of Peace": an immortal god reborn as mortal man (Isaiah), 201-202
  Ten Commandments, not included, 201
  value grasped by *thanatos* (mortal) humans, 202
  value not grasped by *athanatos* (immortal) gods, 202
peace as Original Position. *See* Original Position: state of peace
peace as "time between wars", 1
Peaceful Village 2 (enter robber band), 9-10;
  origin of legitimate violence, 9-10
Peaceful Village as a "where to stand", 6-8
Pitkin, Hanna Fenichel, "blob" analysis, 21-23
Plato;
  justice among thieves, 2
  Republic as model, 2
  sword given to madman, 52
post-traumatic stress disorder (PTSD), 48-50
power, police. *See* legitimate violence, right of, three aspects
power, political;
  collective action (Arendt), 170-71
  force (Weber), 207
  noncooperation (Gandhi), 81-83, 177, 202
  violence (Mao), 173
  See also individual entries
primal war of the state, 7-8, 17-18
Protect, Responsibility to (R2P), 127-29

See also Annan, Kofi;
   Paris, Roland

R
rape;
   as military tactic, 65–68
   as "soldier's right" (spoils
      of war), 66–67
reading, deductive, 152
Remarque, Erich Maria, World War I
   veteran (German army), 46–47, 86
Responsibility to Protect (R2P). See
   Protect, Responsibility to
reverse course, Japan, 149–50
Reves, Henry, peace proposal;
   anti-fascist fascism, 114–15
   policing and war, muddled, 115
   two roads to world
      domination, 114
   war transforms all to
      fascism, 113–14
   See also Hobbes, Thomas, two
      ways to found commonwealth
ridicule, refutation by, 105–106
robber band;
   justice within it (Plato), 10–11
   in Original Position 2, 9–10
   resemblance to kingdom
      (Augustine), 37–38
   See also Original Position 2
Roberts, Adam, 75
Roesler, Hermann;
   Meiji Emperor, powers, 151
Rogers, A. P. V.;
   rules of war, limits, 79
Rome statute. See International
   Criminal Court
Rousseau, Jean-Jacques;
   princes prefer war, why, 105
   ridicule, refutation by, 105
   St. Pierre peace proposal
      "possible but impossible", 105
   state's war against own
      citizens, 105

S
Satyagraha and the logic of war, 184–85
Schmitt, Carl, critique of world
   government, 118–19
   enemy criminalized, 119
   final war of humanity, 119
   "no war, only executions", 119
Self-Defense Forces (SDF), Japan;
   Cambodia PKO commander,
      evaluation, 155
   rules of engagement, unclear, 157
self-defense, individual, 155
   differs from military
      action, 152–53
Self-Limiting Revolution;
   attempted by Congress of India,
      1920–1921, 183
   See also Gandhi, Mohandas,
      both entries
Shakespeare, William, Harfleur speech.
   See Harfleur, Henry's speech at;
   Henry V, king of England, depicted
      by Shakespeare
Shanin, Teodor, on "late Marx";
   compared, "Gandhian
      Constitution", 187
Sharp, Gene, on British "restraint" in
   India, 172
Sherman, Gen. William Tecumseh;
   as "avenger", 84
   critiqued by Walzer, 58–59
   "war is Hell," attributed to, xii, 57
Shiso no Kagaku (Science of Thought),
   Japanese journal, 138, 161
Silko, Leslie Marmon;
   distance-collapse, fictional
      portrayal, 50
social contract, Hobbes;
   as declaration of peace, 2–3
   as declaration of war, 7–8, 18
   as public relations, 7
Somme, Battle of;
   as "well-run slaughterhouse", 76
sovereignty, structural popular, 180

spinning wheel, symbol of self-
sufficiency, India, 181
Stars and Stripes, US military
newspaper, 156
state;
    as blob, 21–23
    defined by Gandhi, 179
    defined by Weber, 13
    as greatest killer, 17–18
    magic of, 14–16
state of nature. *See* Hobbes, Thomas
state of war as state of exception, 94–97
Streit, Clarence K., peace proposal;
    "the fifteen democracies,"
        rule by, 112–13
    influence on Atlantic
        Alliance, 115–16
    institutionalization of
        colonialism, 113
subject to citizen, Japan;
    influence of postwar
        constitution, 158–62
SuperLeviathan as peace
    proposal, 103–104

T

terror, as military tactic;
    area bombing as, 78–80
    Churchill on, 82
    Douhet on, 77
    Trenchard on, 78
    See also bombing
Terror, War on;
    declared September 13, 2001, 130
    institutionalizes muddle, war and
        policing, 130–32
    rules of engagement
        expanded, 131–32
    Schmitt's prediction,
        compared, 131–32
    suspects to be shot, 131
    war against tactic endless, 130
terrorist;
    aka illegal combatant, 130
    compare "Joseph K", 133

    new legal category, 132–34
    rights neither as POWs nor
        criminal suspects, 133–34
Thanatopia, 99–100
    See also war, three phases of
Trenchard, Maj. Gen. Hugh, on terror
    bombing, 78
Tsurumi Shunsuke;
    Japanese Constitution as radical
        democracy, 160–61
    "returning the gaze of the
        state", 161

U

United Nations as aspiring world state;
    incremental expansion of
        power, 123
    lacking right of legitimate
        violence, 123–24
    military action, "posse
        system", 124
    police, judicial action, borrows
        state power, 123–24
    See also Hobbes, Thomas: two
        ways to found commonwealth
United States as aspiring world
    hegemon, 130–32
    four new rights self-granted, 134
    serial war-loser, 170–71
United States Constitution as seizure of
    power, 140
    founders' testimony, 140
    world government,
        model, 103–104

V

village, Indian;
    according to Maine, 88, 109n40
    in Gandhi's Constitution, 185
village, peaceful;
    as model for Original Position, 8
violence;
    compared to *boryoku*, *Gewalt*,
        20–21, 211ff

violence, legitimate. *See*
    legitimate violence
Voiceless Voices Society, 161–62

W

Walzer, Michael, just war scholar;
    on absolute war, 57–59
    critique of Clausewitz, and its
        failure, 80–83
war;
    hell, compared, 84–85
war, alleged pleasure;
    addiction, 91
    comradeship, 93
    the forbidden permitted, 96–97
    looting, 89
    "meaning", 9
    "meaning," liberation from, 93–94
    murder, "getting away
        with", 87, 96–97
    romance, 90
    spectacle, historic, 92–93
    state power flowing
        through body, 97
    vicarious experience.
    See also state of war as state
        of exception
war, holy, described in Old
    Testament, 33–34
war, just;
    closest resemblance to hell, 83
    "treacherous" acts prohibited, 75
    "useless" suffering prohibited, 74
    victory chances not to be
        compromised, 74, 79
    Walzer, defense, 57–59
war, three phases of;
    See also Thanatopia

warriors, Greek;
    illusion of *athanatos*, 30–31
Weber, Max;
    definition of state, 13
    ethics divided, 23, 206
    founding, modern state,
        23–24, 206–207
    "iron cage", 208
    power, political, misdefined, 207
    prophets, 208
    "satanic powers" of politics, 208
    tragedy of politics, 208
Weber, Thomas;
    "creeping
        internationalism", 135–36
what-if: the game, 203
women;
    difficulty receiving equal
        treatment in military, 65–68
Wood, Gordon;
    on township republics, New
        Hampshire, 1777, 186
Wright and Fuller;
    on holy war (massacre), 33–34
    on "sinful civilizations", 35–36

Y

Yahweh, war god;
    firebombs Sodom and
        Gomorrah, 33
    issues rules for massacre, 34
    orders rape of Jericho, 33–34

Z

Zeus, war's spectator;
    mocks Hektor for his *thanatos*
        (mortality), 32

World Social Change

SERIES EDITOR: MARK SELDEN

Perilous Passage: Mankind and the Global Ascendancy of Capital
Amiya Kumar Bagchi

Anarchy as Order: The History and Future of Civic Humanity
Mohammed A. Bamyeh

Water Frontier: Commerce and the Chinese in the Lower Mekong Region, 1750–1880
Edited by Nola Cooke and Li Tana

Empire to Nation: Historical Perspectives on the Making of the Modern World
Edited by Joseph W. Esherick, Hasan Kayali, and Eric Van Young

First Globalization: The Eurasian Exchange, 1500–1800
Geoffrey C. Gunn

Istanbul: Between the Global and the Local
Edited by Caglar Keyder

War Is Hell
Charles Douglas Lummis

China: An Environmental History
Robert B. Marks

The Origins of the Modern World: A Global and Environmental Narrative from the Fifteenth to the Twenty-First Century
Robert B. Marks

The Politics of Greed: How Privatization Structured Politics in Central and Eastern Europe

Andrew Harrison Schwartz

Leaving China: Media, Migration, and Transnational Imagination
Wanning Sun

Masters of Terror: Indonesia's Military and Violence in East Timor
Edited by Richard Tanter, Desmond Ball, and Gerry van Klinken

Through the Prism of Slavery: Labor, Capital, and World Economy
Dale W. Tomich

Politics and the Past: On Repairing Historical Injustices
Edited by John Torpey

The Economic Aspect of the Abolition of the West Indian Slave Trade and Slavery
Eric Williams, edited by Dale W. Tomich, introduction by William Darity Jr.